Corrections in Canada

■ Colin Goff

University of Winnipeg

 anderson publishing co.
2035 Reading Road
Cincinnati, OH 45202
800-582-7295

since 1887

Corrections in Canada

Copyright © 1999
Anderson Publishing Co.
2035 Reading Rd.
Cincinnati, OH 45202

Phone 800.582.7295 or 513.421.4142
Web Site www.andersonpublishing.com

Library of Congress Cataloging-in-Publication Data

Goff, Colin H. (Colin Harford) , 1949-
    Corrections in Canada / Colin Goff.
        p.   cm.
    Includes bibliographical references (p.   ) and index.
    ISBN 0-87084-322-2 (paperback)
    1. Corrections--Canada--History. 2. Corrections--Government policy--Canada. 3. Prisoners--Civil rights--Canada. 4. Prisoners--Rehabilitation--Canada. 5. Probation--Canada.   6. Indian prisoners--Canada. 7. Women prisoners--Canada. I. Title.
    HV9308.G65   1999
    365'.971--dc21   98-31697
                                                                                                              CIP

Cover photo illustration/design: Chris Gliebe/Tin Box Studio
Cover photo credit (figures on city street): Earl Ripling/Photonica

EDITOR Ellen S. Boyne
ASSISTANT EDITOR Elizabeth A. Shipp
ACQUISITIONS EDITOR Michael C. Braswell

To Sarah, Buddy and Robley

Acknowledgments

When writing a textbook on such a topic as corrections, it seems an impossible task to thank everyone for their help and support. As usual, however, there were a number of individuals whose assistance went beyond the normal limits. I am thinking of all the staff at Anderson Publishing, as well as Mickey Braswell. Their patience no doubt wore thin a number of times, but their support and encouragement were tremendous and much appreciated. In Winnipeg, special recognition goes to Anne Champion, Colleen Dell, Buddy Goff, Sarah Goff, Cindy Jarigen and Lesley Murphy. As well, great thanks go to everyone at the University of Winnipeg (especially those at InterLibrary Loan Department who had to deal with me breaking all the rules).

Preface

This text presents the most recent information concerning the federal corrections system in Canada. The decision to exclude in the most part provincial data resulted from the vast amounts of provincial data both available and unavailable. In addition, provinces have undergone so many changes in terms of policies it would have taken two volumes just to describe and analyse them.

The chapters that are included in this book cover such areas as conditional release, women, and the history of corrections. Each chapter is covered as thoroughly as possible. In addition, inserts are provided in most chapters to explore current issues facing corrections today.

Special mention should go to Lesley Murphy, whose hard work made this project seem possible when it didn't appear that it was going to be finished on time. As usual, the comments by Colleen Dell were insightful and refreshing, oftentimes breaking the impasse that had stopped me from proceeding any further in a chapter. In addition, to all those individuals who are still incarcerated or on a conditional release program and who took the time to talk to me—many thanks to you all.

I hope that this text gives the reader an overview of the Canadian correctional system and a greater understanding of some of the issues facing Canadian corrections today, especially at the federal level. It is hoped that in the future greater information about the system will be available, and that more attention will be paid to the social structural dimensions of this issue.

Table of Contents

Acknowledgments   *v*
Preface   *vii*

Chapter 1
Crime and Corrections in Contemporary Canada   1

The Canadian Correctional System   1
The Canadian Correctional Population   3
The Incarcerated Population   3
   The Costs of Incarceration   5
Offenders in Prison   7
   A Demographic Profile of the Typical Inmate   7
      Age   9
      Gender   10
      Education   11
      Employment and Financial Status   11
      Families   12
      Criminal History   13
      Race/Ethnicity   14
   Types of Offences   15
   Why Did the Numbers of Incarcerated Individuals Increase?   16
   Changing Age Composition   18
The Changing Policy Toward Imprisonment   23
Offenders on Remand/Temporary Detention   25
Offenders on Probation   28
Offenders on Conditional Release Programs   29
Summary   30
Discussion Questions   31
References   31

Chapter 2
Correctional Ideologies   35

Correctional Ideologies in Contemporary Society   35
Incapacitation   35
   Does Selective Incapacitation Work?   37

Rehabilitation   41
    Does Rehabilitation Work?   44
Reintegration   48
    Does Reintegration Work?   50
Deterrence   54
    Does Deterrence Work?   56
Summary   59
Discussion Questions   60
References   60

Chapter 3
The History of the Penitentiary and
Correctional Ideologies in Canada   65

The Penitentiary   65
The Prison and Enlightenment   66
The Early History of Prisons in North America   69
The Early Development of the Penitentiary in Canada (1835-1935)   72
The Rehabilitation Era (1935-1960)   78
The Reintegration Era (1960-present)   82
Summary   89
Discussion Questions   89
References   90

Chapter 4
Conditional Release Programs: Parole,
Temporary Absences and Statutory Release   93

Conditional Release Programs   93
    The Use of Conditional Release Programs   95
History of Federal Conditional Release Programs   96
    The Antecedents of Conditional Release Programs   96
    The First Century of Parole in Canada (1868-1958)   99
    The Contemporary Era (1959-Present)   101
The Conditional Release Selection Process   108
    Decision-making Powers   109
    Release or Detention   112
Conditions of Parole, Parole Suspension and Revocation   115
Release, Risk Prediction and Recidivism Rates   116
Parole Eligibility: The "Faint Hope" Clause   118
Intensive Supervision Parole   121
Should Parole be Abolished?   124
Summary   128
Discussion Questions   129
References   129

Chapter 5
Probation   **133**

Probation   133
A Profile of Probationers: Age, Race and Gender   135
The Prevalence of Probation Sentences   136
The History of Probation   140
The Role of Probation   141
Probation Services   143
   The Presentence Report   144
   Probation Supervision   146
Does Probation Work?   148
Intensive Supervision Probation   149
Summary   151
Discussion Questions   151
References   151

Chapter 6
Women and Corrections   **155**

Women Offenders   155
A Profile of Women Offenders in Canada Today   156
The History of Correctional Facilities for Women   160
The Canadian Experience   164
Issues Concerning Federally Sentenced Women   170
   Programs and Services for Federally Sentenced Women   172
   Federally Sentenced Women and Their Children   174
   Employment and Educational Programming   176
   Risks and Needs of Federally Sentenced Women   178
   Long-Term Incarceration for Federally Sentenced Women   180
   Co-Correctional Facilities   182
Summary   183
Dicussion Questions   183
References   184

Epilogue
The Future of Corrections in Canada   **189**

Forecasting the Fate of Corrections in Canada   189
Private Prisons   193
Technology   195
Summary   196

Glossary   **199**

Name Index   **207**

Subject Index   **211**

CHAPTER 1

Crime and Corrections in Contemporary Canada

THE CANADIAN CORRECTIONAL SYSTEM

In Canada, both the federal and provincial/territorial governments are responsible for individuals who are convicted of a criminal offense. Whether an individual becomes the responsibility of either the federal or provincial/territorial correctional system is dependent upon the length of the sentence he or she receives from a judge. Those individuals sentenced to two years or more become the responsibility of the federal government as specified by Section 731(1) of the Criminal Code of Canada. Federal services are then provided to them by the Correctional Service of Canada and the National Parole Board. While both of these organizations operate "under the authority of the federal Ministry of the Solicitor General, the National Parole Board is independent in exercising its parole decision-making authority" (Foran, 1996:3). Offenders sentenced to a period of incarceration in a federal correctional facility are considered to be dangerous or chronic offenders and/or have committed more serious offences than their provincial counterparts.

Adult offenders who receive a sentence of two years less one day serve their terms in a provincial or territorial correctional facility. Provincial authorities are also responsible for all accused persons in a remand facility awaiting trial, those who are incarcerated due to their failure to pay a fine, and all those offenders placed on probation. In addition, those offenders who are to serve a federal sentence are to be admitted to a provincial facility if they wish to appeal their conviction (Section 675(a) of the Criminal Code of Canada) and/or sentence (Section 675(b) of the Criminal Code of Canada). Federally sentenced offenders who decide to waive their right to appeal are sent directly to a federal institution to serve their sentence. Inmates sentenced to a provincial correctional institution are allowed to serve some or all of their period of incarceration in

KEY TERMS		
conditional release	full parole	remand
day parole	probation	statutory release

a federal correctional facility, and vice versa. This system of interchange of inmates is known as the Exchange of Services Agreement. This program was created to allow inmates to maintain their family connections, obtain required treatment services, or ensure that proper levels of supervision are maintained (Foran, 1996).

Many provincial offenders do not serve any period of incarceration in a correctional facility; instead, they serve all of their sentence in the community on supervised probation. Others may be able to spend part of their sentence in the community through a conditional release program, but only after they have served a designated period of incarceration within a correctional facility. In the provincial system, an individual can apply for parole if the sentence imposed is longer than six months. At the present time, only two provinces operate their own parole boards for those sentenced to a provincial facility—Ontario and Quebec. All other provinces and territories now allow the National Parole Board to make parole decisions for them.

Figure 1.1
The Correctional Process for Offenders

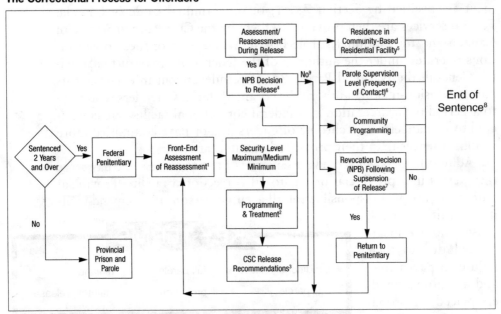

[1] Front-end assessment is comprehensive and integrated evaluation of the offender at the time of the admission. It involves collection and analysis of information on the offender's criminal and mental history, social situation, education, and other factors relevant to determining risks and needs. This provides a basis for deciding the offender's institutional placement and establishing his or her correctional plan.

[2] During the incarceration period, inmates may periodically be outside an institution on a work release program or escorted or unescorted temporary absences.

[3] CSS prepares the cases of inmates eligible for day parole and full parole for review and decision by the National Parole Board (NPB). The CSC recommendation may be either positive or negative.

[4] NPB may impose conditions on the release by CSC or by a private agency under contract.

[5] The residential facility may be operated by CSC or by a private agency under contract.

[6] The purpose of supervision is to monitor the offender's behaviour and adjustment (compliance with conditions) so as to minimize the risk of reoffending. Minimum frequency of contact ranges from four times per month to once per month according to assessed risk and need.

[7] A designate NPB or CSC officer may suspend the release for a breach of conditions, to prevent a breach of conditions, or to protect society.

[8] For offenders who have received a life sentence, the sentence never ends although they can serve part of their sentence in the community. Also, the relatively small number of offenders declared by the courts to be dangerous offenders serve an indeterminate sentence, subject to Parole Board review three years after the declaration and every two years thereafter.

[9] Subject to the detention provisions of the CCRA, an offender not conditionally released by the NPB is entitled to statutory release after having served 2/3 of the term of imprisonment.

CSC = Correctional Service of Canada   NPB = National Parole Board   CCRA = Corrections and Conditional Release Act

THE CANADIAN CORRECTIONAL POPULATION

In Canada, there are four major categories used to distinguish the offender population. The first category is those individuals who are sentenced to a term of imprisonment in either a federal or provincial/territorial correctional facility. The second category includes those individuals who are being held in custody on either remand or temporary detention. The third category is those offenders who are on probation, and the fourth category includes those offenders serving part of their prison sentence while under supervision on parole or statutory release in the community (Reed and Morrison, 1997:4).

The majority of offenders in Canada are not serving their sentence in a correctional facility, but instead are found in the community while serving on probation or are on a conditional release program, such as parole. In 1994-95, 120,261 federally and provincially sentenced offenders were serving their sentence in the community while on probation or on some other type of community release program. Probation is the most popular form of community supervision program, with 84 percent of all offenders during this time period serving all or part of their sentence while on probation. The remaining 16 percent were released into the community on some form of conditional release program (Reed and Morrison, 1997). This continues a trend that has occurred for almost two decades. Since 1980-81 the number of offenders sentenced to serve either probation or conditional release program has increased by 60 percent. Significant increases during this time have occurred in the average numbers of both probationers (59 percent) and offenders placed on a conditional release program (63 percent). When compared on the basis of average daily counts, the number of individuals serving all or part of their sentence in the community has grown at a faster rate than those offenders who are incarcerated. For example, during 1986-87 the total number of offenders placed into the community exceeded those who were incarcerated by three times; in comparison, this ratio had increased to almost four times in 1995-96 (see Figure 1.2).

THE INCARCERATED POPULATION

While the numbers of individuals incarcerated in federal facilities in Canada are much lower than those placed into the community or sentenced to a provincial or territorial correctional facility, during the past 15 years the total number of individuals sentenced to serve all or part of their sentence in a correctional facility in Canada has increased substantially. In 1995-96, the average daily count of inmates under the supervision of both federal and provincial/territorial governments totalled

33,785, or an increase of approximately 50 percent since 1980-81 (see Figure 1.2). This rate of increase has grown faster at the federal level than at the provincial/territorial level. Between 1980-81 and 1995-96, the number of inmates in federal correctional facilities increased at a rate of 61 percent, while the provincial/territorial inmate population experienced a growth rate of 43 percent. If Canada's inmate population continues to increase at this same pace, correctional experts predict the total number of inmates in both the federal and provincial/territorial levels of correctional facilities to increase to 45,000 by the year 2004 (Foran, 1996).

Figure 1.2
Trends in Adult Prison Population Counts, Canada

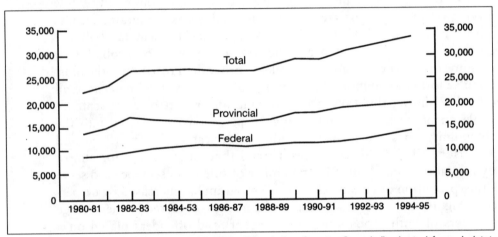

Source: Statistics Canada, "Trends in Adult Prison Population Counts, Canada," adapted from *Juristat*, Catalogue No. 85-002, Volume 16, Number 9, page 15.

The impact of this increase in the number of offenders in custody has placed significant pressures on the federal correctional system. The Correctional Service of Canada (1996) reported that, as of October 1990, "approximately 40 percent of federal institutions housed more inmates than their stated capacities." This meant that 19 of 41 federal institutions were "double-bunked," with most medium-security institutions and almost one-half of the maximum-security institutions reporting overcapacity. A recent Statistics Canada (1997:6) report indicates that this policy of double-bunking continues today. In 1996-97, it was estimated that approximately 26 percent of the cells originally built for one offender in federal institutions were being shared by at least two inmates and, in some cases, three inmates. In terms of real numbers, this translates into more than 5,000 federal offenders being double-bunked during 1994-95 (Correctional Investigator Canada, 1996).

Box 1.1 Measures of Correctional Activity: Admissions and Average Counts

Two different indicators are used to measure the number of inmates in both the federal and provincial correctional sysytems: the number of annual admissions to correctional facilities or to community supervision programs (also referred to as "intakes" when discussing entry into community programs) and the average count of inmates imprisoned or serving a sentence in the community at a given point in time.

While admission data describe and measure the changing caseflow of correctional agencies over time, these data do not indicate the number of individuals using correctional services. A person can be included several times in annual admission totals. For instance, a person held in custody before their trial (remand) could then be sentenced to nine months in prison and later be released on parole to compete their sentence in the community.

In this situation, the offender is counted three times in the admission totals. While it is important to monitor the workload associated with each individual (remand, sentenced to prison, parole), it is also equally important to be able to count the total number of offenders producing the admissions workload.

In order to determine how many offenders are imprisoned or serving a sentence in the community, corrections officials perform daily counts of inmates in their facility and monthly counts of offenders in community supervision. A person sentenced to 25 years in prison for committing a murder in 1990 would appear in the custodial count data for 1995-96, since they would still be in prison on the day or month the count took place. They would not, however, appear as part of the admission data for 1995-96, since they were actually admitted to prison several years earlier.

Source: Statistics Canada, "Measures of Correctional Activity: Admissions and Average Counts," from "Adult Correctional Services in Canada," found in *Juristat*, Catalogue No. 85-002, Volume 17, Number 4, page 3.

The Costs of Incarceration

During the early 1990s, attention was directed toward the increasing costs of supervising the correctional population. At a cost of $1.1 billion per annum, corrections is the second most costly area (after policing) in the Canadian criminal justice system. The cost of operating the federal correctional system was almost $946 million in 1996-97, an increase of 1 percent from 1995-96, while provincial/territorial costs totalled $970 million, a decline of 3 percent for the same time period (Reed and Morrison, 1997; Solicitor General of Canada, 1997). The bulk of the federal costs during 1996-97 were for operations such as the provision for the security and control of inmates (48 percent). The second area of greatest expense was in the area of technical and inmate services (28 percent), followed by 15 percent for administrative purposes, and 12 percent for correctional programming (Foran, 1996; Solicitor General of Canada, 1997). The highest average annual costs were for federal maximum-security facilities ($68,156), followed by minimum-security and correctional farms ($45,170), medium-security ($43,399) and community correctional centres ($32,811). In contrast to the federal government, provincial and territorial governments spent a larger portion of their correctional budgets (83 percent) on custodial services (Statistics Canada, 1997). Despite the fact that most offenders are under community supervision, custodial services accounted for 79 percent of every dollar spent in the area of provincial and territorial corrections during 1994-95 (Foran, 1996).

The average cost of looking after each federal and provincial/territorial inmate during 1995-96 was $42,300. The average annual cost of housing an inmate in the federal correctional system during 1996-97 was $50,375, an 8 percent increase over the previous year. In contrast, the average annual cost of supervising an offender in the community on parole or statutory release was $9,145, or just under 20 percent of the annual cost of keeping an inmate in custody. The average annual cost of incarceration was slightly lower for provincial/territorial governments:

$39,470. This represents an increase of less than 1 percent over the previous year.

A variety of other measures have been implemented by governments in an attempt to control correctional costs. These include an increase in the number of community alternative programs, electronic monitoring of nonviolent adult offenders, reductions in the number of correctional personnel through the use of video surveillance, and the privatization of various functions, such as food services (Statistics Canada, 1997). These measures appear to have had the impact of con-

Kingston Federal Penitentiary, in Kingston, Ontario, was completed in 1835. Kingston was the first penitentiary built in Canada. *Dave G. Houser/Corbis.*

trolling costs at both the federal and provincial levels. Statistics Canada (1997) reported the average cost of housing a federal inmate was $121 per day during 1994-95, a decrease of 18 percent since 1990-91. Provincial facilities also experienced a reduction during 1994-95, when the daily cost per inmate was $107, or a decrease of 11 percent.

OFFENDERS IN PRISON

A Demographic Profile of the Typical Inmate

While the increase in the total of Canada's incarcerated population has led to concern about overcrowding and costs, others have raised a number of other troubling issues, such as the overrepresentation of racial minority groups, concerns about the length of sentences and chances for probation, as well as the large numbers of the poor and young adults in the correctional population. Numerous socioeconomic variables, reviewed below, are considered the main factors that may lead to conditions of disparity (see Boxes 1.2–1.5).

Box 1.2 Incarcerated Male Offenders

What was the Profile of the Incarcerated Male Offender Population on March 31, 1997?

Profile	Number of offenders*	Percent%
Age 20 - 34 yrs	6,574	(46.7)
Single**	8,065	(57.2)
Common law	4.192	(29.7)
Married	1,661	(11.8)
Serving first penitentiary term	7,573	(53.7)
Serving a sentence of less than six years	6,967	(49.4)
Serving a sentence for:		
Murder	2,191	(15.5)
Schedule I offence	8,799	(62.4)
Schedule II offence	1,245	(8.8)
Non Schedule offence	1,863	(13.2)

*The profile was based on an incarcerated male population of 14,091.
**Includes offenders who are separated, divorced, widowed and not stated.

Source: Correctional Service of Canada, Ottawa, "Basic Facts About Corrections in Canada," 1997. Reproduced with permission of the Minister of Public Works and Government Services, Canada, 1998.

Box 1.3 Incarcerated Female Offenders

What was the Profile of the Incarcerated Female Offender Population on March 31, 1997?

Profile	Number of offenders*	Percent%
Age 20 – 34 yrs	184	(51.5)
Single**	201	(56.3)
Common law	69	(19.3)
Married	38	(10.6)
Serving first penitentiary term	265	(74.2)
Serving a sentence of less than six years	207	(58.0)
Serving a sentence for:		
Murder	71	(19.9)
Schedule I offence	163	(45.7)
Schedule II offence	84	(23.5)
Non Schedule offence	39	(10.9)

*The profile was based on an incarcerated female population of 357.
**Includes offenders who are separated, divorced, widowed and not stated.

Source: Correctional Service of Canada, Ottawa, "Basic Facts About Corrections in Canada," 1997. Reproduced with permission of the Minister of Public Works and Government Services, Canada, 1998.

Box 1.4 Incarcerated Aboriginal Offenders

What was the Profile of the Incarcerated Aboriginal Offender Population on March 31, 1997?

Profile	Number of offenders*	Percent%
Age 20 – 34 yrs	1,228	(58.4)
Single**	1,182	(56.2)
Common law	727	(34.6)
Married	175	(8.3)
Serving first penitentiary term	1,126	(53.5)
Serving a sentence of less than six years	1,231	(58.5)
Serving a sentence for:		
Murder	271	(12.9)
Schedule I offence	1,549	(73.7)
Schedule II offence	29	(1.4)
Non Schedule offence	254	(12.1)

*The profile was based on an incarcerated self-identified aboriginal population of 2,103.
**Includes offenders who are separated, divorced, widowed and not stated.

Source: Correctional Service of Canada, Ottawa, "Basic Facts About Corrections in Canada," 1997. Reproduced with permission of the Minister of Public Works and Government Services, Canada, 1998.

Box 1.5 Incarcerated Offender Population by Race

Population by Race on March 31, 1997?

Race	Male	%	Female	%
Caucasian	10,329	(73.3)	205	(57.4)
Aboriginal	2,037	(14.5)	66	(18.5)
Black	840	(6.0)	36	(10.1)
Asiatic	334	(2.4)	9	(2.5)
Other	352	(2.5)	8	(2.2)
Not Stated	199	(1.4)	33	(9.2)
Total	**14,091**	**(100)**	**357**	**(100)**

Source: Correctional Service of Canada, Ottawa, "Basic Facts About Corrections in Canada," 1997. Reproduced with permission of the Minister of Public Works and Government Services, Canada, 1998.

Age

The median age of offenders in Canada has increased during the past decade, reflecting changes in the Canadian population. The median age of a federal offender admitted to custody in 1995-96 was 33 years of age, up from an average of 28 in 1991-92. There is no significant difference between the average age of men and women offenders. The number of offenders age 25 or older admitted into the federal correctional system increased from 59 percent in 1984-85 to 73 percent in 1992-93. During the same time period, the number of federal inmates between the ages of 18 and 24 decreased from 35 percent to 27 percent (Foran, 1995). Inmates serving a sentence in a provincial/territorial institution were slightly younger, at 31 years of age (Reed and Morrison, 1997). When compared to the median age of the Canadian population in 1995, inmates are slightly younger (33 years of age versus 33.8 years of age). For offenders serving a sentence of probation, a similar trend appears, although a slightly larger younger age group is involved. The median age of probationers increased from age 27 in 1989-90 to age 30 in 1993-94 before declining to age 29 in 1994-95 (Reed and Roberts, 1996).

Significant age differentials are found within various subpopulations in the Canadian correctional system. Aboriginal offenders, for example, are younger than all other racial groups. According to Henslin and Nelson (1996:358), this difference can be explained by the fact that aboriginals "have proportionately fewer elderly than any other racial or ethnic group in Canada." Detailed analyses by Frideres (1994) and Wotherspoon (1994) reveal that aboriginals are the "most disadvantaged group with respect to life expectancy and mortality" and they "can expect to live on average about eight to nine years less than other Canadians."

Gender

Crime is largely a male activity in Canada. During 1993-94, 86 percent of all convicted offenders in Canada were male (Birkenmayer and Besserer, 1997). However, this percentage varied by offence type. Men were more likely than women to commit and be convicted of all categories of crime in Canada during 1993-94. In particular, they were responsible for 91 percent of crimes against the person (or violent crimes) and, as a result, were more likely to be sent to a federal correctional facility. In addition, during 1995-96, men made up 97 percent of the federal correctional population and 91 percent of the provincial/territorial population while accounting for just under one-half (49.5 percent) of the Canadian population. In comparison, the highest proportion of women to men were located in the categories of property crimes and morals, a result of the number of women convicted of the crimes of "theft under $1,000" and "soliciting."

During 1995-96, 10,540 women were admitted to a provincial/territorial correctional facility, while another 130 women entered a federal facility. For the same year, 103,982 men were admitted to a provincial/territorial facility and 4,272 to a federal institution. As Boritch (1997) has pointed out, while more men than women are incarcerated each year in terms of absolute numbers, the actual percentage increase has been far greater for women during the past two decades. Between 1978-79 and 1995-96, for example, the number of women admitted to provincial/territorial facilities grew by 57 percent in comparison to a 17 percent increase for males. Moreover, between 1983-84 and 1995-96, women admitted to federal correctional facilities increased by 30 percent, compared to a 2 percent increase for males.

Based upon the rates per 10,000 adults charged with a criminal offence, women are more likely to receive the sentence of probation than men in almost every jurisdiction in Canada. Probation as the most serious sanction accounted for 35 percent of all sentences women received in 1993-94 in comparison to 24 percent for men. Women were more likely to receive probation as the most serious sanction for all offence categories with the exception of "morals" and "other federal statutes"(Birkenmayer and Besserer, 1997:26).

Education

According to Robinson et al. (1997), the National Inmate Survey of federal male inmates conducted by the Correctional Service of Canada revealed that almost two-thirds (64 percent) of the inmates had not finished high school. Approximately 30 percent of the inmates surveyed had attained less than a Grade 8 education, while 16 percent had received a high school diploma and another 8 percent reported that they had attained either a community college diploma or a university degree. These figures are similar to those found by Grant et al. (1996) in their study of offenders who were placed on day parole during 1990-91. They found that 83 percent of their study group had achieved some form of secondary school education while the remaining 17 percent had attained an elementary school education. Another 6 percent of this group were found to be illiterate.

There was a significant difference found for the average amount of education completed by aboriginals and caucasians. For aboriginal women, the mean grade completed was 8.97 while for aboriginal males it was 9.12; in comparison, caucasian women completed an average of 10.31 years of schooling, slightly higher than caucasian males (10.25 years). None of the aboriginal women and only 5 percent of aboriginal males had completed 13 years of education or more, while 12 percent of caucasian women and 15 percent of caucasian males had achieved this level of education.

In their study of 86 women offenders convicted for robbery and assault, Dickie and Ward (1997) report that most had completed Grade 10, although a higher percentage of assault offenders were high school graduates compared to those who had been convicted of robbery (21 percent versus 12 percent, respectively).

Employment and Financial Status

Unstable employment is considered to be a major offender risk and need factor (Andrews and Bonta, 1998). There is a strong relationship with unstable employment and financial problems. Grant et al. (1996) discovered that in the year before their incarceration, 43 percent of the male offenders who received day parole in 1990-91 reported financial problems and 39 percent had relied on some form of social assistance. Individuals with unstable employment patterns are at a much greater risk of reoffending than offenders with a stable employment history (Motiuk and Belcourt, 1997). The Statistical Information on Recidivism scale is used by the federal authorities to establish employment status at the time of arrest. Motiuk (1996) reports that this scale was used to assess the employment status of 12,422 federal offenders. It was discovered that two-thirds of these offenders were unemployed at the time of their arrest.

In their study of male offenders on day parole during 1990-91, Grant et al. (1996) found that at the time of offence, 50 percent were unemployed and 45 percent were employed; the remaining 5 percent were students, retired or already incarcerated. In the year prior to their being incarcerated, 56 percent indicated that they were frequently unemployed. In comparison, only 45 percent of the women offenders sentenced to a federal institution were employed. During the year prior to their current offence, approximately 70 percent were frequently unemployed, 65 percent had financial problems and 40 percent relied on social assistance programs. Only 20 percent of the women offenders reported having any type of vocational training. Aboriginal offenders were more likely to be unemployed (27 percent) at the time of their current offence as well as to be frequently unemployed (74 percent), experience financial problems (56 percent) and to rely on social assistance (49 percent). Only 18 percent indicated having any form of vocational training.

Families

In 1997, the Solicitor General of Canada reported that the most common marital status of all categories of offenders was single. Fifty-seven percent of all incarcerated nonaboriginal male offenders were single, as were 56.3 percent of all nonaboriginal women and 56.2 percent of all aboriginals (both men and women). More aboriginals were living in common-law relationships (34.6 percent) than any other category. The highest rate for individuals legally married was found for nonaboriginals (both men and women), at 11.8 percent

According to a federal inmate survey conducted by Foran (1995), there are several differences between offender and general family structures in Canada. A larger number of the offender population is single, less likely to be married and more likely to be living in a common-law relationship. Offenders were also more likely to be separated from their partner.

A 1990 survey of federally sentenced women discovered that approximately 50 percent of the women incarcerated in the Prison for Women, as well as approximately 67 percent of federally sentenced women serving time in a provincial institution, have children—and that most of these women are the primary caregivers for their children (Shaw, 1991). This has led to the creation of the mother-child program by the federal government; many provincial governments have already instituted such programs.

Criminal History

Many offenders serving a federal sentence have never before served a term of incarceration. In 1997, the Solicitor General of Canada published statistics that indicated that almost 54 percent of all federally sentenced men and 75 percent of all federally sentenced women had never experienced incarceration in a federal correctional facility prior to their current sentence. Many of these offenders had extensive prior criminal involvement but most had received the sentence of probation or two years less one day as the most serious sanction. Many individuals consistently receive sentences that place them into the care of provincial authorities prior to being sentenced to a federal facility. As Birkenmayer and Besserer (1997) reported, in the nine jurisdictions they studied, the average length of incarceration for cases involving one charge was 85 days, while that figure increased to 199 days for cases with two or more charges. This has led to large numbers of offenders continually being sent back to provincial facilities for short periods of time. For example, in 1996 the Solicitor General of New Brunswick reported that 87 percent of individuals in the provincial jail system were repeat offenders (Canadian Press, 1996).

In comparison, federal offenders, whether incarcerated for violent or nonviolent offenses, typically have extensive criminal histories. Motiuk and Belcourt (1997) report that approximately 80 percent of the 6,300 federal inmates they studied had extensive prior records of criminal involvement. They also discovered that almost 70 percent had served a previous term of imprisonment in a provincial or territorial facility, while approximately 30 percent had previously been an inmate in a federal institution.

Not surprisingly, researchers have reported that age is significantly related to prior criminal involvement (Robinson et al., 1997). On the basis of information collected in the federal National Inmate Survey, older offenders were found more likely to have committed more than one prior offense as compared to younger offenders.

A number of focus studies have also inquired about the criminal history of specific incarcerated populations. In their study of 170 women offenders incarcerated in a federal institution for a murder offence, Lavigne et al. (1997) reported that 48 percent did not have any prior conviction. Of the remaining offenders, 17 percent had one or two prior convictions, 17 percent had three to seven, 7 percent had eight to 10, and 11 percent had more than 10 prior convictions. Of those women with prior convictions, almost 67 percent had been convicted for theft-related offences, 60 percent for disturbing the peace, 58 percent for disrupting the process of justice, 46 percent for harm and/or threatening to use harm and 30 percent for substance abuse–related offenses. Six percent of these offenders had a prior conviction for murder.

Hundreds of aboriginals gather outside the Stoney Mountain Penitentiary to show inmates they are not forgotten. Aboriginals make up a large percentage of Canada's prison population. *Canapress Photo Service (Wayne Glowacki).*

Race/Ethnicity

In 1967, in a study titled "Indians and the Law," the Canadian Corrections Association reported that a disproportionate number of aboriginals were found in the Canadian correctional population. Overrepresentation of aboriginal peoples within the federal and provincial correctional systems is now recognized as a significant issue. In comparison to the general population, racial minority groups are overrepresented in the Canadian correctional system. Blacks, for example, comprised 2 percent of the Canadian population in 1995, but they constituted almost 4 percent of inmates in the federal system in 1991. In 1996-97, they represented 6 percent of the total inmates serving a sentence in either a provincial or territorial correctional institution. According to the 1996-97 Correctional Service of Canada's National Inmate Survey, almost three-quarters (72.9%) of all male inmates were white. This is a decrease from 1991 when they comprised 82 percent of the total federal institutional population.

Aboriginal peoples in Canada are more likely to be incarcerated in comparison to any other racial group. The number of aboriginal peoples in the federal inmate population in 1991 stood at 11 percent, although aboriginal peoples represented just 2.5 percent of the total population in 1989 (Solicitor General of Canada, 1989; Grant et al., 1996:42). In 1996-97, their numbers increased to more than 15 percent of the total federal inmate population, while their representation in the Canadian population had increased slightly to 3 percent (National Inmate Survey, 1996; Reed and Morrison, 1997). It has been estimated that "there is an 80 percent probability that they will spend some time in jail at some point in their lives" (Frideres, 1996). The Manitoba Aboriginal Justice Inquiry (1991) and the Law Reform Commission of Canada (1991) both criticized the tendency for the Canadian courts to incarcerate large numbers of aboriginals. Their position largely reflects the attitude of the Standing Committee on Justice and the Solicitor General (1988:211-212), which noted that one reason for aboriginals being "disproportionately represented in the prison population is that too many of them are being unnecessarily sentenced to terms of imprisonment."

The total number of aboriginal inmates serving a sentence in a provincial institution varies markedly across Canada. During 1995-96, aboriginal inmates numbered less than 9 percent of all admissions to provincial facilities east of Manitoba, while, in comparison, they accounted for almost 50 percent of all admissions to provincial facilities in the western provinces. This includes 72 percent of all provincial custody admissions in Saskatchewan, 67 percent in the Northwest Territories, 55 percent in Manitoba, 36 percent in Alberta and 17 percent in British Columbia. In the federal system, there was a significant difference in the numbers of aboriginals serving a sentence in the different federal regions. In the Prairie Region (Alberta, Saskatchewan and Manitoba) of the Correctional Service of Canada, 48.1 percent of the women offenders and 38.3 percent of the male offenders incarcerated were aboriginal.

In terms of probation, aboriginal offenders accounted for 14 percent of all intakes during 1994-95, which represents a 1 percent increase from the previous year. The same geographical differences exist for aboriginal peoples placed on probation programs across Canada. During 1995-96, they represented approximately 5 percent of all new probationers in Ontario and Atlantic Canada, while they accounted for 91 percent of all the number of admissions to probation in the Yukon, followed by 56 percent in Saskatchewan, 47 percent in Manitoba, 22 percent in Alberta and 16 percent in British Columbia (Solicitor General of Canada, 1989). While the western provinces have a higher proportion of aboriginal peoples in their population, Birkenmayer (1995) reports that aboriginals are overrepresented in probation programs.

Types of Offences

According to Birkenmayer and Besserer (1997), in their study of sentencing in nine adult provinicial courts during 1993-94, it is rare for an individual convicted of a single charge to be sent to a federal institution. In 1993-94, only 4 percent of the single-charge cases had a sentence in excess of one year, in comparison to 82 percent of these cases that had a prison term of three months or less. The average prison term was 85 days and the median term was 30 days. Offences against the person received the longest prison sentences, while offences against the administration of justice received the lowest. (See Table 1.1.)

In comparison to single-charge cases, 10 percent of multiple-charge cases had prison as the most serious sanction and 61 percent had terms of three months or less. The average term of imprisonment was approximately 170 days, while the median term was 90 days. Offences against the person had the highest incarceration rate (57 percent), followed by drug offences (56 percent), offences against the administration of justice

(55 percent), property crimes (54 percent) and motor vehicle offences (53 percent). The incarceration rate for individual offences varied from 98 percent (using a firearm during the commission of an offence) to 2 percent (gaming and betting). For 1993-94, 5 percent of all prison terms were for two years or more; the most frequent terms were one month, three months and between one and three months, or 17 percent, 16 percent and 14 percent of all sentences, respectively. (See Table 1.2.)

The most common sentence length for both federally sentenced women and men was three to six years. Seventy-one (or 19.9 percent) of all federally sentenced women are serving a life sentence for murder, while 2,191 (or 15.5 percent of all male offenders) are serving the same sentence. Birkenmayer and Besserer (1997) discovered that for 10 of 12 high-frequency single-charge offences, the incarceration rates were significantly higher for males. The two exceptions found were for possession of drugs (charges were laid under the Narcotics Control Act), for which the sentences for men and for women were approximately the same, and for soliciting, for which women had a much higher rate of incarceration than men (32 percent versus 2 percent, respectively) although men had a longer average prison term (28 days as compared to 26 days).

Why did the Numbers of Incarcerated Individuals Increase?

Despite the fact that the numbers of incarcerated offenders appear to have levelled off during the past few years, the fact remains that Canada incarcerates more people today than it did just 10 or 15 years ago. This pattern of increasing numbers of inmates was not always the case. During most of the twentieth century, the total population of incarcerated offenders in Canada remained relatively constant, with the rate varying between 25 to 35 inmates per 100,000 population. However, starting in the mid-1970s, this rate increased by at least one-third, largely due to policy changes directed toward the incarceration of criminals (see Chapter 2). This increase occurred largely without the construction of new federal and provincial correctional facilities and, as noted above, more male inmates are currently housed in these facilities than existing cells allow. However, the total number of inmates has started to level off and has actually declined since 1995.

Table 1.1
Length of Prison Terms, Single-Charge Cases

Offence Category	Number of Cases 100%=	Distribution of Prison Terms (%)												Average Prison Term (days)
		2-9 days	10-19 days	20-29 days	1 mos	>1 mos <3 mos	3 mos	>3 mos <6 mos	6 mos	>6 mos <1 yr	1 yr	>1 yr <2 yr	>2 yr	
Against Person	18,547	6	11	4	22	17	13	7	5	3	3	4	5	155
Property	29,338	6	12	3	23	16	14	7	7	4	3	3	2	104
Motor Vehicle	21,038	5	30	10	20	11	15	5	3	-	-	-	-	50
Morals	1,211	19	28	6	23	12	6	2	2	-	-	-	-	45
Administration of Justice	32,627	13	23	5	34	13	7	2	2	-	-	-	-	39
Other Criminal Code	1,526	10	15	5	22	13	10	6	7	3	2	3	4	133
Drugs	7,525	9	12	3	19	14	11	8	7	7	3	4	3	142
Other Federal Statutes	1,388	12	21	7	32	15	7	2	3	-	-	-	-	42
Total	113,200	3	19	5	25	14	11	5	4	2	2	2	2	85

Source: Statistics Canada, "Length of Prison Terms, Single Charge Cases," from "Sentencing in Adult Provincial Courts: A Study of Nine Jurisdictions," Catalogue No. 85-513, page 17.

Table 1.2
Length of Prison Terms, Multiple-Charge Cases

Offence Category	Number of Cases 100%=	Distribution of Prison Terms (%)												Average Prison Term (days)
		2-9 days	10-19 days	20-29 days	1 mos	>1 mos <3 mos	3 mos	>3 mos <6 mos	6 mos	>6 mos <1 yr	1 yr	>1 yr <2 yr	>2 yr	
Against Person	14,060	2	5	2	15	14	14	9	9	6	5	7	11	277
Property	22,682	2	5	1	15	14	16	10	12	8	6	7	5	183
Motor Vehicle	11,091	1	14	5	16	13	24	10	9	3	2	2	1	104
Morals	404	4	11	2	28	22	16	7	4	1	-	2	2	93
Administration of Justice	7,811	13	16	5	30	17	10	4	4	1	-	1	1	59
Other Criminal Code	754	2	4	2	12	12	15	7	10	7	5	9	14	350
Drugs	2,774	1	3	1	9	12	15	9	11	11	7	11	11	289
Other Federal Statutes	404	12	11	1	26	22	15	4	4	1	1	1	1	65
Total	59,980	3	8	3	17	14	16	9	9	6	4	5	5	180

Source: Statistics Canada, "Length of Prison Terms, Multiple Charge Cases," from "Sentencing in Adult Provincial Courts: A Study of Nine Jurisdictions," Catalogue No. 85-513, page 17.

Why have the total numbers of incarcerated individuals increased since the mid-1970s? A variety of reasons have been forwarded, including the demand for "get tough" policies by the public and politicians, pressures for the courts to increase the length of sentences in order to protect the public, as well as the growth of the at-risk population of males between 18 and 29 years of age. Other reasons given include the criticisms levelled at so-called "soft" policies, in particular the use of parole, with the result that it is now harder to be released on full parole in Canada. Yet another factor (outside the area of control of correctional and other criminal justice officials) involves changes in social factors such as the employment rate. One common reason given is that the incarcerated population has increased due to more crime being committed, but official crime statistics (the Uniform Crime Reports) indicate that the crime rate in this country started to decrease in 1991.

Changing Age Composition

It is commonly understood that criminal activity is primarily an activity of youth, especially young males. This approach is based partly on the argument that the largest percentage of individuals accused of criminal activity increases from late adolescence to young adulthood before declining. The reasoning behind this position is based on the "age-crime curve"; that is, because younger persons comprise a significant proportion of the total population, they are responsible for the largest amount of crime. This position was supported approximately 25 to 30 years ago in Canada when the "baby-boom" generation was between 15 and 25 years of age and responsible for the bulk of criminal offences committed in Canada. It was further argued that when the "baby-boomers" became older, most would "age out" of crime, that is, they would no longer commit crimes. For correctional policymakers, this meant that the rate of incarceration would significantly decrease. In Canada, Boe (1996) reveals that the Correctional Service of Canada developed a demographic model based on the "age-crime curve." Analysts predicted that if risk rates remained constant, the number of admissions to the federal correctional system would increase until 1982 (the year when the number of 18- to 29-year-olds would peak in the Canadian population). This would be followed by a significant decrease in admissions as the population younger than 30 years of age would decline. However, as Table 1.3 reveals, this did not happen; the actual admissions have increased, most notably during the early 1990s.

Table 1.3
Actual and Predicted Male Federal Corrections Admissions (1982-1992)

Year	Actual Admissions	Predicted Admissions	Difference
1982	5,307	5,307	0
1983	5,655	5,356	+299
1984	5,715	5,366	+385
1985	5,760	5,357	+313
1986	5,916	5,350	+566
1987	6,020	5,359	+661
1988	6,193	5,372	+821
1989	6,151	5,388	+763
1990	6,434	5,387	+1,047
1991	6,331	5,477	+854
1992	7,104	5,478	+1,626

Source: Roger Boe (1996). "Unemployment and Population Aging: Contradictory Trends Affecting Penitentiary Populations." *Forum on Corrections Research*, page 10.

The largest number of offenders per 10,000 population in Canada during 1993-94 were youthful; the peak age for men and women were found in the 20–24 age group. Furthermore, the rate of conviction for men for all age groups was about six times higher than the rate for women. When offender data was combined for both men and women, almost one-half of all individuals accused of property offences in 1995 were 21 years old or younger. Figure 1.3 reveals that 46 percent of all property offenders were 21 or younger and that 33 percent were below the age of 18. According to Figure 1.4, the age curve for individuals accused of violent crimes differed from those accused of property crimes. Violent criminals did not peak for just two or three years and then decline. Instead, they continued to commit such crimes at a stable, although higher, rate of incidence than property criminals (i.e., over a 20-year time span). Thirty percent of all accused individuals were between the ages of 25 and 34, while "only" 25 percent were between the ages of 18 and 24. Because many violent offenders are sentenced to a period of incarceration in a federal correctional facility, the large number of offenders accused of committing violent crimes in their late twenties and early thirties (as opposed to desisting when they grew into their late twenties) had a significant impact upon the higher federal incarceration rates.

Figure 1.3
Persons Accused of Property Crimes, by Age
1995 UCR Research File

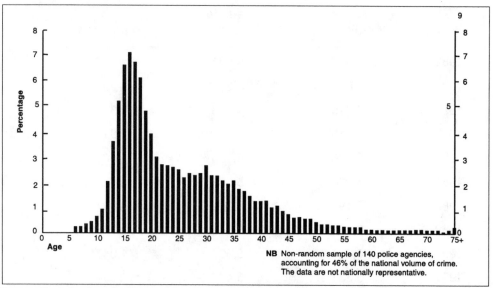

Source: Statistics Canada, "Persons Accused of Property Crimes, by Age," from "Canadian Crime Statistics," found in *Juristat*, Catalogue No. 85-002, Volume 16, Number 10, page 14.

Figure 1.4
Persons Accused in Violent Crimes, by Age
1995 UCR Research File

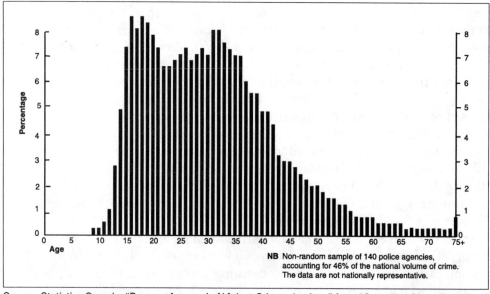

Source: Statistics Canada, "Persons Accused of Violent Crimes, by Age," from "Canadian Crime Statistics," found in *Juristat*, Catalogue No. 85-002, Volume 16, Number 10, page 13.

Boe (1996) reports that significant social factors occurred to counter the predictions made by the Correctional Service of Canada. The increase in the number of young males incarcerated was the result of certain social structural forces, most notably "the general upward drift of unemployment and the emergence of a permanent sector of unemployed youth" (Boe, 1996:9). This finding reinforces other research that has discovered a relationship between joblessness, poverty and criminal behaviour (Hagan, 1993; Schissel, 1992). Correctional Service of Canada admissions and the average count data support this theory, as it was found that during the two major recessions since 1980, significant increases in net and annual admissions to federal correctional facilities in Canada occurred. Some academic researchers (Schissel, 1992) have also discovered a small but significant relationship between changes in the rate of unemployment and the size of the total prison population in Canada.

In 1998, a preliminary research report investigating the issue of the increased prison population in Canada was prepared by the Correctional Service of Canada for the Federal/Provincial/Territorial Ministers Responsible for Justice. It was suggested that there are three reasons why there was such a rapid increase in the provincial and federal prison populations between 1989-90 and 1994-95.

The first issue explored concerned the issue of a rapid increase in admissions to both provincial and federal correctional facilities. Figure 1.5 indicates that the increase in provincial admissions peaked in 1992-93 (a year earlier than the peak in admissions at the federal level), largely because of a huge increase in the remand population. As Boe et al. (1998) argue, if this increase in the remand population had not occurred, the admission trend for the provinces would have remained relatively stable. At the federal level, it was found that admissions under a Federal Warrant of Committal (i.e., inmates serving a sentence of two years or more) increased from 4,004 in 1989-90 to 4,948 in 1993-94, representing an increase of almost 1,000 inmates, or almost 25 percent. By 1996-97, this number had decreased to 4,569. Boe et al. (1998:4) point out that since the provincial and federal systems' admissions were the result of similar sources of social and/or crime forces, "(this) question remains unanswered" (see Figure 1.6).

The second issue explored involved changes in the length of the average sentence given to offenders. Because Canada was experiencing the backlash of the "get-tough" movement and concerns were being raised about dangerous criminals receiving sentences that were too short, it is entirely plausible that this increase in correctional populations occurred because the police, crown prosecutors and judges felt public pressure to increase sentences. There was an 11 percent increase in sentences at the provincial level (representing an increase from 28 to 31 days), but this occurred between the years of 1984-85 to 1988-89. Since that time, Boe et al. (1998) discovered the mean aggregate sentence for inmates in

Figure 1.5
Annual Admissions to Provincial Custody

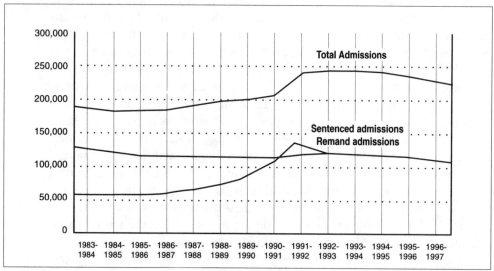

Source: Roger Boe et al. (1998). "Recent Statistical Trends Shaping the Corrections Population in Canada." *Forum on Corrections Research* Volume 10, Number 1, page 4.

Figure 1.6
Annual Admissions to Federal Custody on Warrant of Committal

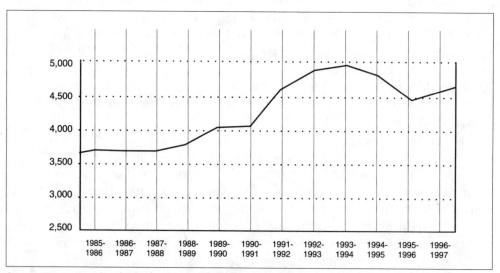

Source: Roger Boe et al. (1998). "Recent Statistical Trends Shaping the Corrections Population in Canada." *Forum on Corrections Research* Volume 10, Number 1, page 4.

provincial custody remained constant between 1988-89 to 1996-97, with the exception of a one-year increase of two days (to 33 days on average) of provincial sentences that occurred during 1994-95. This two-day increase in average sentence length in 1994-95 was largely attributable to a larger than average number of remands for that particular year. Since that time, the average length of custody has returned to 31 days. At the federal level, it was discovered that the mean aggregate sentence at admission decreased substantially. From a high of 47 months as the average sentence in 1988-89 there has been a decrease to 43 months during 1996-97.

The third reason explored involved the changes in the average length of time served in custody by offenders. Boe et al. (1998) report that the average sentence served at the provincial level is now 25 days, or about 75 percent of the sentence. While aggregate sentences have remained largely stable over the past 10 years, the average time served has slowly increased, thereby contributing to the growth of provincial correctional populations. For federal offenders, the average amount of time served has largely remained constant from 1986-87 until the present.

In general, Boe et al. (1998:7) indicated they could provide no specific reasons to this increase in prison population of Canada, concluding that this "question cannot be answered from these data . . ." However, they did suggest that major changes in corrections legislation (e.g., changing the time before an inmate could apply for day and full parole at the federal level) contributed to this growth. They also mentioned a number of economic factors, such as the recession experienced in the late 1980s and early 1990s as well as the restructuring of the economy, at both the national and regional levels.

THE CHANGING POLICY TOWARD IMPRISONMENT

The concern over the cost of incarceration led the federal government to explore less costly alternatives to imprisonment. In 1993, the Standing Committee on Justice and the Solicitor General noted that if Canada were to continue using incarceration as its main technique to fight crime, it was headed toward circumstances similar to those found in the United States. This meant an ever-increasing prison population serving longer prison terms and, as a result, new and costly facilities having to be constructed to house this ever-increasing number of inmates. However, the committee recognized the limitations of the American approach, noting that "if locking up those who violate the law contributed to safer societies, then the United States would be the safest country in the world." Realizing that the United States "affords a glaring example of the limited impact that increased incarceration may have on crime" and recognizing the "inherent inadequacy of the criminal justice system as a

Table 1.4
Provincial Custody Admissions, Aggregate Sentence and Time Served

Annual admissions to provincial custody, sentenced and remand

	1983-84	1984-85	1985-86	1986-87	1987-88	1988-89	1989-90	1990-91	1991-92	1992-93	1993-94	1994-95	1995-96	1996-97
Sentenced admissions	129,748	123,771	119,299	116,269	117,325	116,051	115,100	114,834	120,733	121,817	119,789	117,938	114,562	107,997
Remand admissions	60,885	61,042	63,772	67,638	72,816	82,202	84,797	92,893	123,014	123,929	120,945	120,922	115,768	117,462
Total admissions	190,633	184,813	183,021	183,907	109,141	198,253	199,897	207,727	243,747	245,746	240,734	238,860	230,330	225,459

Median aggregate sentence for inmates in provincial custody (days)

	1983-84	1984-85	1985-86	1986-87	1987-88	1988-89	1989-90	1990-91	1991-92	1992-93	1993-94	1994-95	1995-96	1996-97
Median aggregate sentence	28	28	30	30	30	31	31	31	31	31	31	33	31	31

Median time served by inmates in provincial custody (days)

	1983-84	1984-85	1985-86	1986-87	1987-88	1988-89	1989-90	1990-91	1991-92	1992-93	1993-94	1994-95	1995-96	1996-97
Sentenced releases	24	14	20	22	23	23	22	20	19	18	26	27	27	24
Remand releases	11	5	6	6	6	5	6	6	5	4	6	6	6	7
Total releases	19	9	12	13	9	9	12	10	11	10	11	8	12	16

Source: Roger Boe et al. (1998). "Recent Statistical Trends Shaping the Corrections Population in Canada." *Forum on Corrections Research* Volume 10, Number 1, 9.4.

response by society to stop crime and the fear it inspires," the Committee recommended the development of a national crime prevention strategy that would incorporate crime prevention into the mandates of all federal agencies responsible for criminal justice. The responses to these recommendations have led to significant changes in the criminal justice system, in particular the use of corrections. Instead of lengthening the punishments for most offences, a number of changes have been introduced that focus upon the use of greater prevention programs, particularly pretrial programs such as the Community Justice Forum program that was initiated by the Royal Canadian Mounted Police (RCMP). Other changes have reformed the sentencing system, which is now designed to promote alternatives to imprisonment when the offender has committed a nonviolent crime. The courts in Canada are now required to consider all available alternatives to imprisonment and only incarcerate an offender when it is believed that no other course of action will protect the community (Reed and Morrison, 1997).

Other factors concerning the impact of crime control policy upon the correctional population also need to be considered. For example, Reed and Roberts (1996) report that while the use of incarceration of adults has levelled off in Canada during the past few years, it has actually occurred independently of changes in the annual crime rate. They suggest that a number of other factors have led to this situation, including high rates of public fear of crime, changes in the administration of correctional policies such as greater restrictions on conditional release programs, as well as the increased prosecution, conviction and incarceration of certain offenders (e.g., sex offenders). In addition, they believe revisions to the Criminal Code, changing policing practices (e.g., mandatory arrest policies) as well as the elimination of capital punishment have all had an effect, potentially contributing in a variety of ways to the growth of the total number of individuals incarcerated and under community supervision.

OFFENDERS ON REMAND/TEMPORARY DETENTION

Remand to custody refers to nonsentenced admissions, which includes those individuals admitted on remand while awaiting trial or other kinds of temporary detention such as immigration hold (Reed and Morrison, 1997:10). During 1995-96, 115,768 individuals were placed on a nonsentenced admission, with the largest category being remand (106,467 individuals, or 92 percent of the total figure). The remand population has slowly decreased throughout the 1990s; the 1995-96 total represents a decrease of 6 percent from the previous year and 9 percent since 1991-92. As Reed and Morrison (1997:10) explain, most of the remand population spend only a brief period of time in custody, with six days being the median length of stay during 1995-96.

Box 1.6 How Many Inmates?

Average Number of Inmates by Custody Status, Correctional Service Canada and the Provinces/Territories, 1992-93 to 1996-97

Jurisdiction		Average actual-in count			% change from previous year	Incarceration rate/10,000 adults	% change from previous year
		Sentenced/ Other	Remand	Total			
Newfoundland	1992-93	373	37	410	14.1	9.6	12.2
	1993-94	379	34	413	0.8	9.6	−0.5
	1994-95	355	39	394	−4.7	9.1	−5.2
	1995-96	315	36	350	−11.0	8.1	−11.1
	1996-97	280	32	311	−11.2	7.2	−10.9
Prince Edward Island	1992-93	83	12	95	−5.5	9.9	−6.5
	1993-94	79	8	86	−9.5	8.8	−10.8
	1994-95	76	12	88	1.8	8.8	0.4
	1995-96	74	13	87	−0.4	8.7	−1.5
	1996-97	66	13	79	−10.0	7.7	−11.5
Nova Scotia	1992-93	335	60	395	0.7	5.7	0.5
	1993-94	363	73	437	10.4	6.2	9.4
	1994-95	373	66	439	0.5	6.2	−0.2
	1995-96	345	61	406	−7.5	5.7	−8.1
	1996-97	326	78	405	−0.3	5.6	−1.0
New Brunswick(1)	1992-93	422	42	464	11.3	8.2	10.0
	1993-94	420	46	466	0.3	8.2	−0.6
	1994-95	386	43	429	−7.9	7.5	−8.7
	1995-96	363	48	411	−4.2	7.1	−5.0
	1996-97	346	54 4	00	−2.7	6.8	−3.4
Quebec	1992-93	2,674	1,285	3,959	—	5.8	4.7
	1993-94	2,725	1,218	3,943	—	−0.4	−107.1
	1994-95	2,726	1,305	4,031	—	2.2	−641.1
	1995-96	2,579	1,241	3,821	—	−5.2	−333.7
	1996-97	2,163	1,264	3,427	—	−10.3	97.6
Ontario(2)	1992-93	5,638	1,786	7,424	0.8	9.2	−0.9
	1993-94	5,265	1,782	7,047	−5.1	8.6	−6.6
	1994-95	5,405	1,881	7,285	3.4	8.8	2.2
	1995-96	5,510	1,850	7,360	1.0	8.7	−0.5
	1996-97	5,748	2,014	7,762	5.5	9.1	3.9
Manitoba(3)	1992-93	673	271	944	−1.6	11.4	−2.3
	1993-94	654	244	897	−4.9	10.8	−5.7
	1994-95	705	245	950	5.9	11.3	5.2
	1995-96	696	276	972	2.3	11.5	1.6
	1996-97	640	345	985	1.3	11.6	0.6
Saskatchewan	1992-93	1,042	156	1,198	−8.9	16.6	−9.3
	1993-94	1,060	154	1,214	1.3	16.7	0.8
	1994-95	1,076	164	1,240	2.1	17.0	1.8
	1995-96	1,088	179	1,267	2.2	17.2	1.4
	1996-97	980	196	1,175	−7.2	15.8	−0.8

Box 1.6—*continued*

Jurisdiction		Average actual-in count			% change from previous year	Incarceration rate/10,000 adults	% change from previous year
		Sentenced/ Other	Remand	Total			
Alberta	1992-93	2,112	472	2,584	6.4	13.5	4.3
	1993-94	2,238	478	2,716	5.1	13.9	3.3
	1994-95	2,215	497	2,713	−0.1	13.7	−1.5
	1995-96	2,084	466	2,550	−6.0	12.7	−7.5
	1996-97	1,741	487	2,228	−12.6	10.9	−14.1
British Columbia	1992-93	1,548	379	1,927	1.9	7.3	1.4
	1993-94	1,665	449	2,114	9.8	7.7	6.5
	1994-95	1,875	487	2,362	12.0	8.4	8.6
	1995-96	1,934	501	2,434	3.0	8.4	0.3
	1996-97	1,961	623	2,584	6.3	8.7	3.4
Yukon	1992-93	63	17	79	−4.4	36.7	−7.5
	1993-94	60	18	77	−2.5	35.4	−3.4
	1994-95	54	15	69	−10.4	32.4	−8.3
	1995-96	72	21	93	34.5	42.6	31.4
	1996-97	64	17	81	−13.3	35.7	−16.4
Northwest Territories	1992-93	252	26	278	7.2	71.1	5.2
	1993-94	244	38	282	1.5	70.9	−0.3
	1994-95	255	42	297	5.3	73.4	3.5
	1995-96	278	39	317	6.5	76.7	4.5
	1996-97	301	42	343	8.4	81.9	6.8
Provincial and territorial total	1992-93	15,216	4,543	19,759	2.5	9.2	4.4
	1993-94	15,151	4,541	19,692	−0.3	9.0	−1.9
	1994-95	15,499	4,797	20,297	3.1	9.2	1.8
	1995-96	15,338	4,730	20,068	−1.1	8.9	−2.5
	1996-97	14,615	5,164	19,780	−1.4	8.7	−2.8
CORRECTIONAL SERVICE CANADA(4)	1992-93	—	–	12,362	5.0	5.7	3.6
	1993-94	—	–	13,018	5.3	6.0	3.6
	1994-95	—	–	13,952	7.2	6.3	5.9
	1995-96	—	–	14,020	0.5	6.2	−0.1
	1996-97	—	–	14,155	1.0	6.2	−0.4

Note: Due to rounding, figures may not add to totals. The data on this table represent yearly averages whereas the data on Table 15 are reported as monthly averages.

(1)   New Brunswick: The category of "other" includes police holdings, persons held for immigration reasons and those on mixed status, i.e., remand/sentence.

(2)   Ontario: "Remand status only" counts are not available. Ontario reports "remand" counts which include inmates on remand status only and those on remand/sentenced dual status. Historically, remand inmates represent about 75% of these reported counts. The percentage is used to estimate "remand status only" counts. The remaining 25% have been included in the "sentenced/other" counts.

(3)   Manitoba: Some lock-up inmates may be included in the remand counts.

(4)   Correctional Service Canada: Actual-in counts also include persons designated as having temporary detention status. Counts exclude federal inmates held in provincial institutions under the Exchange of Services Agreement. Counts also exclude inmates held in Her Majesty's Penitentiary at Newfoundland, by statute, retains jurisdiction over all offenders sentenced in the province.

Source: Statistics Canada, "Average Number of Inmates by Custody Status, Correctional Service Canada and the Provinces/Territories, 1992-93 to 1996-97," from "Corrections Key Indicator Report for Adult and Young Offenders," Catalogue No. 85-222, pages 10-11.

OFFENDERS ON PROBATION

The majority of offenders in Canada who are under the control of the correctional system are not in prison, but instead are released into the community on probation. **Probation** is the most popular community-based sanction used by the provincial and territorial justice systems, largely because it is consistent with the principle of least restraint in the use of punishment. It is believed that probation can be more effective in terms of the rehabilitation of offenders, thereby leading to lower recidivism rates (Reed and Roberts, 1996). While the exact nature of probation varies from offender to offender, probationers are given conditions to follow, and these conditions usually require them to keep the peace, refrain from becoming involved with a variety of substances, such as alcohol, and not coming into contact with designated individuals. A probation order may also include special conditions as specified by a judge, such as making restitution to a victim. Probation can be combined with a suspended sentence, fine or jail sentence; these are typically referred to as "split sentences." Currently, the maximum length of a probation order in Canada is three years, although the most common length is one year.

During 1995-96, the number of admissions to probation across Canada decreased by 2.5 percent. Since 1991-92, however, all provinces have increased their use of probation, with the exception of Prince Edward Island, Quebec and the Yukon; and these provinces reported decreases of 4 percent, 18 percent and 39 percent, respectively. There is considerable variation in the use of probation across Canada. The province of Ontario was responsible for approximately 40 percent of all new offenders admitted to probation. Six other provinces reduced their use of probation during 1995-96 compared to the previous year, with Manitoba, Newfoundland and Prince Edward Island registering decreases in excess of 10 percent. Of the four provinces reporting increases, the largest occurred in New Brunswick (6.4 percent).

Five provinces utilize probation in excess of the national average of 1,430 probationers per 10,000 adults charged. The highest probation rate per 10,000 adults was found in Nova Scotia (2,394:10,000), followed closely by Newfoundland (2,365:10,000), the Yukon (2,364:10,000), Prince Edward Island (2,054:10,000) and British Columbia (2,037:10,000). Quebec (554:10,000) used probation the least, far below the rate of the next lowest province, Saskatchewan (1,113:10,000).

Part of the popularity of probation is its relatively low cost when compared to imprisonment in either a provincial/territorial jail or federal correctional facility. While it is less costly, not as much funding goes into probation services compared to the incarceration of offenders. As a result the resources used for the supervision of probationers are stretched to their limit, making it difficult to maintain adequate supervision for all offenders. Probation and parole services receive little more than 10 percent of all correctional expenditures although they are responsible for almost three-quarters of all convicted offenders. During 1994-95, only 13 percent of the provincial/territorial operating costs were spent on probation services, compared to approximately 77 percent for custodial services (Foran, 1996).

OFFENDERS ON CONDITIONAL RELEASE PROGRAMS

In Canada, there are three types of **conditional release** programs currently in practice: full parole, day parole and statutory release. All of these attempt to encourage law-abiding behavior among inmates as well to provide an "escape valve" for overcrowded correctional facilities. Most conditional release programs in Canada are operated by the federal authorities (i.e., the National Parole Board) but, until recently, three provincial governments (British Columbia, Ontario and Quebec) have operated their own parole boards, giving them jurisdiction over all offenders serving a sentence of two years less one day.

Full parole allows inmates to serve part of their prison sentences in the community. Most inmates serving a federal sentence become eligible for full parole after serving the lesser of one-third of their sentence or after seven years of incarceration. Offenders serving life sentences are considered to be dangerous offenders and have to wait for a longer period of time before they can apply for full parole. If granted parole, they are required to follow specific conditions designed to enhance their reintegration back into the community and reduce the risk of reoffending.

The next type of parole is **day parole**. The purpose of this program is to provide offenders with the opportunity to participate in community activities in preparation for release on either full parole or statutory release. Day parolees are required to stay in a supervised facility such as a halfway house in which they must stay at night. All federally sentenced inmates may apply for day parole six months prior to the date of first application of full parole if they were sentenced to a period of incarceration of three years or more. However, if they received a sentence of between two and three years, they are eligible for day parole after serving six months of their sentence. Offenders serving a life sentence are permitted to apply for day parole three years before their full parole eligibility date.

As of March 1996, the average count of offenders on full parole was 8,943. While this figure is 8 percent higher than in 1991-92, it represents a decrease of 16 percent since 1993-94. The number of federally sentenced offenders granted full parole in 1995-96 was 34 percent, a rate that has remained constant since 1991-92. In contrast to the federal parole full grant rate, the three provincial parole boards granted parole at a much higher rate for 1995-96. In Ontario, the grant rate for full parole was 42 percent, while in British Columbia it was 48 percent and in Quebec it was 68 percent. The full parole grant rate for federal offenders is lower than for provincial offenders due to the more serious nature of their offences (Reed and Morrison, 1997).

The use of day parole, which only occurs at the federal level, decreased in 1995-96, continuing a decline that started in 1991-92. Fifty-nine percent of the day parole applications were granted in 1995-96, continuing the decline from a high of 67 percent during 1991-92. **Statutory release**, another conditional release program operated only by the federal authorities, has also been used less frequently in recent years. Statutory release requires, by law, most federally sentenced offenders to serve the final one-third of their sentence in the community under supervision. Conditions of release are similar to those given to those individuals on full parole. Certain offenders are not eligible for statutory release. For example, offenders serving a life sentence or those defined as dangerous offenders will be detained by the National Parole Board because of the concern that they pose a high-risk of committing a new offence causing death or serious harm prior to the expiry of their term (Reed and Morrison, 1997:11). Inmates placed on statutory release are individuals who did not apply or were denied release for full parole. In addition, some inmates refuse to be placed on statutory release because they do not wish to be subject to the conditions that they would have to exist within the community. In 1995-96, approximately 2,700 offenders were released on statutory release, a 2 percent increase over the previous year.

SUMMARY

Across Canada, provincial/territorial and federal correctional facilities are completely full. The costs of incarceration are high and, as a result, governments are looking at ways to reduce their spending on corrections. During the 1990s there has been an attempt to utilize alternatives to incarceration in an attempt to lower costs. This has led to the growth of community corrections and an increase in policies that emphasize reintegrating offenders into a community setting as quickly as possible.

The profile of the typical federal inmate in Canada includes a number of socio-demographic traits. In contrast to the general population, very few inmates have completed their high school education. Given their lower levels of educational attainment, it is perhaps not surprising to learn that most inmates were either unemployed or only partially employed at the time of their offence and had low incomes in comparison to the Canadian population. In addition, members of racial minority groups are incarcerated at a higher rate than dominant groups and are, thus, overrepresented in the correctional population. The average offender is older than in the past, with the median age of those incarcerated in the federal and provincial/territorial systems now being about 33 years of age.

DISCUSSION QUESTIONS

1. Is it possible to reduce dramatically the costs of incarceration in Canada today? If so, how?

2. Should we incarcerate more white-collar offenders?

3. Why do you think there is an overrepresentation of certain racial groups in the Canadian correctional system today? What can be done to reduce the overrepresentation of aboriginals and blacks in the federal correctional system?

4. Do you think conditional release programs are overused in Canada today?

5. Do you agree with the current change of policy toward incarceration at the federal level? Do you think it will be successful in the future?

REFERENCES

Amoretti, Ana and Pierre Landreville (1996). "Recycling Offenders: Re-incarceration Trends in Quebec Federal Penitentiaries." *Critical Criminology: An International Journal*, Volume 7, 20-42.

Birkenmayer, Andy (1995). *The Use of Community Corrections in Canada: 1993-94.* Ottawa: Canadian Centre for Justice Statistics.

Birkenmayer, Andy and Sandra Besserer (1997). *Sentencing in Adult Provincial Courts. A Study of Nine Jurisdictions: 1993 and 1994.* Ottawa: Statistics Canada.

Boe, Roger (1996). "Unemployment and Population Aging: Contradictory Trends Affecting Penitentiary Populations." *Forum on Corrections Research*, Volume 8, 8-11.

Boe, Roger, Larry Motiuk, and Michael Muirhead (1998). "Recent Statistical Trends Shaping the Corrections Population in Canada." *Forum on Corrections Research*, Volume 10, 3-7.

Boritch, Helen (1997). *Fallen Women: Female Crime and Criminal Justice in Canada.* Toronto: ITP Nelson.

Campbell, Gayle (1990). *Women and Crime.* Ottawa: Canadian Centre for Justice Statistics.

Canadian Press (1996). "N.B. to Close Four of 10 Jails." *Winnipeg Free Press*, April 11, 1996.

Correctional Investigator Canada (1996). *Annual Report of the Correctional Investigator 1995-1996.* Ottawa: Minister of Public Works and Government Services Canada.

Correctional Service of Canada (1990). *1990/91 Institutional Profiles.* Ottawa: Operational Planning and Resource Analysis Branch.

Council of Europe (1995). "International Statistics." In *Corrections Population Growth: First Report on Progress.* Ottawa: Solicitor General of Canada.

Dickie, Ida and Leanne Ward (1987). "Women Offenders Convicted of Robbery and Assault." *Forum on Corrections Research, 9,* 29-32.

Faith, Karlene (1993). *Unruly Women: The Politics of Confinement and Resistance.* Vancouver: Press Gang Publishers.

Foran, Tim (1996). *Government Spending on Adult Correctional Services.* Ottawa: Canadian Centre for Justice Statistics.

Foran, Tim (1995). "A Descriptive Comparison of the Demographic and Family Characteristics of the Canadian and Offender Populations." *Forum on Corrections Research,* Volume 7, 3-5.

Foran, Tim and Micheline Reed (1996). "The Correctional System." In Leslie W. Kennedy and Vincent F. Sacco (eds.) *Crime Counts: A Criminal Event Analysis.* Scarborough, Ontario: Nelson Canada.

Frideres, James S. (1994) "Health Promotion and Indian Communities: Social Support or Community Disorganization." In B. Singh Bolaria and Rosemary Bolaria (eds.) *Racial Minorities, Medicine, and Health.* Halifax: Fernwood Press.

Frideres, James S. (1996). "Native Canadian Deviance and the Social Control of Race." In Bernard Schissel and Linda Mahood (eds.) *Social Control in Canada: Issues in the Social Construction of Deviance.* Toronto: Oxford University Press.

Grant, Brian A., Larry Motiuk, Louis Brunet, Linda Lefebvre and Pierre Couturier (1996). *Day Parole Program Review: Case Management Predictors of Outcome.* Ottawa: Correctional Service of Canada.

Hagan, John (1993). "Structural and Cultural Disinvestment and the New Ethnographies of Poverty and Crime." *Contemporary Sociology,* Volume 22, 327-332.

Hendrick, Diane (1996). *Canadian Crime Statistics, 1995.* Ottawa: Canadian Centre for Justice Statistics.

Henslin, James and Adie Nelson (1996). *Sociology: Canadian Edition.* Scarborough: Allyn and Bacon.

Johnson, Holly and Karen Rodgers (1993). "A Statistical Overview of Women and Crime in Canada." In Ellen Adelberg and Claudia Currie (eds.) *In Conflict With the Law: Women and the Canadian Criminal Justice System.* Vancouver: Press Gang Publishers.

Lavigne, Brigette, Lana Hoffman, and Ida Dickie (1997). "Women Who Have Committed Homicide." *Forum on Corrections Research,* Volume 9, 25-28.

Law Reform Commission of Canada (1991). *Report on Aboriginal Peoples and Criminal Justice.* Ottawa: Law Reform Commission of Canada.

Manitoba Aboriginal Justice Inquiry (1991). *The Justice System and Aboriginal People: Public Inquiry into the Administration of Justice and Aboriginal People.* Province of Manitoba: Queen's Printer.

Motiuk, Larry and Ray Belcourt (1997). "Profiling Federal Offenders with Violent Offences." *Forum on Correctional Research,* Volume 9, 8-13.

Reed, Micheline and Peter Morrison (1997). *Adult Correctional Services in Canada, 1995-96.* Ottawa: Canadian Centre for Justice Statistics.

Reed, Micheline and Julian V. Roberts (1996). *Adult Community Corrections in Canada: 1994- 95.* Ottawa: Canadian Centre for Justice Statistics.

Robinson, David, Michael Muirhead and P. Lefaive (1997). "An Inmate Survey: A Profile of Violent and Non-Violent Offenders." *Forum on Corrections Research,* Volume 9, 52-56.

Schissel, Bernard (1992). "The Influence of Economic Factors and Social Control Policy on Crime Rate Changes in Canada: 1962-1988." *Canadian Journal of Sociology,* Volume 17, 405-428.

Shaw, Margaret (1991). *Survey of Federally Sentenced Women: Report of the Task Force on Federally Sentenced Women on the Prison Survey.* Ottawa: Corrections Branch.

Solicitor General of Canada (1997). *Basic Facts About Corrections in Canada.* Ottawa: Solicitor General of Canada.

Solicitor General of Canada (1989). *Task Force on Aboriginal Peoples in Federal Corrections—Final Report.* Ottawa: Solicitor General of Canada.

Standing Committee on Justice and the Solicitor General (1988). *Taking Responsibility (Report on its Review of Sentencing, Conditional Release and Related Aspects of Corrections).* Ottawa: Solicitor General of Canada.

Standing Committee on Justice and the Solicitor General (1993). *Crime Prevention in Canada: Toward a National Strategy.* Ottawa: Solicitor General of Canada.

Statistics Canada (1997). *Justice Spending in Canada.* Ottawa: Canadian Centre for Justice Statistics.

Statistics Canada (1996). *The Justice Data Factfinder.* Ottawa: Canadian Centre for Justice Statistics.

Walker, Samuel (1989). *Sense and Nonsense About Crime: A Policy Guide,* Second Edition. Pacific Grove, CA: Brooks/Cole.

Wotherspoon, Terry (1994). "Colonization, Self-Determination, and the Health of Canada's First Nations Peoples." In B. Singh Bolaria and Rosemary Bolaria (eds.) *Racial Minorities, Medicine, and Health.* Halifax: Fernwood Press.

CHAPTER 2

Correctional Ideologies

CORRECTIONAL IDEOLOGIES IN CONTEMPORARY SOCIETY

Before the history and operation of corrections in Canada is presented, one central question needs to be examined: What should we do with offenders? The answer to this question involves exploring correctional ideologies, or those ideas and practices that are associated with the confinement and treatment of offenders. As Allen and Simonsen (1998:54) mention, ideologies are important to our understanding of corrections because they "have supplied both the basis and rationalization for the broad range of efforts—vengeful to semihumane—aimed at getting criminals off the streets."

Since the later stages of the eighteenth century when the modern approach to corrections was first developed, four major punishment ideologies have guided correctional practices. These ideologies are usually referred to as incapacitation, rehabilitation, reintegration and deterrence. Their use has varied according to prevailing social and political factors, and their success or failure often reflects changing attitudes about punishment and corrections in society. This chapter overviews these different approaches to punishment, exploring them in terms of their philosophical backgrounds as well as some of the contemporary research associated with their operation and impact upon corrections in Western nations.

KEY TERMS		
collective incapacitation	marginal deterrent effect	reintegrative shaming
deterrence	parsimony	selective incapacitation
general deterrence	proportionality	shock incarceration
incapacitation	recidivism rate	specific deterrence
intensive supervision probation (ISP)	rehabilitation	suppression effect
	reintegration	

INCAPACITATION

Incapacitation is the custodial control of convicted offenders that ensures their inability to commit crimes that affect the general public (van Dine et al., 1979:125). Put more simply, this approach believes that a small group of offenders will commit a large number of crimes over a given time period if they are not incarcerated. It argues that incarcerating these high-rate offenders will prevent them from committing more crimes, an action that will have the impact of lowering the crime rate. According to James Q. Wilson (1983), the following three assumptions are essential to the incapacitation approach to corrections:

(1) Some criminals commit a large number of repeat offenses.

(2) Those repeat offenders taken off the street are not immediately and completely replaced by other offenders.

(3) Prison does not increase crime by changing inmates in ways that offset the reduction of crime from incapacitation.

According to Wilson, the first point has largely been found to be true, at least for a small group of offenders who have been found to commit crimes repeatedly. These individuals are referred to as "career criminals" and their existence has been documented for more than a quarter of a century. Peterson and Braiker (1981), in their study of 624 California inmates, discovered that 25 percent of the offenders they studied committed approximately 60 percent of the total number of armed robberies, burglaries and auto thefts as well as about 50 percent of the assaults and drug offences.

The second assumption is considered to be applicable for only some offences. Replacement of offenders is thought to occur more frequently in well-planned (i.e., rational) crimes, such as drug selling, white-collar crime and auto theft, while it occurs less often with spur-of-the-moment (i.e., irrational) offences. The third assumption holds that many offenders punished by long periods of incarceration will not commit crime again despite being exposed to other criminals and their illegal techniques while in prison because their prison experiences are so negative.

Whether these assumptions are valid has been vigorously debated. However, the main issue surrounding incapacitation is whether the impact of incarcerating offenders lowers the crime rate. This is difficult to assess directly because it is hard to predict how many offences a criminal would have committed while he or she is incarcerated. The answer to this question tends to vary according to a number of issues. One approach has been to study such variables as the type of offence and the age of the offender in the belief that such variables can determine offending patterns in the future and assist in the prediction of future criminal behaviour (Visher, 1987). It has been argued that one does not know when criminals will stop committing crimes. They may have been at the end of their criminal career and may have stopped committing crime even if they had not been incarcerated. As a result, incarcerating them will have little effect on the crime rate.

There are two strategies for incarcerating offenders that are affiliated with the incapacitation approach. The first is **collective incapacita-**

tion, which refers to the amount of crime reduction achieved through "traditional offense-based sentencing and imprisonment policies or changes in those policies, such as imposing mandatory minimum sentences" (Visher, 1987:514-515). In such a system, offenders are sentenced according to prior record and the seriousness of the act. The second strategy, and the one that concerns us here, is **selective incapacitation**. In this case, offenders who are predicted to be the greatest risk of committing future crimes are incarcerated for the longest prison sentences. As Visher (1987:515) states, the ability to identify offenders who will commit serious crimes in the future and predict the actual number of offences they will commit is the most common form of the incapacitation approach used today in the correctional system.

Does Selective Incapacitation Work?

Selective incapacitation is a policy that has emerged in recent years in an attempt to identify and separate high-risk from low-risk offenders and then detain the former for lengthy periods of time. High-risk offenders are considered to be the most likely to commit dangerous crimes once they are released. This group, often referred to as "career offenders" or "career criminals," has been the subject of increasing research during the past 20 years. The classic study in the area of selective incapacitation was conducted by the RAND Corporation almost 20 years ago. RAND researchers requested that more than 2,000 prison and jail inmates in three states of the United States (California, Michigan and Texas) furnish self-report data about seven types of crimes they committed prior to their current incarceration (Chaiken and Chaiken, 1982). They reported wide fluctuations among offenders in terms of the number of crimes they committed each year. Most inmates stated they were involved with a small number of offences in any given year; 50 percent of the inmates indicated they committed fewer than five crimes each year for each of the seven crimes. For all offenders, the mean number of offences was just less than 15 crimes each year. However, the most active 10 percent of the inmates who were serving a period of incarceration for a robbery reported committing at least 58 robberies each year while they were on the streets. For those who were convicted of a burglary, the corresponding number was 187. The obvious conclusion was that although the most active offenders constitute a minority, they commit the majority of crimes.

In 1982, one of the researchers involved in the RAND study, Peter Greenwood, created a system he felt would distinguish those offenders who should be "selectively incapacitated" from those who could be released after serving shorter sentences. He discovered that the incarcerated robbers and burglars who had committed the greatest number of crimes had the following characteristics:

(1) An earlier conviction for the same offence;

(2) Imprisonment for more than one-half of the past two years prior to the current arrest;

(3) A conviction before the age of 16;

(4) Previous commitment to a juvenile institution;

(5) Use of heroin or barbiturates during the previous two years;

(6) Use of heroin or barbiturates as a juvenile; and

(7) Employment for less than one-half of the preceding two years.

The robbers who had four or more of these characteristics committed an average of two robberies each year, compared to those who had either none or one of the criteria. The researchers claimed that by implementing a program of selectively incapacitating the high-rate offenders, crime rates would decrease and prison space could be used more effectively.

Greenwood classified offenders with scores between 4 and 7 as "high-rate" offenders, those with scores between 2 and 3 as "medium-rate" offenders and those with scores of 0 or 1 as "low-rate" offenders. He then developed a statistical model that allowed him to estimate the amount of crime prevented by incarcerating these offenders. Significant reductions in the crime rate could be achieved if the high-rate offenders were incarcerated for the longest period of time. For example, if all high-rate robbers in California were incarcerated for eight years and all others served a one-year term, Greenwood predicted the robbery rate would be reduced by 20 percent without increasing the prison population.

The RAND study received a significant amount of attention from both researchers and criminal justice policymakers. Some (Bernard and Ritti, 1991; Visher, 1986) reported that the potential of using this seven-item scale to reduce crime is actually less than originally predicted and that, in addition, the number of individuals incarcerated would have to increase dramatically in order to attain a minimal reduction in crime. According to Visher (1987), this led to important qualifications being made about the length of an offender's career and the type of offenders being incarcerated. First, it is argued that the RAND researchers implicitly assumed that a criminal career is longer than the period of incarceration. However, this is not always the case, as researchers have discovered, because offenders vary significantly according to how long they offend before terminating their criminal activities (Blumstein et al., 1988). This means that if a selective incapacitation policy is implemented, many offenders sentenced to lengthy periods of incarceration may have terminated their offending after their current offence or during the next few years anyway. Secondly, the significant reduction in crime due to the implementation of a selective incapacitation model found in the study was specific only to robbers in California. Visher (1987) explains that the reason for this significant impact of a selective incapacitation policy was the fact that robbers were treated most harshly in California and thus greater crime reductions occurred in that state as compared to either Michigan or Texas. In addition, criticisms have been directed at the seven-point scale. Von Hirsch (1985) argued that the scale does not reflect the seriousness of the crime committed by the offender and therefore ignores the amount of harm. Others have argued that employment should not be used as a predictor for selective incapacitation because offenders generally have only limited control over this factor in their lives. In response to these criticisms, Greenwood (1984) replied that the information supplied by his scale is vital to prosecutors, judges and parole boards in terms of their decisions on sentence lengths and release dates because it would enable them to make more efficient decisions.

Studies that have attempted to clarify and explore Greenwood's arguments empirically have been few in number. One recent research effort was conducted by Miranne and Geerken (1991), who studied offenders in New Orleans using an improved self-report survey. Their findings support Greenwood's conclusion that a small number of offenders commit a significant proportion of the crimes. However, the authors note that the jurisdiction they studied—Louisiana—incarcerates its offenders for lengthy periods of time and the results may not be the same for jurisdictions that sentence similar offenders to shorter terms.

Despite these issues, the impact of the RAND study upon the criminal justice system has led to a number of significant new policies, in particular in the United States, which seems to be the country most concerned with selective incapacitation as a correctional device. One policy change entails the career criminal programs that have been established by many prosecutors' offices. According to Chaiken and Chaiken (1991), these programs are designed to concentrate resources on those offenders who have numerous convictions for serious offences. The goal of these programs is to prosecute offenders identified as "high-risk" as quickly as possibly with the intention of incarcerating them for longer periods of time once convicted. In order to achieve this, career criminal prosecution programs usually emphasize cooperation between the police and prosecutor, a screening process whereby suspects with prior records are identified and then designated for priority prosecution, and the assignment of experienced prosecutors to these cases. In addition, the other activities of these prosecutors are reduced. The prosecutors are responsible for each case from beginning to end, and for all prosecutions of the same offender and they rarely engage in plea bargaining. As a result, career criminal prosecution programs have increased conviction rates, the rate of incarceration and the length of sentences, although all these increases have been modest. The areas of greatest increase have been the frequency of conviction and length of sentence. One New York career criminal program that focused on those offenders who had at least one prior felony conviction and who were charged with a major felony attained convictions 95 percent of the time. Nearly 80 percent of those classified as high-risk offenders were convicted of the highest charge (Fowler, 1981).

Perhaps the highest-profile selective incapacitation programs are those resulting from what are commonly referred to as "three strikes and you're out"" laws (which impose mandatory punishments for three-time offenders). Between 1993 and 1995, 23 states and the United States federal government enacted "three strikes" legislation for high-risk repeat offenders. These laws are overwhelmingly approved of by the public, with 86 percent of a national sample contacted in 1994 favoring the law and only 12 percent opposing it. This reflects a perception that existing laws are not protective of public safety in their enforcement and/or punishment and that these new laws are needed to bolster existing sanctions by incarcerating the most serious offenders for lengthy periods of incarceration.

It should be noted that the early evidence indicates that for most states these laws have had minimal impact on their prison population because they were enacted only to apply to the most violent repeat offenders. In the state of Washington, for example, only 85 offenders were admitted to the state prison system under these laws in the first three years. An exception to this trend is found in California, which has admitted in excess of 26,000 offenders under their "three strikes" law since April 1994. Most of these individuals have been sentenced for nonviolent crimes. In comparison, all but one of the 85 offenders in Washington state have been sentenced for violent crimes (Clark et al., 1997). The meaning of "three strikes and you're out" varies considerably from jurisdiction to jurisdiction. While most states define violent crimes such as murder, rape, robbery, arson, aggravated assault and carjacking as an offence under a "three strikes" law, some states also include the sale of drugs, escape from a state correctional facility, treason, and embezzlement and bribery. In addition, some states differ in terms of the sentence when sufficient "strikes" have accumulated against an offender. Twelve states impose mandatory life sentences with no

Pete Wilson, Governor of the State of California, has been an outspoken proponent of that state's "three strikes and you're out" law. *Jacques M. Chenet/Corbis.*

possibility of parole, while others allow parole but only after a lengthy period of incarceration (for example, 30 years).

Most attention has been focused on the California "three strikes and you're out" law, which was enacted in 1994. It specifies that a minimum of 25 years must be served before an offender is eligible for parole. In addition, an offender can be sentenced under this law after being convicted of only one felony if he or she has a prior conviction from a list of "strikeable" offences. If an offender has two prior felony convictions from the list of "strikeable" offences and commits another felony, he or she receives a mandatory indeterminate life sentence with no chance of parole for 25 years. The California legislature holds that incapacitating career criminals will reduce the crime rate; yet it may have the opposite effect, at least in some respects. Reports have been received that the "three strikes" law has caused some offenders to use excessive violence against arresting police officers in order to avoid capture and charges that would place them under the law. In addition, offenders charged with a third felony conviction are apparently refusing to negotiate pleas that would result in lengthy prison sentences, thereby leading to court backlog. Many of the offenders sentenced under these laws are older, raising the issue of whether they are near the end of their criminal careers. In addition, it has been reported that "some victims and witnesses have refused to testify and some juries have refused to convict because of the long prison terms that defendants would face if convicted" (Conklin, 1998:495). So far, then, it appears that the success of selective incapacitation is debatable at best—its impact upon crime remains to be documented in a meaningful way.

REHABILITATION

Rehabilitation is a difficult ideology to define because it encompasses so many different programs and policies. As a result, it is best to offer a generic definition, specifically that rehabilitation involves the application of "correctional resources in such a way as to improve the condition of offenders so that they no longer need or want to commit crimes" (Schwartz and Travis, 1997:11). To accomplish this goal, punishments (i.e., treatment) are implemented so that they fit the needs of the individual offender (Cullen and Gilbert, 1982). Today, the ideology of rehabilitation focuses upon the development and implementation of programs designed to target the needs, risks and responsivity of criminals in order to reduce crime.

The traditional measure of the success or failure of treatment programs is the **recidivism rate**. This rate is determined by taking the number of offenders who, during a designated time period after being released from a correctional facility, are rearrested for committing another offence or violating the conditions of their parole (i.e., a technical violation). Another technique for measuring the success of a rehabilitation program is the **suppression effect.** This means that there is a reduction in the number and seriousness of crimes although the offenders usually continue to participate in criminal activity. The effectiveness of treatment methods has been debated frequently, but the most famous discussion of this issue was by Martinson (1974:25), who wrote after systematically examining more than 200 treatment programs that with "few and isolated exceptions, the rehabilitative efforts that have been reported so far have had no appreciable effect on recidivism." According to Martinson, rehabilitation is ineffective because of problems intrinsic in its "theory." In his opinion, treatment programs fail because they are based on a medical model perspective that sees criminal behaviour as a "disease,"

> . . . that is to say, as something foreign and abnormal in the individual which can presumably be cured. This theory may well be flawed, in that it overlooks—indeed denies—both the normality of crime in society and the personal normality of a very large proportion of offenders, criminals who are merely responding to the facts and conditions of our society.

Martinson's critique had an incredible impact upon the prevailing correctional ideology of rehabilitation of the day. Rehabilitation went from being the dominant ideology to almost a state of nonexistence between 1975 and 1981. Since the early 1980s, however, a number of supporters of rehabilitation have argued that many treatment-based programs work for certain kinds of offenders (Andrews et al., 1990; Cullen and Gilbert, 1982; Gendreau and Ross, 1987; Lipsey, 1991). However, their approach differs from earlier ideologies of rehabilitation by stressing the risks, needs and responsivity of offenders. Palmer (1991:340) summarized this new approach to rehabilitation by claiming that, by the late 1980s, "the emerging picture or perhaps new implicit consensus among many skeptics, sanguines, and others was that 'something' apparently works, although no generic method or approach . . . especially shines." Palmer (1994:xviii) later reported that some rehabilitation programs were successful, although none were "simultaneously very successul and widely applicable."

Those who, like Cullen and Gilbert, seek to reaffirm rehabilitation argue that the critics of rehabilitation have used suspect methodological approaches when evaluating the success or failure of treatment programs, a practice that led them to the erroneous conclusion that "nothing works" (Gottfredson, 1979). A predominant technique employed by critics to show the limits of rehabilitation is to question how the success of a program is operationalized. Conklin (1998:521) points out that a standard way of measuring success is to look at the total number of parole revocations. This approach is deemed inappropriate because revoking parole is a discretionary decision and reflects the beliefs held by probation or parole officers as much as it does the actions of the parolee.

Rehabilitation is the contemporary theoretical basis of correctional treatment and it is largely based upon risk prevention. Basically, this means that no one program can be successful for every offender. The most effective rehabilitation programs today include behavioral therapy, social skills training, life skills enrichment such as educational and vocational programs, family interventions and multimodal programs. Combining a few or many of these programs into a multiple-prevention strategy is recognized as the most appropriate way to treat offenders and reduce recidivism. Ineffective approaches include individual and group counselling, diversion and area-wide delinquency programs.

Underlying the most successful treatment programs today are four general principles that are used to classify offenders for the purpose of giving them effective treatment. According to Andrews and Bonta (1998:242-248), these principles are (1) risk, (2) need, (3) responsivity, and (4) professional discretion. The risk principle consists of two components: (1) that criminal behavior can be predicted, and (2) that this involves the process of matching different types and levels of treatment services to the risk level of the offender. A proper analysis of risk leads to the differentiation between risk levels of different offenders. Andrews and Bonta (1998:243) note that for high-risk offenders "we need to deliver more intensive and extensive services if we are to hope for a significant reduction in the probability of recidivism." Alternatively, low-risk offenders need very little, if any, services.

The need principle is a subset of an offender's risk level and involve the identification of the criminogenic needs of the offender. These are the "dynamic attributes of the offender that, when changed, are associated with changes in the probability of recidivism" (Andrews and Bonta, 1998:243). Noncriminogenic needs need not be the focus of correctional intervention, as altering them will unlikely reduce recidivism unless they impact upon a criminogenic need. A significant amount of criminogenic needs are associated with procriminal attitudes, as researchers have found significant associations in both adult and youthful offenders (Bonta, 1990; Shields and Ball, 1990).

The responsivity principle refers to the idea of "delivering treatment programs in a style and mode that is consistent with the ability and learning style of the offender" (Andrews and Bonta, 1998:245). Successful correctional programming involves delivering services that involve both social learning and cognitive approaches as they relate to individual offender traits. According to Andrews (1989:16), there are five dimensions of effective correctional supervision and counselling. These are:

(a) Authority: "firm but fair," distinguishing between rules and requests, monitoring progress, rewarding compliance with treatment . . .

(b) Anticriminal modelling and reinforcement: demonstrating and reinforcing vivid alternatives to procriminal styles of thinking, feeling and acting.

(c) Concrete problem solving: skill building and removal of obstacles in order to increase the rewards associated with anti-criminal behaviour in settings such as home, school, and work.

(d) Advocacy and brokerage: referring the offender to other helping agencies, as long as the receiving agency offers appropriate correctional service.

(e) Relationship factors: relating in open, enthusiastic, caring ways.

Professional discretion refers to the principle that not all offenders can be treated in exactly the same way although they may share similar risk and need factors. Professionals can "override" the principles of assessment as long as it is done in a way that improves assessments and it is not conducted in a haphazard manner. Discretionary decisions have to reflect "ethical, humanitarian, legal and effectiveness considerations. Principles of treatment, no matter how solid the research base, must be applied by an informed and sensitive professional" (Andrews, 1989:16).

Does Rehabilitation Work?

How is it possible to decide whether rehabilitation "works" to reduce the amount of recidivism of offenders? Martinson (1974) used the "vote-counting" method as his methodological approach in evaluating treatment programs. This method involves giving one vote to each study's findings on the basis of whether it is favorable or unfavorable on the basis of successful treatment outcomes. According to Cullen and Applegate (1997:xvii), this approach contains at least three limitations. The first limitation is that there is no agreed-upon standard on which to base decisions about whether treatment "works." Andrews (1994:7), for example, found that 40 to 80 percent of treatment programs did in fact reduce recidivism, although most of the original authors and evaluations stated that they did not. Furthermore, Gendreau and Goggin (1996:38) state that more than 700 research studies exist that indicate successful reductions in recidivism after treatment. They note that the average reduction in criminal reoffending is between 25 and 30 percent, although some have reported up to 50 percent reductions when appropriate treatment programs are developed.

Box 2.1 Maximizing Predictive Accuracy

Maximizing the Predictive Accuracy of Offender Risk/Needs Assessment

1. Standardized and structured risk assessments are more valuable than those based on unstructured professional or clinical judgment. Professional discretion is helpful, but in combination with systematic assessment.

2. The best risk assessment instruments measure the presence of several major risk factors. However, even a composite measure of minor risk factors will not maximize predictive accuracy.

3. Staff training, management support, professional standards and ongoing clinical supervision also affect the reliability and consistency of risk assessment.

4. Risk assessment should rely on more than one information source.

5. Broadly assess reoffending through the use of longer follow-up periods and different measures of reoffending.

6. Assess both fixed and dynamic risk factors, and reassess these factors periodically to detect any changes in risk.

7. False positive and negative errors can be influenced by the careful selection and cross-validation of the scores used to separate lower- and higher-risk offender groups.

Source: *Forum on Corrections Research*. September 1996, Volume 8, Number 3.

The second limitation of the vote-counting method involves a Type II statistical error—specifically when a study finds that no treatment effect exists when one does in fact exist. This is particularly true when small sample sizes are used, because they reduce "the power of the test to detect real differences . . ." (Cullen and Applegate, 1997:xvii). According to Gendreau and Goggin (1996:38), the average offender treatment program found in the 700 studies they identify is about 10 percent. They note that while 10 percent may appear to be modest, it "is comparable to what is acceptable for many medical interventions and represents substantial cost savings." The third limitation of the vote-counting approach is that it is imprecise. Simply by counting those studies that support rehabilitation and those that do not "does not tell us the strength of the relationship between treatment and recidivism" and "makes it difficult to proceed to the next step of discerning what makes treatment effective in some instances but not in others" (Cullen and Applegate, 1997:xvii).

Supporters of the rehabilitation approach have countered the vote-counting method with a technique known as "meta-analysis." A meta-analysis computes the "effect size" (i.e., recidivism) for each study. The effect size could be negative (i.e., treatment increases crime), zero (i.e., no effect) or positive (i.e., treatment reduces crime). These meta-analyses of rehabilitation programs have found support for the approach (e.g., Andrews et al., 1990; Lipsey, 1991; Lipsey and Wilson, 1997). Meta-analyses focusing on offender treatment programs indicate that those offenders who receive some kind of psychosocial treatment do much better in terms of reduction in recidivism rates than those who do not (Losel, 1996).

Lipsey (1991:134) conducted a meta-analysis of 443 studies of juvenile delinquency treatment and found that interventions reduced recidivism by 20 percent, a figure that "could be quite large enough to have practical significance." He also evaluated which treatment approaches were more effective, reporting that certain types of treatments (e.g., behavioural, multimodal) "seem to be more effective than the less structured and focused approaches" (e.g. counselling), leading to recidivism reductions of between 20 to 40 percent (Lipsey, 1991:134). Gendreau and Goggin (1996) add that better results can be derived from studies that are conducted under conditions of optimal therapeutic integrity. Therapeutic integrity refers to programs that are properly constructed, operated by qualified and well-trained staff who provide intensive treatments, and are evaluated by an individual who understands behavioral interventions. Gendreau and Goggin (1996:40) state that programs that have therapeutic integrity and those that do not have it show significant differences in recidivism:

> In the case of prison-based programs that fall within the minimum criteria of the appropriate category (such as behavioral treatment), reductions in recidivism of about 5 percent to 16 percent are the norm. Prison programs with, in our opinion, a great deal of therapeutic integrity, can produce reductions in recidivism in the range of 20 percent to 35 percent . . . with regard to contemporary community-based interventions, the Ohio and South Carolina programs for high-risk juveniles are especially noteworthy. Reductions in recidivism of at least 30 percent are typical of these programs. In one South Carolina comparison, a 50 percent reduction was reported. . . . One of the truly impressive features of these programs is that they are multi-faceted. They are also based in the offenders' natural environment (home, peers, school).

Recently, Lipsey and Wilson (1997) have contributed new evidence to the belief that appropriate treatment interventions reduce criminal reoffending. In their meta-analysis of 200 studies evaluating the impact of intervention on juvenile offenders classified as "serious," they reported an average reduction of 12 percent in recidivism. However, they note that the best programs reduced recidivism by as much as 40 percent. The authors note that, given the clientele, these programs' positive impact on recidivism was "an accomplishment of considerable practical value in terms of the expense and social damage associated with the delinquent behavior of these juveniles" (Lipsey and Wilson, 1997:29-30).

The success of these programs has led many researchers to point out that imprisoning large numbers of offenders has a marginal incapacitative effect (e.g., Clear, 1994; Spelman, 1994). They also argue that the savings from using a "lock 'em up" strategy are not substantial and, in most cases, such a strategy is more costly. A recent study compared the reduction in crime and cost savings of rehabilitation and selective incapacitation programs such as the "three strikes and you're out" laws (Greenwood et al., 1996). It was estimated that both the incapacitation and treatment approaches would reduce crime by approximately 20 percent. The cost savings, however, were substantial—the incapacitation approach would cost about $5.5 billion per year, while the rehabilitation approach would cost less than one-fifth of that. Other researchers have noted that short- and long-term reductions in victimization would be significantly greater if rehabilitation programs were introduced as opposed to "get tough" policies. Petersilia (1992) notes that most offenders return to society and, if not treated, will in all probability commit more serious crimes than they did prior to their incarceration. Genuine concern for public safety "would justify using rehabilitation programs, designed according to principles of effective treatment, to reduce the recidivism of offenders returned to the community" (Cullen and Applegate, 1997:xxiv).

In addition, supporters of rehabilitation argue that the success of treatment intervention in terms of reducing recidivism far surpasses deterrence-based programs and reintegrative correctional programs such as intensive supervision and home confinement. Problems associated with such programs are largely due to faulty program implementation. Many "get tough" programs fail to achieve certainty of punishment and, as a result, failed to attain deterrence. For example, Jones and Goldkamp (1993) found that in the jurisdictions they studied many offenders failed drug tests but were not sanctioned due to crowded courts and crowded prisons. Because there was a lack of certainty of punishment, high levels of deterrence did not occur.

Perhaps the most basic reason deterrence programs fail to have a significant impact on recidivism rates is that they do not focus on the known predictors of recidivism, such as antisocial values and peer groups (Andrews and Bonta, 1998). Cullen and Applegate (1997:xxi) comment that "the deterrence approach ignores the criminological evidence showing that the roots of crime among serious offenders typically extend to childhood or early adolescent activities, where youths develop propensities and associations that stabilize their involvement in crime." Threats and sanctions can have little impact on these factors that lead to continued criminal activity. Deterrence-based programs have been found to be successful, however, but only when they include rehabilitation-based treatment programs implemented with therapeutic integrity (Cullen et al., 1996; Petersilia, 1997).

REINTEGRATION

For the supporters of the **reintegration** ideology the two overriding concerns are the placement of only the most serious offenders in correctional facilities and the development of community corrections. Community corrections options are to operate as alternatives to incarceration. They involve a variety of programs, such as community service orders, probation and fines in order to allow offenders to live in their communities while they are serving their sentences. Reintegration is a correctional ideology that, like rehabilitation, has to be defined in broad terms because it involves many different programs. Latessa and Allen (1997:28) define reintegration as "a broad correctional ideology stressing acquisition of legitimate skills and opportunities by criminal offenders, and the creation of supervised opportunities for testing, using, and refining those skills, particularly in community settings." This involves the use of probation orders as well as conditional release programs.

The reintegration ideology justifies punishing offenders on the basis of their criminal actions, that is, lawbreakers deserve to be punished according to their crime(s) and the harm(s) they inflicted upon their victim(s). The core of the reintegration ideology involves the ideas of proportionality and parsimony. The doctrine of **proportionality** refers to the idea that there has to be a rank ordering of crimes on the basis of their relative seriousness proportionate to the rank ordering of the severity of punishments. Both the seriousness of crimes and the severity of punishments can be determined by subjective decisions about the degree of harm and the blameworthiness of the offender. To date, considerable agreement has been found between the seriousness of crimes and the corresponding amount of punishment considered to be necessary to indicate societal disapproval (Cohen, 1988; Evans and Scott, 1984). To achieve this relationship, jurisdictions have implemented sentencing guidelines that employ determinate sentences that are designed so inmates will serve all of their sentence before being released. In addition, parole boards will usually be eliminated or have their decision-making powers severely restricted to reduce the chance of them shortening the sentences handed out by the judge. Sentences imposed by judges, therefore, specify the actual amount of time an offender serves. Offenders can be let out early, usually on the basis of "good time," a policy involving the reduction of an inmate's sentence by a certain amount (e.g., one-third) for obeying institutional rules.

One of the defining aspects of the reintegration ideology is support for a whole range of community sanctions. This means that those offenders convicted of what are classified as "lesser" offences, or even those who commit certain types of violent crimes as their first offence, may serve their sentences in the community. This belief in the widespread use of community

Inmates from the Quinte Detention Centre in Napanee serve the community by cleaning up litter along a highway. *Canapress Photo Service (Michael Lea).*

sanctions is referred to as **parsimony**, meaning that a punishment should involve a sentence that places the least restrictive control on the offender. This idea is based on the idea that too much social control can be harmful to the offender. Offenders who are unjustly dealt with by giving them harsh sentences "may be propelled by circumstances or an altered self-concept toward further deviance" (Pfohl, 1985:304). One important implication of using parsimony is that judges follow a policy that dictates that a sentence should always be placed at the "lower end of the range of 'deserved' punishments as a starting point and should increase that penalty only if . . . one or more of his other 'guiding' factors requires increased severity in the particular case" (Frase, 1997:374).

Reintegration involves individuals becoming law-abiding citizens as they become involved in the community. The community is the source of opportunities for the offender. By taking advantage of these opportunities, offenders should learn to make use of legitimate resources and services that allow them to reintegrate. As part of this process, offenders are expected to develop new attitudes and lifestyles that enable them to function in a law-abiding manner. A number of characteristics have now been identified as essential for successful community-based programs within the reintegration ideology. These include

(1) A location within, and interaction with, a meaningful community.

(2) A nonsecure environment.

(3) Community-based education, counselling and support services (these are provided by noncorrectional public and private agencies as well as by correctional staff and are organized into a comprehensive service-delivery network).

(4) Opportunities (for the offenders) to assume the normal roles of citizen, family member, student or employee.

(5) Opportunities for personal growth.

(6) Efforts to change the community by encouraging tolerance for non-conforming behavior that is nevertheless law-abiding and developing opportunities for self-sufficiency and self-realization (McCarthy and McCarthy, 1984:8).

The logic of reintegration as a correctional ideology has been particularly appealing over the past 40 years, and many programs have been developed in its context. This appeal is largely the result of the perceived financial benefits of not having to keep offenders locked up and the use of volunteers and private agencies to assist in the reintegration of the offenders into the community.

Does Reintegration Work?

One of the most complete reintegration correctional systems was introduced by the state of Minnesota in 1980 when they implemented a sentencing guidelines grid system. A significant aspect of this approach was the fact that the Minnesota Sentencing Guidelines Commission decided that prison sentences should be used primarily for violent offenders as opposed to property offenders. After the first two years of operation, it was found that Minnesota's guidelines did not increase the prison population although judges lost their discretion to sentence individuals to community sanctions. Judges had to follow the sentencing grid system, which largely predetermined the sanction they were to give to the offender. Miethe and Moore (1989:3-4), in their study on the effect of the sentencing guidelines, discovered that:

(1) Imprisonment rates increased slightly during the transition period but remained lower than they had before the implementation of the guidelines.

(2) Judges were more likely to depart from the guidelines as the number of years increased from the time of the implementation. However, most judges were staying within the guidelines in more than 90 percent of their sentencing decisions.

(3) Judges increased the number of cases in which they gave jail sentences as a condition of probation, from 44 percent to 66 percent. The result was an increase in the number of offenders incarcerated in local jails.

(4) Judges initially increased both the uniformity and proportionality of their sentences, but both of these slipped slightly over the years.

(5) Prosecutors changed their plea bargaining practices in order to avoid following the guidelines when they felt they were unreasonable.

(6) Violent offenders were more likely to be imprisoned under the guidelines than before, and without any additional increase on the correctional resources of the state.

Perhaps the greatest success of the reintegration ideology has been the use of community corrections. Following the principle of parsimony and the policy of least restrictive control, community corrections have proliferated in North America since the late 1960s and include the pre-adjudication level of the justice systems (such as diversion and pretrial release programs) as well as rehabilitation programs that attempt to reintegrate offenders living in semi-secure facilities in the community. The programs are usually classified into three categories: (1) preconviction, (2) post-conviction, and (3) intermediate punishments.

Preconviction community corrections are alternatives to formal prosecution and most typically involve diversion and pretrial release. Diversion has been defined as "formally acknowledged and organized efforts to utilize alternatives to initial or continued processing into the justice system. To qualify as diversion, such efforts must be undertaken prior to adjudication and after a legal proscribed action has taken place" (National Advisory Commission on Criminal Justice Standards and Goals, 1973:73). Examples of diversion programs include alternative measures for young offenders and some types of family group conferencing/community justice forums. Diversion can be both informal and formal in its orientation. Informal diversion refers to the application of diversion by an individual criminal justice official, such as a police officer who may decide that it is better to send an offender to a mediation program than to prosecute the offender. Formalized diversion involves the formal screening of cases to determine the accused's suitability for diversion, specific diversion workers and formal, established arrangements that link community programs to the diverted offender.

Post-conviction programs, generically referred to as diversion, include probation, parole, restitution and community-service programs. These programs are thought to be beneficial to many individuals because they allow them to continue to work and maintain family ties. They also permit them to avoid the cost of hiring a lawyer as well as the establishment of a criminal record and the stigma of being labelled a "criminal" if convicted. In addition, any treatment costs may be incurred by the criminal justice system, allowing members of all social classes to participate. Diversion programs include a wide variety of different forms. Governments and private agencies have large amounts of discretion to develop diversion programs. Generally they involve the formal processing of an offender through at least some part of the criminal justice system until they reach a point at which they are offered the option of attending a treatment program. In most cases, prosecutorial approval is given prior to the offender being placed into a program.

A number of internationally respected articles exploring the reintegration ideology have been published about the Canada experience. Hylton (1981; 1982) and Chan and Ericson (1981) have published reviews of the operation of the operation of community corrections in Saskatchewan and Canada as a whole, respectively. Both research efforts indicated that community corrections did not reduce the prison population; rather, they contributed to a substantial increase in provincial correctional populations, thereby negating the presumed benefits of the reintegration ideology. This increase in the offender populations has been called "net-widening," a term introduced to refer to the social control system actually increasing its power over larger numbers of the population.

Hylton studied the implantation of the provincial community correctional system in Saskatchewan between 1962 and 1979. He argues that although community corrections were largely designed to reduce the population of incarcerated offenders and maintain a limit on the number of persons involved with the provincial correctional system, this is not what actually occurred. His data reveal that throughout the time period studied there were "steady increases in the number and rate of admissions to prison and in the number of persons incarcerated on any given day were observed" (Hylton, 1982:345). In his analysis, Hylton (1981) reports that the average daily count per 100,000 population in Saskatchewan's correctional facilities increased from 55 in 1962 to almost 85 in 1979. The total number of admissions per 100,000 population in Saskatchewan increased from 434.85 in 1962 to 688.72 in 1979, an increase of almost 58 percent. He also found offenders were being sentenced to about the same length of time over the period of analysis, but that the system expanded "by institutionalizing more offenders for about the same period of time" (Hylton, 1981:199).

Chan and Ericson's (1981:42) analysis came to a similar conclusion that "none of the evidence appears to support that fewer people are being imprisoned today." Their central argument is that alternative community-based programs continually add to the prison population instead of controlling or reducing it. Their arguments have been countered by McMahon (1992), who argued, after analysing the Ontario provincial offender data between the 1950s and 1980s, that admissions to the provincial system declined by approximately 31 percent and prisoner counts by 20 percent per 100,000 population. She concluded that "net-widening did not occur in Ontario during the postwar period (in Ontario): in 1961, prison plus probation admissions represented a total of 1,622 per 100,000 population; in 1984, the rate stood at 1,402" (McMahon, 1992:207-208). However, her conclusions are in the minority. An overview of numerous diversion programs in the United States by Krisberg and Austin (1980) found that the majority of the programs "widened the net," largely because most were not able to target offenders correctly.

Large increases in offender populations in the United States as well as overcrowded prisons and concern about dangerous offenders on probation during the 1980s led to the creation of intermediate criminal sanctions, the most notable development within the reintegration ideology. These sanctions are so named because they fit between incarceration and probation, thereby allowing the state to maintain surveillance over offenders in much increased numbers but at the same time at a great cost reduction.

The first—and most common—intermediate punishment to appear was **intensive supervision probation (ISP)**, which increased the community surveillance of offenders considered "too good" to be incarcerated and yet "too serious" for regular probation programs. Generally, ISP involves the close monitoring of convicted offenders by parole or probation officers. These offenders are required to follow specific conditions while on such a program, most typically:

(1) Some combination of multiple weekly contacts with a supervising officer;

(2) Random and unannounced drug testing;

(3) Stringent enforcement of probation or parole conditions;

(4) Required participation in relevant treatment programs, employment, and perhaps community service (Petersilia and Turner, 1993).

By the early 1990s, ISP programs were so popular that Camp and Camp (1993) were able to report that more than 70 percent of United States jurisdictions were using them, with a total caseload of approximately 60,000 offenders. These programs are popular because they offer many attractions to correctional officials, including diversion from prison, "getting tough" on crime, increasing control over marginal offenders and avoiding large expenditures for new prisons. However in a rigorous evaluation of 14 ISPs in nine states, Petersilia and Turner (1993:310-311) discovered that these programs did not reduce recidivism. According to the researchers, "At no site did ISP participants experience arrest less often, have a longer time to failure, or experience arrests for less serious offenses." They also found that one year after intake into the program, arrests for criminal reoffending were higher among ISP offenders (37 percent) than among the control group (33 percent). For technical violations, the average ISP violation rate was 65 percent, compared to 38 percent for the control groups. Of the 14 sites studied, 12 had violation rates above 50 percent, with four of the sites having rates in excess of 80 percent.

Based on these data, what is it possible to say about the effectiveness of ISPs as a crime reduction strategy? According to Cullen et al. (1996), the increased surveillance and control of offenders, so essential a component of ISP, appear to have little impact on offender recidivism. For example, Byrne and Pattavina (1992:296) reviewed 18 ISP programs and concluded that the "majority of ISP program evaluations do not support the notion that 'intensive' supervision significantly reduces the risk of offender recidivism." ISPs that do work have been found to include significant rehabilitation components. This finding also applies to studies investigating the success of shock incarceration (i.e., boot camp) programs as well as home confinement programs.

DETERRENCE

Deterrence is defined as "the inhibition of criminal activity by state-imposed penalties . . . it is based on the idea that punishment should be used to prevent crime" (Conklin, 1998:475). Another definition is supplied by Gibbs (1975:2), who described it as "the omission of an act as a response to the perceived risk and fear of punishment for contrary behavior." It is the oldest of all the correctional ideologies, dating back to the work of Cesare Beccaria and Jeremy Bentham in the latter stages of the eighteenth century. In the opinion of Beccaria and Bentham, the existing systems of punishment were characterized as cruel, harsh and inequitable. Both men attempted to develop policies that would reform the criminal justice system based on utilitarian principles and hedonistic psychology. They felt that the system should operate on the basis of providing the greatest good to the greatest number of people. A central component of their approach was the idea of rational actors, meaning that the majority of individuals in a society would act to maximize the benefits of their behaviour by obeying the law and minimizing the punishment. In their opinion, punishments should be severe, but only enough to counter the rewards of lawbreaking.

This model of punishment is typically divided into three different categories: (1) specific deterrence, (2) general deterrence, and (3) the marginal deterrent effect. Specific deterrence refers to the contention that those individuals who are punished for a crime will not commit that particular offence again because their tendency to commit a crime has been reduced. Offenders, through punishment, learn that the risk is greater than they originally perceived and, as a result, the rewards of their illegal behaviour are reduced, with the result that they will tend to avoid criminal behaviour in the future.

Specific deterrence traditionally has been measured by the recidivism rate of offenders released from prison. However, recidivism rates can be high for many offenders, leading to the argument that those who have been punished in the past are the most likely to reoffend (Beck and Shipley, 1989). Most of the research in the deterrence ideology has focused on two variables that are felt to determine the effectiveness of punishment—the certainty (i.e, the likelihood that an individual will be punished) and the severity of punishment.

General deterrence refers to the inhibition of the desire to become involved in criminal behaviour among the general population as a result of the punishment of offenders (Blumstein et al., 1978:3). More specifically, general deterrence holds that crime rates will be influenced and subsequently controlled by the threat of criminal punishment. As Siegel (1995:119) points out, an inverse relationship should exist between crime rates and the severity, certainty and speed of legal punishments. This means that if the punishment for a crime is increased and that if the effectiveness and efficiency of the justice system in enforcing the law is improved, the number of individuals involved in that criminal act should decline. Results of research on general deterrence have been divided on this issue. For example, Tittle and Rowe (1974) found that if the police made an arrest in 30 percent of all reported crimes, the crime significantly declined. However, more recent research by Yu and Liska (1993) found support for the general deterrence hypothesis but also concluded that it was race-specific. That is, black arrest probabilities influences black offence rates, while white arrest probabilities affect the offending patterns of whites. In addition, Zedlewski (1983) concluded that the threat of punishment works better for some types of crimes (e.g., burglary) than others (e.g., theft).

A guard stands in the hallway of a segregation unit at Kingston Penitentiary. *Canapress Photo Service (Michael Lea).*

The **marginal deterrent effect** of punishment is the extent to which crime rates respond to incremental changes in the threat of sanctions (Nagin, 1978). Large increases in the rate at which police arrest offenders would be likely to deter many offenders, whereas small increases would no doubt have little or no impact. Jacobs (1993) studied marginal deterrence by identifying the strategies used by drug dealers to reduce the risk of selling drugs to undercover police officers. He discovered that dealers filter their clientele by trying to avoid those individuals who are unfamiliar, evaluating physical appearance as well as body language, and paying attention to verbal clues such as insufficient price bartering. Any evidence of these factors deters drug dealers from selling to strangers, leading Jacobs to conclude that marginal deterrence is a regular feature of illegal drug dealing.

Does Deterrence Work?

According to deterrence theory, crime rates are inversely related to the risk of imprisonment, with crime being more usual when there is less threat of incarceration. However, as Conklin (1998:487) states, "the problem of simultaneity plagues much of this research: it is unclear if the risk of imprisonment affects crime rates, if crime rates influence the risk of imprisonment, or if both are true." Perhaps one of the clearest examples of deterrence programs are the "Scared Straight" programs in which young people visit prisons to listen to inmates serving life sentences talk about prison life and the realities of being incarcerated while their families are suffering in the outside world. These group discussions are vividly and graphically presented to the young people in the hopes that a short, two-hour program will deter them from committing crimes in the future. Original guesses estimated that this program kept in excess of 80 percent of all participants from committing another crime. However, a systematic evaluation by Finckenauer (1982) revealed that this was not the case. His research at the Rahway State Prison in New Jersey found that youths who participated in the program were arrested more often than those who had not been involved. A second evaluation reported that 85 percent of the participants continued to commit delinquent acts after their involvement in the program.

A popular contemporary approach to deterrence is **shock incarceration** (i.e., boot camps), which is patterned after the military-style discipline used in armed forces boot camps, in the hope that youths and young adults will be frightened from committing crime by exposure to harsh discipline and work activities. The typical offender is an individual who has never been incarcerated before and has been convicted only for nonviolent crimes. The average length of stay is short, with 107 days being the norm across the United States in 1993. Numerous evaluations have been made of the deterrent effect of shock incarceration, and the results have been disappointing for advocates of deterrence. Researchers have found it unlikely that shock incarceration programs actually deter participants from engaging in criminal activity in the future. In addition, these programs have actually been found to increase correctional costs by incarcerating those offenders who have traditionally been placed on probation (MacKenzie, 1993; Morash and Rucker, 1990).

A number of studies have been conducted during the past 20 years that have attempted to study whether certain offenders commit crimes after assessing the risk of getting caught and being punished. Tunnell (1992) and Shover (1996) have studied chronic property offenders in the hopes of determining the deterrent effect of punishments or the threat of sanctions. Both report that harsher penalties were unlikely to deter the offenders they studied. They feel this is because offenders rarely think they will be caught and that they expect the rewards to be significant. Tunnell and Shover also report that the offenders are not deterred by the possibility of being imprisoned, especially if they have already been incarcerated and know how to survive the prison system.

Are high-status offenders such as white-collar criminals more easily deterred? After all, one can argue they are more rational and, because they tend to have high-paying jobs, enjoy the material aspects of life. Braithwaite and Geis (1982) reviewed the literature and concluded that white-collar criminals should be more easily deterred because they have little if any commitment to crime as a significant part of their life. Clinard (1983), in his research of retired middle-level executives, found that many middle managers were concerned about the threat of government sanctions and that these sanctions acted as a major deterrent when they considered taking illegal actions. Yet, Weisburd et al. (1995) found no specific deterrent effect of incarceration over a 126-month follow-up period of white-collar offenders convicted in the federal courts. While imprisonment obviously had profound effects on their lives, it was mostly upon their personal, as opposed to their professional, lives. They reported that incarceration had no marginal deterrent effect in terms of arrest, conviction or sentence.

Many of the above studies are plagued by measurement problems. It has proved to be difficult to obtain accurate measures of key variables, such as arrest rates, incarceration rates and indicators of deterrence (Siegel, 1995:120). Critics argue that any deterrent effect may reflect some other phenomenon as opposed to the fear of punishment. For example, a reduction in the crime rate may follow an increase in the number of people incarcerated in prison. However, this may be an incapacitation effect; that is, it may mean that the fear of being incarcerated does not reduce crime, but it is taking the most serious criminals off the street and sentencing them for a long period of time that actually brings about the reduction in the crime rate.

Some criminologists argue that deterrence theory is also supported if people who perceive they will be caught and punished if they become involved in a criminal activity therefore do not participate in criminal acts. However, if perceptions of punishment have little or no effect on behaviour, then deterrence does not work (Green, 1989). Studies in this area have found that the certainty (as opposed to the severity) of punishment may have the most significant deterrent effect on behaviour. Grasmick and Bursik (1990) discovered that when people expected to be caught and punished for such crimes as theft, tax cheating and drunk driving, they were unlikely to commit these crimes in the future. Horney and Marshall (1992) decided to look at the perceived deterrence of active or known criminals and discovered that the criminals' perceptions of arrest risk were inversely related to offence participation. That is, the greater the perceived risk of apprehension, the less likely criminals would risk any criminal activity.

The research described above raises questions about the ability of the fear of the certainty of punishment to reduce criminal activity. This is largely due to the fact that many offenders reoffend after they have been punished, indicating that prior experience with the law and formal sanctions will decrease the perception of deterrence and reduce criminal activity. This is so because the severity of sanctions can vary for offenders. For example, Apospori et al. (1992) discovered that offenders who were punished with light sanctions lowered their estimates of risk in committing crimes. Those sanctioned the most severely appear to be the most likely to be deterred (Apospori and Alpert, 1993). Apospori et al. (1992) discovered that offenders who were punished lowered their estimates of the risk in committing crimes. Apospori and Alpert (1993) reported that criminals who receive the most severe punishments are most likely to be deterred.

Interest in deterrence has also included how the fear of informal sanctions (such as the humiliation of telling parents that one has been caught by the police) may have an impact on crime reduction. For example, Williams and Hawkins (1989) reported that the fear of being arrested can deter spousal abuse but that social costs (e.g., disapproval by and loss of friends) were more significant in deterring such actions than formal legal sanctions. This interest in the role of informal criminal sanctions in deterrence has made many investigators take note of the importance of embarrassment, guilt and shame. This is the key argument in John Braithwaite's book, *Crime, Shame, and Reintegration* (1989). Brathwaite makes the point that the crime rate might be reduced in the United States by utilizing shaming. He believes that shame is a powerful deterrent in many countries and cultures and that it may be a more significant way to achieve higher levels of deterrence. In Braithwaite's opinion, shame can be divided into two components. The first type involves stigmatization; it involves a continual process of degradation, thereby separating the offender from society but maintaining his or her visibility to the law-abiding segment of society in order to present a clear example of what would happen to them if they, too, broke the law. Braithwaite is more favourable toward the second type of shaming, which he calls "reintegrative shaming," a process whereby offenders are shamed but are also accepted back into the community. This process would have the victim meet the offender in a controlled environment in which the community could display its feelings of displeasure about the criminal act before deciding how best to re-accept the offender back into the community. According to Braithwaite (1995), this process shows disapproval for the action in question, followed by a showing of respect for the offender. Studies to date (e.g., Braithwaite and Mugford, 1993) have found this approach to be successful for many types of offenders. As a result, shaming programs have now started in many Western jurisdictions in the hope that offenders dealt with in this manner will be deterred from future criminal activity.

SUMMARY

At the core of the correctional enterprise lay four models of punishment: deterrence, incapacitation, rehabilitation and reintegration. These four models generally coexist with each other, as governments might find it necessary to incapacitate certain types of offenders (e.g., sexual predators) for lengthy periods of time while releasing low-risk offenders back into the community after they have served only brief amounts of time within an institution.

Deterrence remains a central form of punishment. It is hoped the pains of punishment will prevent offenders from committing crimes after they are released. However, studies related to the severity and certainty of punishment reveal that deterrence is a complex phenomenon and that people respond differently to legal sanctions. Selective incapacitation is related to deterrence in the sense that it focuses on a select group of individuals who are at high risk to reoffend in the area of violent crimes. As a result, "three strikes and you're out" laws have become popular in the hope that these high-risk offenders will stay behind bars for a longer period of time, thereby substantially reducing the crime rate.

In contrast to deterrence and selective incapacitation are the reintegration and rehabilitation models of punishment. Reintegration is the dominant ideology in use today in Canada, as the government searches for ways to lower costs within the correctional system. The emphasis in reintegration is upon placing low-risk offenders into the community prior to the end of their sentences so authorities can assist offenders in their efforts to reintegrate into society as law-abiding citizens. Rehabilitation attempts to isolate the various factors correlated with the criminal actions of offenders and, ultimately, to assist these individuals in improving their skills in these areas. This approach emphasizes the social learning approach, which allows correctional authorities to teach offenders the requisite skills necessary to live crime-free lives.

DISCUSSION QUESTIONS

1. Can we make deterrence more successful? How?

2. Do you think "three strikes and you're out" laws really work? What do you think of the way in which California has used these laws? What do you think the impact on the criminal justice system has been?

3. Why do you think the doctrine reaffirming rehabilitation is becoming more popular?

4. Do you think there is too much emphasis on the reintegration model today? Do you think it has flaws? If so, what are they?

5. What correctional ideology do you think should be the primary model to guide the Canadian correctional system today? Why?

REFERENCES

Allen, Harry E. and Clifford E. Simonsen (1998). *Corrections in America*, Eighth Edition. Upper Saddle River, NJ: Prentice-Hall.

Andrews, D.A. (1994). "An Overview of Treatment Effectiveness: Research and Clinical Principles." Unpublished paper, Carleton University.

Andrews, D.A. (1989). "Recidivism is Predictable and Can be Influenced: Using Risk Assessments to Reduce Recidivism." *Forum on Corrections Research,* Volume 1, 11-18.

Andrews, D. A. and James Bonta (1998). *The Psychology of Criminal Conduct*, Second Edition. Cincinnat: Anderson.

Andrews, D.A., Ivan Zinger, Robert D. Hoge, James Bonta, Paul Gendreau and Francis T. Cullen (1990). "Does Correctional Treatment Work? A Clinically Relevant and Psychologically Informed Meta-Analysis." *Criminology*, Volume 28, 369-404.

Aspospori, Eleni and Geoffrey Alpert (1993). "Research Note: The Role of Differential Experience with the Criminal Justice System in Changes in Perceptions of Severity of Legal Sanctions Over Time." *Crime & Delinquency*, Volume 39, 184-194.

Aspospori, Eleni, Geoffrey Alpert and Raymond Paternoster (1992). "The Effect of Involvement with the Criminal Justice System: A Neglected Dimension of the Relationship Between Experience and Perceptions." *Justice Quarterly*, Volume 9, 379-392.

Austin, James and Barry Krisberg (1982). "The Unmet Alternatives to Incarceration." *Crime & Delinquency*, Volume 28, 374-409.

Beck, Allen J. and Bernard E. Shipley (1989). *Recidivism of Prisoners Released in 1983.* Washington, DC: Bureau of Justice Statistics.

Bernard, Thomas J. and R. Richard Ritti (1991). "The Philadelphia Birth Cohort and Selective Incapacitation." *Journal of Research in Crime and Delinquency,* Volume 28, 33-54.

Blumstein, Alfred, Jacqueline Cohen and David P. Farrington (1988). "Criminal Career Research: Its Value for Criminology." *Criminology,* Volume 26, 1-35.

Blumstein, Alfred, Jacqueline Cohen and Daniel Nagin (1978). *Deterrence and Incapacitation: Estimating the Effects of Criminal Sanctions on Crime Rates.* Washington, DC: National Academy of Sciences.

Bonta, James (199). "Antisocial Attitudes and Recidivism." Paper presented at the Annual Convention of the Canadian Psychological Association, Ottawa, Canada.

Braithwaite, John (1995). "Reintegrative Shaming, Republicanism, and Policy." In Hugh Barlow (ed.), *Crime and Public Policy.* Boulder, CO: Westview.

Braithwaite, John (1989). *Crime, Shame, and Reintegration.* Cambridge, England: Cambridge University Press.

Braithwaite, John and Gil Geis (1982). "On Theory and Action for Corporate Crime Control." *Crime & Delinquency,* Volume 28, 292-314.

Braithwaite, John and Stephen Mugford (1993). "Conditions of Successful Reintegration Ceremonies: Dealing with Juvenile Offenders." *British Journal of Criminology,* Volume 34, 139-171.

Byrne, James M. and April Pattavina (1992). "The Effectiveness Issue: Assessing What Works in the Adult Community Corrections System." In James M. Byrne, Arthur J. Lurigio and Joan Petersilia (eds.), *Smart Sentencing: The Emergence of Intermediate Sanctions.* Newbury Park, CA: Sage.

Camp, George M. and Camille Graham Camp (1995). *The Corrections Yearbook 1995: Probation and Parole.* South Salem, NY: Criminal Justice Institute.

Camp, George M. and Camille Graham Camp (1993). *The Corrections Yearbook: Probation and Parole.* South Salem, NY: Criminal Justice Institute.

Chaiken, Marcia R. and Jan M. Chaiken (1991). *Priority Prosecution of High-Rate Dangerous Offenders.* Washington, DC: U.S. Department of Justice.

Chaiken, Marcia R. and Jan M. Chaiken (1982). *Varieties of Criminal Behavior.* Santa Monica, CA: RAND.

Chan, Janet and Richard V. Ericson (1981). *Decarceration and the Economy of Penal Reform.* Toronto: University of Toronto Press.

Clark, John, James Austin and D. Alan Henry (1997). "'Three Strikes and You're Out': A Review of State Legislation." *NIJ Research in Brief.*

Clear, Todd R. (1994). *Harm in American Penology: Offenders, Victims, and Their Communities.* Albany, NY: State University of New York Press.

Clinard, Marshall (1983). *Corporate Ethics and Crime: The Role of Middle Managers.* Beverly Hills, CA: Sage.

Cohen, Mark A. (1988). "Some New Evidence on the Seriousness of Crime." *Criminology,* Volume 26, 343-353.

Conklin, John E. (1998). *Criminology*, Sixth Edition. Needham Heights, MA: Allyn & Bacon.

Cullen, Francis T. and Brandon K. Applegate (1997). "Introduction." In F.T. Cullen and B.K. Applegate, *Offender Rehabilitation*. Aldershot, UK: Ashgate.

Cullen, Francis T. and Karen E. Gilbert (1982). *Reaffirming Rehabilitation*. Cincinnati: Anderson.

Cullen, Francis T., John P. Wright and Brandon Applegate (1996). "Control in the Community: The Limits of Reform." In Alan J. Hartland (ed.), *Choosing Correctional Options that Work: Defining the Demand and Evaluating the Supply*. Thousand Oaks, CA: Sage.

Evans, Sandra S. and Joseph E. Scott (1984). "The Seriousness of Crime: The Impact of Religiosity." *Criminology*, Volume 22, 39-59.

Finckenauer, James O. (1982) *Scared Straight! and the Panacea Phenomena*. Englewood Cliffs, NJ: Prentice-Hall.

Fowler, Glenn (1981). "More 'Career Criminals' Convicted in State Effort." *New York Times*, January 8, B7.

Frase, Richard (1997). "Sentencing Principles in Theory and Practice." In M. Tonry (ed.) *Crime and Justice: A Review of Research*, Volume 22. Chicago: The University of Chicago Press.

Gendreau, Paul and Claire Goggin (1996). "Principles of Effective Correctional Programming." *Forum on Corrections Research*, Volume 8, 38-41.

Gendreau, Paul and Bob Ross (1987) "Effective Correctional Treatment: Bibliotherapy for Cynics." *Crime & Delinquency*, Volume 25, 463-489.

Gibbs, Jack (1975). *Crime, Punishment, and Deterrence*. New York: Elsevier.

Gottfredson, Michael R. (1979) "Treatment Destruction Techniques." *Journal of Research in Crime & Delinquency*, Volume 16, 39-54.

Grasmick, Harold and Robert Bursik (1990). "Conscience, Significant Others and Rational Choice: Extending the Deterrence Model." *Law and Society Review*, Volume 24, 837-861.

Green, Donald (1989). "Past Behavior as a Measure of Actual Future Behavior: An Unresolved Issue in Perceptual Deterrence Research." *Journal of Criminal Law and Criminology*, Volume 80, 781-804.

Greenwood, Peter W. (1984). "Selective Incapacitation: A Method of Using Our Courts More Effectively." *NIJ Reports*, 4-7.

Greenwood, Peter W. with Alan Abrahamese (1982). *Selective Incapacitation*. Santa Monica, CA: RAND.

Greenwood, Peter W., K.E. Model, C.P. Rydell and J. Chisea (1996). *Diverting Children From a Life of Crime: Measuring Costs and Benefits*. Santa Monica, CA: RAND.

Horney, Julie and Ineke Haen Marshall (1992). "Risk Perceptions Among Serious Offenders: The Role of Crime and Punishment." *Criminology*, Volume 30, 575-594.

Hylton, John H. (1981). "Community Corrections and Social Control: The Case of Saskatchewan, Canada." *Contemporary Crises*, Volume 5, 193-215.

Jacobs, Bruce A. (1993). "Undercover Deception Clues: A Case of Restrictive Deterrence." *Criminology,* Volume 31, 281-299.

Jones, Peter R. and John S. Goldkamp (1993). "Implementing Pre-trial Drug Testing Programs at Two Experimental Sites: Some Deterrence and Jail-Bed Implications." *The Prison Journal,* Volume 73, 199-219.

Langer, Sidney (1979). *The Rahway State Prison Lifer's Group: A Critical Analysis.* Union NJ: Kean College Department of Sociology.

Latessa, Edward J. and Harry E. Allen (1997). *Corrections in the Community.* Cincinnati: Anderson.

Lipsey, Mark W. (1991). *Juvenile Delinquency: A Meta Analytic Inquiry into the Visibility of Effects.* New York: Russell Sage.

Lipsey, Mark W. and David B. Wilson (1997). *Effective Intervention for Serious Juvenile Offenders.* Washington, DC: OJJDP Study Group on Serious and Violent Juvenile Offenders.

Losel, Frederich (1996). "Effective Correctional Programming: What Empirical Research Tells Us and What It Doesn't." *Forum on Corrections Research,* Volume 8, 33-37.

MacKenzie, Doris Layton (1993). "Boot Camp Prisons in 1993." *National Institute of Justice Journal,* 21-28.

Martinson, Robert (1974) "What Works?—Questions and Answers About Prison Reform." *The Public Interest.* Volume 35, 22-54.

McCarthy, Belinda R. and Bernard J. McCarthy (1984). *Community Based Corrections.* Pacific Grove, CA: Brooks /Cole.

McMahon, Maeve W. (1992). *The Persistent Prison? Rethinking Decarceration and Penal Reform.* Toronto: University of Toronto Press.

Miethe, Terance and Charles A. Moore (1989). *Sentencing Guidelines: Their Effect in Minnesota.* Washington, DC: U.S. Department of Justice.

Miranne, Alfred C. and Michael R. Geerken (1991). "The New Orleans Inmate Survey: A Test of Greenwood's Predictive Scale." *Criminology,* Volume 29, 497-518.

Morash, Merry and Lila Rucker (1990). "A Critical Look at the Idea of Boot Camp as a Correctional Reform." *Crime & Delinquency,* Volume 36, 204-222.

Nagin, Daniel (1978). "Crime Rates, Sanction Levels, and Constraints on the Prison Population." *Law and Society Review,* Volume 12, 341-366.

National Advisory Commission on Criminal Justice Standards and Goals (1973). *Corrections.* Washington, DC: U.S. Government Printing Office.

Palmer, Ted (1994). *A Profile of Correctional Effectiveness and New Directions for Research.* Albany, NY: State University of New York Press.

Palmer, Ted (1991). "The Effectiveness of Intervention: Recent Trends and Current Issues." *Crime & Delinquency,* Volume 37, 330-346.

Petersen, Mark A. and Harriet Braiker with Suzanne M. Polich (1981). *Who Commits Crimes: A Survey of Prison Inmates.* Boston: Oelgeschalager, Gunn and Hain.

Petersilia, Joan (1997). "Probation in the United States." In Michael Tonry (ed.), *Crime and Justice: A Review of Research,* Volume 22. Chicago: The University of Chicago Press.

Petersilia, Joan (1992). "California's Prison Policy: Causes, Costs, and Consequences." *Prison Journal*, Volume 72, 8-36.

Petersilia, Joan and Susan Turner (1993). "Intensive Probation and Parole." In Michael Tonry (ed.) *Crime and Justice: A Review of Research*, Volume 17. Chicago: University of Chicago Press.

Pfohl, Steven J. (1985) *Images of Deviance and Social Control: A Sociological History*. New York: McGraw-Hill.

Schwartz, Martin and Lawrence F. Travis III (1997). *Corrections: An Issues Approach*, Fourth Edition. Cincinnati: Anderson.

Shields, I.W. and M. Ball (1990). "Neutralization in a Population of Incarcerated Young Offenders." Paper presented at the Annual Meeting of the Canadian Psychological Association, Ottawa, Ontario.

Shover, Neal (1996). *Great Pretenders: Pursuits and Careers of Persistent Thieves*. Boulder, CO: Westview.

Siegel, Larry L. (1995). *Criminology: Theories, Patterns and Typologies*, Fifth Edition. St. Paul, MN: West.

Spelman, W. (1994). *Criminal Incapacitation*. New York: Plenum.

Tittle, Charles and Allan R. Rowe (1974). "Certainty of Arrest and Crime Rates : A Further Test of the Deterrence Hypothesis." *Social Forces*, Volume 52, 455-462.

Tunnell, Kenneth (1992). *Choosing Crime: The Criminal Calculus of Property Offenders*. Chicago: Nelson-Hall.

van Dine, Steve, John P. Conrad and Simon Dinitz (1979). "The Incapacitation of the Chronic Thug." *Journal of Criminal Law and Criminology*, Volume 70, 125-135.

Visher, Christy A. (1987). "Incapacitation and Crime Control: Does a 'Lock 'Em Up' Strategy Reduce Crime?" *Justice Quarterly*, Volume 4, 513-544.

Visher, Christy A. (1986). "The RAND Inmate Survey: A Reanalysis." In Alfred Blumstein et al., (eds.) *Criminal Careers and "Career Criminals,"* Volume 2. Washington, DC: National Academy Press.

von Hirsch, Andrew (1985). *Past or Future Crimes: Deservedness and Dangerousness in the Sentencing of Criminals*. New Brunswick, NJ: Rutgers University Press.

Weisburd, David , Erin Waring and Ellen Chayet (1995). "Specific Deterrence in a Sample of Offenders Convicted of White-Collar Crimes." *Criminology*, Volume 27, 163-181.

Williams, Kirk and Richard Hawkins (1989). "The Meaning of Arrest for Wife Assault." *Criminology*, Volume 27, 163-181.

Wilson, James Q. (1983). *Thinking About Crime*, Revised Edition. New York: Basic Books.

Yu, Jiang and Alan Liska (1993). "The Certainty of Punishment: A Reference Group Effect and Its Functional Form." *Criminology*, Volume 31, 447-464.

Zedlewski, Edwin (1983). "Deterrence Findings and Data Sources: A Comparison of the Uniform Crime Rates and the National Crime Surveys." *Journal of Research in Crime and Delinquency*, Volume 20, 262-276.

CHAPTER 3

The History of the Penitentiary and Correctional Ideologies in Canada

THE PENITENTIARY

It is accepted among most historians that the **penitentiary** was created by humanitarian reformers for two reasons: (1) to protect offenders from moral contamination, and (2) to restore them to the proper way of living by improving their character. These reformers were part of the period of Western history referred to as the Enlightenment. They considered the penitentiary as a grand and noble experiment, as an alternative to existing systems that inflicted great physical pains upon offenders. Contemporary prisons, they argued, should represent a different system that would limit the pains of incarceration so that offenders would return to society reformed, that is, ready to integrate into society as law-abiding citizens. In reality, Western correctional systems practised punishments that gradually became more psychologically brutal, a far cry from those correctional systems that reformers envisioned as fair, just and beneficial to both inmates and society. Correctional facilities of every type are now so common that their existence is considered to be a foregone conclusion and their place in our criminal justice system unquestioned.

KEY TERMS

Archambault Commission	false negatives	penitentiary
	false positives	reform era
Auburn system		rehabilitation era
Brown Commission	Fauteux Report	reintegration era
congregate system	Great Law	separate system
doctrine of free will	Kingston Penitentiary	utilitarianism
doctrine of the social contract	Ouimet Report	
	panopticon	

THE PRISON AND ENLIGHTENMENT

Prisons in the Western world did not exist as we know them today until the late eighteenth and early nineteenth centuries. To the leading thinkers of the Enlightenment, the doctrine of the social contract and the doctrine of free will were the essential ingredients of this new way of thinking. In general, reason and experience replaced faith and superstition as the basis of the new society.

The **doctrine of the social contract** was based on the idea that society was held together by a bond between citizens and government. To achieve this contract, governmental authority had to protect all citizens but, at the same time, citizens had to relinquish some degree of their individuality in order for the government to create, administer and enforce laws in the name of the common interest. The government would protect the natural liberties and rights of individual citizens through the "rule of law."

The **doctrine of free will** was based on the idea that all humans rationally and freely choose to engage in the social contract. This perspective, referred to as **utilitarianism,** held that those who challenged the social contract in reality broke its laws and must be punished for their actions. The best known statement of this approach to punishment is found in Cesare Beccaria's *On Crimes and Punishments* (1765). Beccaria (1738-1794) recommended that punishment "fit" the crime and that it be prompt and certain and should contain a certain amount of deterrence. Beccaria's major recommendations have been summarized by Beirne and Messerschmidt (1995:336):

(a) The right of governments to punish offenders derives from a contractual obligation among its citizens not to pursue their self-interest at the expense of others.

(b) Punishment must be constituted by uniform and enlightened legislation.

(c) Imprisonment must replace torture and capital punishment as the standard form of punishment.

(d) Punishment must fit the crime. It must be prompt and certain, and its duration must reflect only the gravity of the offence and the social harm it caused.

Another prominent figure during the Enlightenment was Jeremy Bentham (1748-1832). It was Bentham who invented the idea of an Inspection House, the facility that was the forerunner of the prison. He envisioned the prison as a type of **panopticon,** a Greek word that means "all-seeing," an institution where offenders would be placed and given the time to contemplate their criminal actions and how they would become stalwart citizens in the future. In the introduction to his book, *Panopticon* (1787), Bentham wrote that he foresaw the role of the panopticon as disciplining all those individuals who broke the law. The explicit purpose of the panopticon was "to punish the incorrigible, guard the insane, reform the vicious, confine suspects, employ the idle, maintain the helpless, cure the sick, and offer training in any branch of industry and education" (Beirne and Messerschmidt, 1995:338). Bentham believed that the panopticon was to become the permanent institution within the criminal justice system for these lawbreakers, replacing the many temporary facilities that existed at the time. It was his hope that anyone sent to the panopticon would reform their morals and, upon their release, be a model, law-abiding citizen. Despite initial interest in his ideas, Bentham's panopticon was never built in England or Western Europe, and the two that were built in the United States during the nineteenth century were deemed impractical and soon abandoned. In place of the panopticon, short-term facilities were built that were largely designed to hold small numbers of accused persons until their trials. If convicted, most individuals were sent to workhouses and other similar, nonsecure facilities with little, if any, reforming capabilities.

Competing or alternative ideas about prisons and their role as a permanent institution in the criminal justice system did not resurface until the Restoration (1814-1830). During this brief period, it was widely recognized that existing facilities housing offenders and suspects of criminal activity were inadequate. In particular, there were concerns that they were failing in their ability to control the "dangerous classes." The term "dangerous classes," as Beirne and Messerschmidt (1995:341) point out, was a derogatory term used by some law-abiding citizens to refer to the working class, the unemployed and the unemployable, who were all viewed as a major threat to law and order. Criminals were thought to be a large component of the dangerous classes and largely uncontrollable through the use of the then-existing correctional facilities. Beirne (1987) documents how the very institutions built as houses of corrections failed to control the criminal activities of the dangerous classes for three reasons. The first reason was the continuing and increasing presence of large numbers of the poor, the unemployed and the criminal in the cities. For many of these individuals, the main source of income was robbery. Second, the continuing existence of these so-called "dangerous classes" resulted in great fear about crime among citizens. Moral panics over criminal activities consistently broke out and, as a result, the fear about crime escalated. The third reason involved continuing increases in the official crime rate, an issue that alarmed the public and fuelled their concern over crime and what should be done about it. A common statement was that many of the offenders were, in fact, recidivists. This led to claims that the institutions used to incarcerate offenders were, in fact, failing in their stated goal of reforming criminals. By 1820 "it was already understood that the prisons, far from transforming criminals into citizens, serve only to manufacture new criminals and drive existing criminals even deeper into criminality" (Foucault, 1980:40).

A significant factor in the early development of the penitentiary was the growth of capitalism. In the eighteenth century there was no need for an elaborate correctional system, for in its place was a policy of transportation whereby offenders were transported to a colony that needed laborers. This approach to dispensing with criminals was eroded after the American Revolution. The result was that offenders had to be dealt with locally. It was at this point that the concept of the "modern" penitentiary emerged, an institution "created to tighten and extend control over the laboring poor" and hopefully reform them into hardworking and productive laborers (Dobash, 1983:7). As Johnson (1996) points out, the penitentiary emerged as a major institution of punishment in large part because there were no other cheap alternatives.

Penitentiaries gained a strong foothold in the institutional fabric of Western societies during the mid-nineteenth century, at the same time the factory "was also beginning to use rigorous procedures to bring an unprecedented discipline to workers lives. . . . Both organizations were among the first to try to take people from casual routines to rigid ones" (Rothman, 1971:107). Factory owners required a large labor pool that was disciplined; the penitentiary had the ability to produce large numbers of such individuals. The relationship between these two institutions was close, as the type of reformation techniques used in the penitentiary "mimicked the discipline necessary for the factory system" by "instilling the virtues of bourgeois rationality into those segments of the population least amenable to them" (Scull, 1977:26). This idea is reinforced by Foucault (1977), who wrote that imprisonment during the mid-nineteenth century represented a system of power and dominance over the dangerous classes. However, this power was not derived from direct force but rather from regulation, surveillance and discipline. Then, for Foucault, the rise of the penitentiary was not the result of reformist zeal but rather a way to organize and train people into "normalcy." These ideas are echoed in large part by Melossi and Pavarini (1981), who note that the prison emerged as a central institution of the capitalist economic system. As the number of factories increased, the penitentiary was able to supply them with employable, disciplined workers. Accordingly, the prison "has as its basic aim education in discipline and obedience" and is "like a factory producing proletarians not commodities" (Melossi and Pavarini, 1981:95, 145).

By all accounts, a significant transformation in correctional facilities and ideologies occurred between the end of the eighteenth century until the middle of the nineteenth century in Western European nations and North America. According to Cohen (1985:13), there were four significant changes during this time period. First, the state became more involved in controlling crime and criminals. This eventually led to the creation of centralized, rationalized and bureaucratic apparatuses designed to control crime and punish criminals as well as to cure and reform those who were incarcerated. Second, it was realized that not all criminals were the same; this led to the differentiation and classification of criminals into separate groups and types. Based upon a variety of psychological criteria, three general categories of offenders were created: high-risk, medium-risk and low-risk. Third, offenders were increasingly placed into institutions, be they prisons, mental health facilities or other types of closed institutions. In terms of holding criminals and attempting to change their behavior, the prison emerged as the favorite type of facility. Finally, the mind replaced the body as the object of penal repression. Efforts were made to reform individuals through a variety of techniques, including rules that forbade talking among inmates, the extensive use of solitary confinement and the liberal use of physical punishments such as whipping (which was also thought to have redeeming features for the reformation of the inmates' minds).

THE EARLY HISTORY OF PRISONS IN NORTH AMERICA

The early history of prisons in North America followed many of the principles laid out by the early social contract reformers. Offenders were viewed as possessing the freedom to choose between right and wrong. For those individuals who broke the law primarily due to their confused morality, the reformist approach attempted to teach them the "proper" morality, that is, how to live as a law-abiding citizen. This involved removing the offender from society and "teaching" him or her new values through a disciplinary system "that would promote a model of 'the good life' within the prison" (Clear, 1994:79). This was to be accomplished through a regime of discipline, because reformers were not as concerned with the quality of

The state penitentiary at Auburn, New York, was the forerunner of the congregate system of prison organization. *Gleason's Pictorial Drawing Room Companion/Corbis.*

prison life as they were in producing "the right thinking citizen ready for work" (Hudson, 1987:5). This is best represented by ticket-of-leave policies (later known as parole) that allowed inmates to be released when they "earned" their freedom by demonstrating their intent to live a law-abiding livelihood. This era was based largely on the ability of the prison to "harm" the offender by making the conditions psychologically painful.

The first significant efforts that brought about the **reform era** occurred in the United States. William Penn, the head of the Quakers and founder of the state of Pennsylvania in 1681, introduced the Great Law of the Quakers into the area of punishment. The **Great Law** was more humanitarian compared to other laws of the day, stipulating that hard labour be an effective punishment for serious crimes and that capital punishment be abolished (with the exception of for premeditated murder). Significantly, it was under this law that a correctional facility, where hard punishment was the norm, was first built. The Great Law was in force between 1682 and 1718. It was replaced by the English Anglican Code, which prescribed capital punishment as well as mutilation, branding and an assortment of other corporal punishments (Allen and Simonsen, 1998). In 1790, the first correctional facility for long-term offenders (which became the basis of the modern prison system) was built in the United States. With the recent success of the War of Independence, the Quakers once again focused upon the treatment of convicted offenders (Barnes and Teeters, 1959). They were able to use their influence with the Pensylvania State Legislature to declare one wing of the Walnut Street Jail in Philadelphia as a facility to house long-term inmates with the exception of those sentenced to death. This was the first time that a prison (or, really, a part of a prexisting prison) was used exclusively for the correction of long-term offenders (Taft, 1956).

The Walnut Street Jail originally operated on many of the practises established one century earlier by the Great Law. Although these were not practised when the English Anglican Code was in force, they once again became the basis of the correctional system after the War of Independence. Some of these practises were: (1) all prisoners were to be bailable; (2) prisons were to be free as to fees, food and lodging; and (3) all countries were to provide houses to replace the pillory, stocks, and the like (Barnes and Teeters, 1959:158).

The fundamental core of this approach was solitary confinement without work because it was believed that this practice would lead to more inmates being reformed. Offenders were to reflect on their actions and then repent for their sins once they had decided they were reformed. As the negative effects of the approach became apparent, the Quakers introduced moral and religious instruction and made the inmates work for eight to 10 hours a day.

By the end of the 1820s, numerous problems, including overcrowding, lack of funding, idleness and vice, led to a concern that this form of punishment was largely a failure. The first prisons built in the United States reflected two different models of how prisons should operate. Certain similarities existed between them—isolation, silence, obedience and the need for some type of reformation on the part of the offender, yet there were significant differences between them that enabled them to become competing models for prison design and operation during the nineteenth century. The first system, the **separate system**, was an outgrowth of the Walnut Street Jail. It emphasized solitary confinement, manual inmate labour in the cells and the separation of inmates not only from the outside world but also from each other. This penal system was, as Johnson (1996:38) describes it, "a complete and austere system of moral quarantine . . . the aim of punishment was penance resulting in purity and personal reform." The problem with this system was that it was expensive to operate. While the cost of operating it was relatively low, in that only a small staff was required, a policy of solitary confinement was interpreted as requiring large (and therefore expensive) cells. In terms of product output from the inmates, it is best described as much industry but little profit (Conley, 1980:257). This system employed a unique architectural design. Rows of cells were built extending from a central hub, with each inmate being assigned a single cell with an attached exercise yard. Inmates were blindfolded when moved to and from their cells and were not allowed to come into contact with any of the other prisoners. Prisoners were not assembled, not even for religious services; instead, religious leaders stood in the central area while inmates remained in their cells.

The alternative system is referred to as the silent system, **congregate system** or, most typically, the **Auburn system**. Like the separate system, it required solitary confinement of offenders, but only at night. Penance of the inmates was the object of this system as well, but instead of requiring the inmates to contemplate their crimes and future in Christian terms, it favoured a system that enforced an "alteration of habit, of character-in-action . . ." Inmates were allowed to congregate for meals and while working; however, they were not allowed to talk, following a policy of "no communication and hence no contamination" (Johnson, 1996:39-40). When being moved around the prison, inmates were required to walk in lockstep, all the while having to look down at the floor. A unique aspect of the Auburn system was its architectural design, which utilized tiers. Each wing of cells was built on top of another wing of cells, a design that was called a tier system. Regimentation was the key aspect of this system:

> With daybreak, a bell gives the sign of rising; the jailors open
> the doors. The prisoners range themselves in a line, under the
> command of their respective jailors, and go first into the yard,
> where they wash their hands and faces, and from thence into
> the workshops, where they go directly to work. Their labor is
> not interrupted until the hour of raking food. There is not a
> single instant given to recreation . . . In the evening, at the set-
> ting of the sun, labor ceases, and the convicts leave the work-
> shops to retire into their cells (Beaumont and de Tocqueville,
> 1964:65-66).

The merits of each system were hotly debated among reformers, citizens and government officials. Which system would bring about the
greatest change in inmates? Even more fundamentally, could either system change a person from a lawbreaker to a law-abiding citizen? A central component of this debate revolved around the issue of economic
self-reliance. Earlier correctional institutions were characterized in part
by high costs, and this issue was of great concern to reformers. It was
deemed that economic inefficiency stemmed from two factors, "the high
cost of supervision and the non-productiveness of institutional labour"
(Melossi and Pavarini, 1981:125). The separate system attempted to
reduce administrative costs (it did), while the congregate system attempted to increase the productivity of inmate labor. Neither system brought
about the hoped for savings, but the Auburn system proved to be less
costly. Supporters of the separate system argued that the complete separation of inmates allowed them to reform on an individual basis. In their
opinion, the congregate system was problematic because it allowed
inmates to come into physical contact with each other, had too many
rules, most of which led to harsh punishment if broken. Advocates of the
Auburn system criticized the separate system on the basis of higher costs,
lack of vocational training, and the fact that it did not contribute any
money toward its operation. The Auburn approach ultimately became
the template of penitentiaries in North America because it was slightly
cheaper and because it provided a better model of what law-abiding citizens thought inmates ought to be doing while incarcerated.

THE EARLY DEVELOPMENT OF THE PENITENTIARY
IN CANADA (1835-1935)

Canada's first penitentiaries were built by provincial authorities. The
first penitentiary was located in Kingston, Ontario, and was completed
in 1835. The New Brunswick Penitentiary was built in St. John and
accepted its first inmates in 1841, while Nova Scotia opened its Provin-

cial Penitentiary in Halifax in 1844. The largest of these correctional facilities was the **Kingston Penitentiary**. It contained approximately 150 cells, with each approximately eight feet long, seven feet high and 30 inches wide. Each cell contained a bed hinged to the cell wall and a bucket that served as a toilet. These spartan conditions were accompanied by a system of harsh discipline.

All these facilities were modelled on the Auburn system, reflecting "the most up-to-date thinking in penology and . . . philosophy of reform" (Carrigan, 1991:327). Discipline, order and authority were mainstays in this approach to reforming offenders. Prison guards were trained to strictly enforce all rules and inmates were not allowed to "exchange looks, winks, laugh, nod, gesticulate to each other" (Beattie, 1977:121). These rules were to be strictly enforced by guards, who were informed that the reform of inmates was based "on the absolute prevention of intercourse among the Convicts" (Beattie, 1977:118). Any infraction of the rules was to be punished by whipping; guards were allowed to administer anywhere from six to 12 lashings to those inmates who broke the rules. Inmates could also be placed in solitary confinement, where they lived on bread and water.

This approach to reforming inmates led to serious problems for provincial officials within a very short time. There were so many rules and regulations that prisoners were constantly being punished for infractions. During 1846, 14 inmates in Kingston were whipped at least 20 times, with one inmate being whipped 60 times. The number of inmates punished increased dramatically each year. Carrigan (1991:330) reports that there were 770 punishments handed out during 1843; 2,102 during 1845; 3,445 during 1846; and 6,063 during 1847.

Questions about the ability of this approach to "reform" inmates arose throughout the 1840s. In particular, concerns were raised about the ability of the threat and use of harsh punishments to deter inmates from committing crimes once released. High recidivism rates, which hovered around 25 percent annually, were thought to be indications that such punishments were failing in their intended effects. Great concerns were directed toward these reports. Beattie (1977:30) points out that the Kingston Penitentiary was an institution constructed as "the key to social order and social discipline," but these reports seemed to indicate it was "contributing to social disorder. . . ." Efforts were then made to study and analyse the extent of the problems and then to make efforts to introduce the necessary changes to make it an effective place for reform.

In 1848, a Royal Commission of Inquiry into the conditions at the Kingston Penitentiary was created. The chairperson was George Brown, editor of the influential Toronto newspaper, *The Globe*, which had published many articles about the poor conditions at the provincial facility. Brown and the other five commissioners were given the mandate of investigating the charges of "mismanagement, theft, cruelty, conspiracy to defraud the government and starving the convicts" (Shoom, 1972-73:260). The commissioners discovered that these charges were true, finding numerous examples of mismanagement. In their report they substantiated the reports that punishments were used excessively, much to the detriment of reform. The **Brown Commission** submitted two reports, with the first one (released in 1848) describing the general conditions at Kingston Penitentiary. This led to the removal of the warden and to changes in the internal operations of the prison. The second report, released in 1849, made recommendations for improving the conditions and treatment of inmates. The recommendation was that while the Auburn system should be maintained, the separate system should be introduced so that all new inmates would be segregated for six months. During these months, they would receive instruction and counselling, and be given work to start their reformation as early as possible. Overall, the Brown Commission favoured "moral persuasion" over physical punishment. To achieve this, it was proposed that an improved classification system of inmates be introduced, moral and secular instruction be introduced along with better job training, and that punishment be administered fairly and uniformly (Carrigan, 1991). Although their suggestions appeared to recommend sweeping changes in operation at Kingston, the Brown Commission did not necessarily represent a fundamental change in penal philosophy. Baehre (1977:206-207) notes that neither whipping nor prison labor was eliminated, and as a result "did little to change the existing principles of discipline as carried out in Kingston except to make the system run more smoothly in the years to come."

The impact of the Brown Commission is best seen through the plethora of legislation passed by the Ontario provincial government during the following 18 years. The first piece of legislation, the Penitentiary Act of 1851, allowed for the building of the cells that would hold new inmates during their period of solitary confinement and established the policy that governed the use of punishment. The Prison Inspection Act (1857) and subsequent legislation passed in 1859 created a Board of Inspectors for Asylums and Prisons. As Carrigan (1991) summarizes, this approach still did not lead to the reform of inmates. Conditions continued to be poor, punishments harsh, and interaction nonexistent. In this context they were supposed to change their behaviour and become law-abiding citizens. In addition, few, if any, reformative programs were offered. At the time "when reform was seen in moral and religious terms, very little of what went on in prison might be construed as values or character building" (Carrigan, 1991:335).

One year after Confederation, Parliament enacted the Act Respecting Penitentiaries and the Directors Thereof. This legislation placed all three existing provincial penitentiaries under federal authority, with the newly created Department of Justice being given the power to administer them. Over the next 12 years, the federal government undertook a building program that saw the construction of four new federal facilities. These were largely built to replace the overused and poorly managed provincial facilities as well as to incarcerate the growing number of individuals convicted of committing crimes. In 1873, the St. Vincent de Paul Penitentiary (located near Montreal) was opened, followed four years later by the Manitoba Penitentiary (later known as Stoney Mountain Penitentiary), just north of Winnipeg. The British Columbia Penitentiary (located in New Westminster) opened in 1878, and Dorchester Penitentiary (located in Dorchester, New Brunswick), which replaced the two penitentiaries in St. John and Halifax, opened in 1880.

The first chairperson of the Board of Directors of Federal Penitentiaries (1867-1869) was James Moir Ferres. Characterized as in "the forefront of reform-minded officials" at the time, he cancelled all punishments, allowed inmates to sing during church services and write their own letters, and reduced the number of infractions which led to the use of corporal punishment" (Carrigan, 1991:347). Perhaps the most influential figure in the federal system was James G. Moylan, who was appointed Inspector of Penitentiaries for Canada in 1875, a position held until 1895. He was an avid supporter for prison reform, and believed that "the cardinal object to be effected in our penal institutions is the reformation of the criminal. This is above and beyond every consideration" (Carrigan, 1991:347).

Despite his support of the reform ideology, during the 20 years of his tenure there were only a few improvements in the federal penitentiaries. Moylan continued to be a supporter of reducing the number of punishments as well as a supporter of the Auburn model. As Jackson (1983) notes, Moylan was an avid supporter of using solitary confinement for all new inmates for a period of eight to nine months and those who persistently disobeyed the infractions for at least 18 months. It was his belief that such treatment was an advancement over using whipping as a punishment. This was based largely on the information he received from European prison administrators who maintained that solitary confinement was responsible for lower recidivism rates. As a result of his efforts, a new cell block was built at Kingston that ultimately became the home for "third term men, incorrigibles, and prisoners who had been sentenced for unnatural offences" (Jackson, 1983:36). The new wing contained 108 cells that were slightly larger than those that housed the other prisoners. They were 13 feet long, nine feet wide and 10 feet high, with the larger area designed for inmates not only to live but also to work in their cells. The new cell block was completed in 1894, and three years later it was hailed as a success in the treatment of those inmates sent there. In 1897, the Inspector of Prisons reported that it "has fully demonstrated (its) superiority . . . as regards to the treatment of incorrigibles and criminal crooks" (Jackson, 1983:38-39). Throughout the 1890s, discipline and hard work continued to be the guiding principles for federal corrections. Ekstedt and Griffiths (1988:44) note that the Penitentiary Branch Report of 1895 criticized prison officials for allowing inmates to pursue their education during the time normally set aside for work, stating that these efforts "afford too frequent opportunity for conversation and plotting."

During the first decades of the twentieth century, major changes were introduced to the correctional system in Canada. These changes included the introduction of parole and probation, training for prison officials as well as guards, and the introduction of rationality into the operation of prisons. More significant were the types of program changes directed toward inmates. The new types of programs introduced into prisons included classification systems. This separation of inmates into categories based on the diagnostic analysis of the personal history of the offender as well as the needs of the offender ultimately resulted in

the minimum-, medium- and maximum-security designations used to distinguish prisons. It also included the policy of normalization, that is, the design of programs inside prisons that would place inmates in an environment that was controlled but not oppressive, thereby representing as closely as possible conditions that existed in the outside world. Education programs were also implemented to combat illiteracy, which was viewed as an important source of criminal behaviour. In addition, vocational training programs were introduced in order to train inmates for employment once they had completed their sentences (Stojkovic and Lovell, 1997).

A prison nurse teaches a nursing course for inmates. The twentieth century witnessed the addition of vocational and educational programs for inmates. *Ted Streshinsky/Corbis.*

As a matter of policy, inmates were allowed to take higher education courses in their cells during their leisure time. In addition, the rule of silence was relaxed, and conversation between inmates was permitted during meals and in cells until 7:00 P.M. (although the rule of silence was still strictly enforced at work). Representatives of aftercare services (e.g., the Salvation Army) were permitted to interview inmates prior to their release to determine whether these services could assist with the inmates' reintegration into the community. Recreation, considered a fringe benefit, was permitted, but only on a limited basis. Inmates were allowed to paint and draw, although the subjects had to be approved beforehand and every piece of paper had to be numbered and accounted for (Subcommittee on the Penitentiary System in Canada, 1977:12-13).

Despite these changes, abuses of inmates at the hands of prison employees continued. Examples of punishments included hosing inmates by a powerful stream of cold water (used until 1913); balls and chains worn as the inmates engaged in labor activities (used until 1933); handcuffing inmates to bars from 8:00 A.M. to noon and 1:00 P.M. to 5:00 P.M. (used during the 1930s) and dunking inmates diagnosed as mentally ill in troughs of ice and slush (a practice abolished in the 1930s) (Subcommittee on the Penitentiary System in Canada, 1977:12). The quality of guards did not improve, as the Royal Commission to Investigate the State and Management of Kingston Penitentiary discovered in 1914. In their report, they noted that many guards "are not qualified by education or character for the positions they fill. . . ." It was also reported that when they carried "an illicit traffic in tobacco and rob the convicts in doing so," this would lead to "an evil effect which nothing can overcome" (Ekstedt and Griffiths, 1988:49).

Overall, the years between 1900 and 1935 saw very little change in the federal penitentiary system in terms of ideology or daily operations. Gosselin (1982:74) concluded that, despite the numerous studies made during this time period into the operation and administration of the correctional system, "no major changes were in fact made."

Beginning around 1935, the federal government slowly started to change its treatment of inmates. Perhaps the most fundamental change was made to the rule governing silence. Inmates were now allowed to talk prior to working in the morning, when at lunch and from the end of work until 7:00 P.M. This rule change was viewed with some reluctance on the part of prison officials. Edmison (1970:535-536) describes the reaction of the federal Superintendent of Penitentiaries to this rule change as mixed. According to Superintendent General D.M. Ormond, this change did not lead to "any greater dangers to the security of the institutions . . . however . . . the average conversation is of no reformative value to those taking part." In 1935, federal inmates were paid five cents per day for labor. Changes were also made to the living conditions of inmates as a reward for good behaviour. These rewards included the provision of lighting in cells, permission to write a letter to the inmate's immediate family once every three months, and a 30-minute visit by approved relatives every month. However, recreational activities were still considered a "fringe benefit" (Subcommittee on the Penitentiary System in Canada, 1977:13). Despite these progressive (but limited) reforms, serious problems plagued the federal correctional system.

THE REHABILITATION ERA (1935–1960)

The rehabilitation ideology emerged as the dominant correctional ideology in Canada starting in about 1935. As Clear (1994:80) points out, the **rehabilitation era** was formally supported for a number of reasons. First, correcting offenders was now a science, leading to trained specialists taking control of the correctional system from the philanthropic reformers. Second, this approach called for the creation of specialized roles in the correctional system for these new specialists, including case management workers, psychologists and psychiatrists. Finally, the belief that offenders could be treated, released and become law-abiding citizens led to more money being spent on corrections. This led to an unprecedented number of federal institutions being built so that corrective techniques could be applied to as many offenders as possible. To achieve the goal of rehabilitation successfully, better trained personnel were employed to offer a wide array of treatment programs.

Despite the introduction of this new philosophy, remnants of the older, more coercive policies continued to exist. The result was "a paradox that still plagues corrections today—should corrections treat or control its charges?" (Schwartz and Travis, 1997:29). Ever-increasing numbers of inmates made conditions in the correctional system volatile. In 1920, there were approximately 1,800 inmates; by 1937, this figure had more than doubled to 4,000. Inmates faced an increasingly elaborate system of rules and regulations, making it all but impossible not to commit an infraction. By 1933, overcrowding was rife in the federal correctional system. In 1934, the number of prison regulations increased from 194 to 724, with many of these so petty "that prisoners could not possibly know all the rules or avoid breaking them" (Carrigan, 1991:366). As a result of these policies, inmates rebelled across Canada. Between 1932 and 1937, 16 riots occurred in the Canadian federal correctional system. An investigation into theses riots led to changes in policy, probably the most notable of which permitted inmates to voice their issues and grievances to investigators. Some of their complaints included lack of recreation, insufficient open-air exercise, insufficient lighting, harsh treatment by officers, insufficient medical and dental treatment and punishments improperly handed out for rule infractions. These concerns, as well as a concern about the general conditions at penitentiaries, led the delegates at the first Canadian Penal Congress to request a reorganization of the Remission Services and to demand a Royal Commission that would investigate the practices, nature and place of the penitentiary in contemporary Canadian society.

Box 3.1 Federal Prison Construction

Federal Prison Construction in Canada

Before the 1940s
- Kingston Penitentiary – 1832
- Laval Penitentiary – 1837, closed in 1989
- Dorchester Penitentiary – 1880
- Saskatchewan Penitentiary – 1911
- B.C. Penitentiary – closed in 1976
- Stony Mountain Institution – 1920s and 1930s
- Collins Bay Institution – 1930s
- Prison for Women – 1934

The 1950s
- Federal Training Centre
- Leclerc Institution
- Joyceville Institution

The 1960s
- Springhill Institution
- Correctional Development Centre (Quebec)
- Archambault Institution
- Cowansville Institution
- Millhaven Institution
- Warkworth Institution
- Drumheller Institution
- Matsqui Institution

The 1970s
- Regional Reception Centre (Quebec)
- Regional Psychiatric Centre (Prairies)
- Edmonton Institution
- Kent Institution
- Mission Institution

The 1980s
- Atlantic Institution
- Drummond Institution
- Donnacon Institution
- Port Cartier Institution
- Special Handling Units
- La Macaza Institution
- Bowden Institution

Source: Chris Posner (1991). "An Historical Overview of the Construction of Canada's Federal Prisons." *Forum on Corrections Research*, Volume 3, Number 2, page 4.

In 1936, the first of many Royal Commissions to inquire into the state of the federal correctional system in Canada was created. The Royal Commission on the Penal System, under the supervision of Justice Archambault, held its first hearings in 1936. This commission visited federal correctional facilities across the country and tabled its report in 1938. It described a prison system that focused on punishment, strong-armed custodial practices and cruelty. Inmates usually were placed in their cells for 16 hours each day and privileges were rarely granted. If a prisoner requested any privilege, the request usually had to be processed through a lengthy bureaucratic process. In addition, living conditions were decrepit. Some prisons still used buckets for human waste, some did not have lighting in all cells or proper heating. They also found inadequate skills-training programs and limited reformative educational systems operating, and a shortage of skilled instructors and counselling staff. All these factors contrasted against a backdrop of the official policy of reforming inmates—what the investigators discovered was a system that had little, if any, positive or rehabilitative impact upon those incarcerated. In addition, they found an extremely high recidivism rate; in 1936-37, it exceeded 70 percent.

Given these findings, it is not surprising that the **Archambault Commission** produced a report that was critical of the existing federal correctional system. The commissioners recommended that the focus of the system remain upon the "the individual's personal and emotional rehabilitation." As for the specific problems it found, the Archambault Commission made 88 recommendations to correct them. They proposed that the federal and provincial correctional systems be combined and operated by the federal government. Provincial governments would continue to be responsible for those individuals placed on remand, sentenced to very short sentences, or who broke provincial statutes. The commissioners also recommended that existing staff be retrained and that new staff be better qualified. They also wanted to see a completely new system of classifying inmates, an end to the segregation of many inmates, and better medical and psychiatric services and facilities. In addition, the report called for the provision of better educational services and vocational training, the end of minor regulations, and overhauls to both probation and parole systems. Before any of these recommendations could be introduced in any meaningful way, World War II started, negating most concerns about the correctional system. Some changes were introduced, however, particularly in the area of personal liberties. Inmates were now granted greater visiting privileges as well as increased recreational activities and much improved library facilities. Earned remission was made easier, reflecting perhaps the most significant policy change that emerged from the recommendations of the Archambault Commission.

According to Jaffray (1963:86), 1946 "marks the real beginning of penal reform in Canada." It was in this year that the federal government

created a new position, the Commissioner of Penitentiaries, and empow-
ered the appointee to review the operation of the entire federal correctional system. By 1949, the commissioner was able to report that
"progress has been made in the development of facilities necessary to
carry out an effective programme of rehabilitation in the Canadian penitentiaries (*Annual Report of the Commissioner of Penitentiaries*,
1950:7). An important aspect of this change included improvements in
the classification system, as greater attempts were now made to obtain
social histories and psychological testing of all federal inmates. In addition, educational and vocational programs improved both qualitatively
as well as quantitatively. This approach ushered in a more progressive
stage of Canadian corrections, as the federal system began to formally
embrace a rehabilitative approach.

In 1953, a Committee of Inquiry was formed by Parliament to study
the operation and activities of the remission service. This committee,
with Justice Fauteux serving as chairperson, took the position that the
purpose of the correctional system was the reformation of the offender.
This was to be achieved by training rather than punishing offenders.
Carrigan (1991:374) points out that this committee popularized the
usage of the word "corrections" in Canada, a word they defined as
describing "the total process by which society attempts to correct the
anti-social attitudes or behaviour of the individual." According to the
committee, treatment was now to be accomplished by training as
opposed to punishment. Treatment was to be accomplished through specialized techniques devised by specialized personnel. Aftercare programs,
particularly for addicts, psychopaths and sex offenders, were recommended, as was the construction of medium-security institutions. Other
recommendations included liberalizing parole and probation, automatic
review of parole, increased use of presentence reports and the creation
of a national federal board.

The significance of the **Fauteux Report** upon the Canadian corrections system cannot be overstated, as it introduced the medical model of
corrections into the federal correctional system. This policy was associated with the use of the "therapeutic state," where control proliferated in
the name of treatment (Kittrie, 1971). In this approach, medical solutions
are recommended for almost every human problem. Treatment is prescribed as a cure for virtually every type of nonconformity and most typically administered by physicians or other professionals such as psychiatrists, social workers or trained staff. In the medical model, treatment is
mandatory and is forced upon inmates and other nonconformists.

While the Fauteux Report ushered in an important phase of the
Canadian correctional system with the introduction of rehabilitation as
the guiding philosophy, this approach was also heavily criticized as being
oppressive and antihumanitarian. A major issue is the belief that the subjects (in this case, inmates) have no real choice in behaving the way that

they do. Another is the separation of moral judgments from scientifical-ly informed treatment, thereby allowing professionals to experiment on inmates with mind-altering drugs, even though the benefits of this tech-nique are dubious, as drugs were no doubt used more for controlling and managing inmates rather than "curing" them. It also individualized complex social problems, ignoring social forces that can influence peo-ple's behavior. It also significantly increased the powers of the "experts," whose careers are largely based on the idea that nonconforming behav-ior is a problem found in abnormal individuals. Professional-enhancing approaches such as these are largely founded upon corporate businesses, whose profits in such endeavors can easily be in the tens of million dol-lars. Such issues have largely been unexamined in Canada.

Despite these limitations, the impact of the Fauteux Committee was unparalleled in Canadian correctional history. In 1957, eight federal prisons were in existence; by 1961, there were 34. In addition, these pris-ons were classified into distinct security classifications—maximum, medi-um and minimum. In addition, the Parole Act was passed in 1959, cre-ating the National Parole Board. However, the support for rehabilitation waned, and by the mid-1960s significant criticisms were aimed at this approach. The long-term result was the demand for greater use of incar-ceration with reduced treatment programs for offenders.

THE REINTEGRATION ERA (1960–PRESENT)

As the rehabilitation era waned in its dominance, it was replaced by the **reintegration era**. The reintegration approach emerged and became dominant during a time of great social unrest, with much emphasis being placed upon the relationship between conditions in society and criminal behaviour. This change toward community-based corrections was based on a philosophical change that viewed corrections as improving the lives of offenders by keeping them in the community. As a result, the correc-tional system went through fundamental changes to assist offenders in reintegrating back into the community. This reflected a fundamental reorientation of the role of the correctional process vis-à-vis the offender:

> Correctional agencies in an era of reintegration should be advocates for offenders. Correctional officials should bend their efforts toward securing social services and advantages for offenders that would give them non-criminal alternatives. Offenders were seen as full participants in the correctional process, not merely as the subjects of well-intentioned rehabil-itative interventions (Schwartz and Travis, 1997:30).

This approach differed from the reform and rehabilitation eras in two ways—first, the coercive aspect of treatment was de-emphasized, as it was realized, through a series of court decisions, that such policies invaded the legal and personal rights of offenders. Second, the focus of corrective tactics and strategies was expanded to include the community as well as the offender. As O'Leary and Duffee (1970:5) note, a key focus of this approach was to reduce the stigma associated with criminality "because that stigma is a block to entrance to the community." Clear (1994:83) points out that the reintegration agenda gave corrections "a distinctly moral overtone—its leaders were not simply trying to control the errant citizen, but were in fact bonded with them, charged with the responsibility for enriching the quality of their lives and their community."

Reintegration represented the second major transformation in penal policy. According to Cohen (1985:31), the original approach to punishment in the Western world now changed in a fundamental manner:

(1) Away from the state: Instead of the state incarcerating all offenders in heavily secured institutions, the emphasis was now upon "decentralization" and "nonintervention." The state divested itself of a number of control functions and created structures that are community-based, only partially sponsored by the state, and less bureaucratic and accountable than the state-run facilities.

(2) Away from the experts: A distrust of professionals emerged as well as questions about their classification criteria and treatment programs. As a result, there occurred an "anti-psychiatric" and "antiprofessional" movement that stressed that serious harms resulted from the activities of experts.

(3) Away from the institution: Closed facilities were now seen as harmful, and "open" facilities, most notably community-type facilities and programs, replaced them. "Deinstitutionalisation," "decarceration" and "community control" were born.

(4) Away from the mind: Concerns about treating the minds of offenders were replaced by an emphasis on the body rather than the mind as well as the act rather than the actor. The "back to justice" movement was created as an alternative, leading to a concern with prisoners rights.

In Canada, the reintegration era can be said to have formally started with the Canadian Committee on Corrections (Ouimet) Report, which appeared in 1969. In keeping with the reintegration model, the **Ouimet Report** supported the idea that offender change "might more profitably be pursued within a community setting than inside correctional institutions." Community facilities were to be shared by both federal and private agencies, such as the Elizabeth Fry Society and the John Howard Society, in order to minimize the use of imprisonment. They proposed a wider range of sentencing alternatives made to reduce the use of incarceration as a punishment. The Ouimet Committee (Ouimet, 1969) noted that "the existence of (certain) restrictions upon the power of a court to sentence otherwise than to imprisonment all too frequently leads to a practice of imposing a sentence of imprisonment in the absence of mitigating factors." Alternatives were necessary to allow offenders to serve their sentence in the communities. In their final report, the Ouimet Committee (Ouimet, 1969:204) recommended imprisonment or confinement "be used only as an ultimate resort when all other alternatives have failed, but subject to its other recommendations concerning different types of offenders and different categories of dispositions."

To achieve this end, various alternatives were explored. Diversion programs, community residential centres, group homes and fine option programs are examples of reintegrative policies introduced at this time. The Report of the Task Force on Community-Based Residential Centres (Outerbridge, 1972:ix) specified the goals to be employed under the reintegration model:

(1) to divert persons entirely from the criminal justice system and incarceration;

(2) to shorten the length of incarceration; and

(3) to provide temporary relief from incarceration.

This led to the development and implementation of diversion programs and the greater use of probation (both of which fulfill the first directive), changes in parole and the creation of mandatory supervision (which are associated with the second directive) and temporary absences and day parole (the third policy directive).

One of the major changes during this era was that prison inmates were recognized as having certain fundamental legal rights. Prisoners rights groups emerged, and lawyers took their cases to court in order to establish and secure these rights (Fogel, 1975). These cases brought about changes in the correctional system, with inmates being given the legal protection to fair hearings, impartial tribunals and the right to vote, among many other rights.

A variety of interest groups with diverse philosophies and goals joined forces to bring about the demise of those ideologies that focused upon offender change. Throughout the 1970s, a series of popular books published in the United States and Europe brought attention to the limits of the offender change models. George Jackson's *Soledad Brother* (1970) and Jessica Mitford's *Kind and Usual Punishment* (1975) were popularized accounts of prisoners descriptions of the coercive conditions within the California State Correctional System and a biting criticism on the use of the indeterminate sentence in California, respectively. Critical monographs were also written by members of the judiciary, most notably Judge Marvin Frankel's *Criminal Sentences* (1973), in which he charged that the sentencing of criminals had virtually become "law without order." Perhaps the most famous critique was offered by Martinson's (1974) study, which analysed more than 200 evaluations of treatment programs conducted between 1945 and 1967. According to Martinson (1974:6), treatment programs have "no appreciable effects on recidivism," leading to the conclusion that "nothing works" in terms of rehabilitating offenders. The impact of this evaluation was significant, for, as Blumstein (1997:352) mentions, Martinson's article "created a general despair about the potential of significantly affecting recidivism rates of those presented to the criminal justice system." In part, this article supported that harming offenders in the name of rehabilitation is unsuccessful and that individualized treatment gave state and prison too much discretionary power, which led to unjust and coercive programs and policies. Mathiesen, in his *The Politics of Abolition* (1974), charged that the prison was nothing more than a mechanism for class control and any reforms introduced simply continued to legitimate such an approach. As a result, he called for the abolition of prisons because imprisonment is an inhumane and ineffective way to control crime and criminals.

In terms of implementing the reintegration ideology, a successful approach was proposed by David Fogel (1975) in his *"We Are the Living Proof": The Justice Model for Corrections*. This text advocated the "justice model" for corrections, maintaining that inmates should be protected from harm through legal rights and the right to choose whether they want to participate in a limited number of programs that could possibly assist them in society after release. The following year, Andrew von Hirsch published *Doing Justice: The Choice of Punishments* (1976), which took a similar position. These texts laid the basis for a new approach in correctional programming that emphasized fair practices and policies within correctional institutions, the elimination of coercive rehabilitation in favour of voluntary and more limited programs, and the increased use of alternative sanctions. This approach was accepted almost immediately by Canadian agencies concerned with the operation of the correctional system.

The Law Reform Commission of Canada, in its first report to Parliament, outlined the nature of the reintegrative ideology. This involved a proposed reduction in the use of imprisonment as a sanction, an approach that also suggested that imprisonment be used as minimally as possible. According to the Law Reform Commission of Canada (1976:24), for

hard core real crimes needing traditional trials and serious
punishments . . . we need restraint. For one thing, the cost of
the criminal law to the offender, the taxpayer and all of us—
must always be kept as low as possible. For another, the dan-
ger with all punishments is that familiarity breeds contempt.
The harsher the punishments, the slower we should be to use
it. This applies especially to punishments of last resort. The
major punishment is prison. This is today the ultimate weapon
of the criminal law. As such it must be used sparingly . . .

On the next page, the Law Reform Commission of Canada outlined
what the alternatives to imprisonment should be, providing insight into
what was gradually to take form as official federal policy:

Restricting our use of imprisonment will allow more people for
other types of penalties . . . Positive penalties like restitution
and community service orders should be increasingly substituted for the negative and uncreative warehousing of prison (Law
Reform Commission of Canada, 1976:25).

The next year the Sub-Committee on the Penitentiary System in
Canada published the Report to Parliament about the conditions in the
federal system, proposing that legal rights be an essential condition of
the correctional system. They stated:

. . . justice for inmates is a person's right and also an essential
condition of their socialization and personal reformation. It
implies both respect for the persons and property of others and
fairness in treatment. The arbitrariness traditionally associated
with prison life must be replaced by clear rules, fair disciplinary procedures and the providing of reasons for all decisions
affecting inmates (Subcommittee on the Penitentiary System in
Canada, 1977:77).

Throughout the early 1980s, the federal government maintained its
interest in a variety of community sanctions. For example, they were an
essential component of the proposed sentencing policy in the Criminal
Law Reform Act of 1984 (Bill C-19). It was proposed that community
alternatives to imprisonment be expanded and understood as sanctions
in their own right. According to the proposals,

. . . emphasis would be given to non-custodial sanctions, with
imprisonment reserved for cases where such non-custodial
sanctions are appropriate. The provisions would also expand
or create sanctions to allow for tough and effective penalties to
be imposed without having to resort to imprisonment.

While these policies were being implemented across Canada, questions remained about the nature of reintegration. While community corrections did increase, it was argued that they did so in addition to segregative control, as opposed to a replacement of it. Prisons were still extensively used, leading to the argument that the penal system in Canada had expanded. According to critics, the phenomena of "net-widening" occurred, that is, the entire social control system expanded. Cohen (1985) argues that far from decreasing the total number of in-

A minister stands in front of a halfway house. Halfway houses are residential programs in the community in which offenders are housed and provided various treatments. *Ed Eckstein/Corbis.*

mates in Canada, the reintegrative ideology was used to expand the correctional system. Based upon studies mentioned in Chapter 1, as well as data from both the United States and Britain (which were experiencing similar changes), Cohen (1985:37) concluded that the "reach and intensity of state control have been increased; centralization and bureaucracy remain; professions and experts are proliferating dramatically and society is more dependent on them; informalism has not made the legal system less formal or more just."

Other analysts (e.g., Austin and Krisberg, 1982; Clear, 1994) believe that while new policies were implemented they were not large in number and, in reality, never allowed to develop to their full potential. One of the problems with the reintegration approach was that offenders and community residents were not always compatible. According to Clear, the reintegration movement of the late 1960s and early to mid-1970s failed largely due to the fact that empowerment of offenders lay at the core of reintegration, while the penal system still continued to rely on harm to offenders as its main focus. As a result, the correctional policies introduced during this era "could be thought of as integrative in the main" (Clear, 1994:84).

By the late 1970s the support for reintegration was declining, largely due to a shift toward more "get tough" correctional policies. This shift involved a change from a service approach to one that emphasized the risk that offenders posed to the community (Clear and O'Leary, 1981). This change was facilitated by improvements in scales designed to predict the risk presented by offenders. In the 25 years during which the reintegration ideology dominated policy, officials and researchers focused on **false positives**, that is, the incorrect placement of offenders who did not recidivate. By the mid-1980s, however, improvements in the accuracy of risk scales shifted the focus to **false negatives**, that is, those offenders who were released on conditional release programs and who subsequently committed a crime in the community. As a result, researchers reanalysed their risk-measuring scales to identify those offenders with the best potential for successful reintegration (Motiuk and Serin, 1998).

In the opinion of Schwartz and Travis (1997:158-159), the risk prediction ideology consisted of three main tenets. First, there was a shift in focus from assisting the offender to reintegrate back into the community to a protection of community residents from the potential harmful behaviour of offenders released into the community (Zedlewski, 1995). Second, new methods of control and surveillance, such as electronic monitoring, were perfected and implemented. The third, and perhaps most important, change is to be found in the purpose and role of community correctional workers. No longer was it acceptable for such workers to work in a supportive role; instead, they became "no-nonsense" enforcers who were trained in the legalities of enforcement as well as identifying the potential risks an inmate posed for the community. So while community corrections are used just as frequently as before, their nature has changed. Greater surveillance and control are now commonplace and correctional workers perform tasks to ensure that offenders are complying with the conditions of their release. This is accomplished with the assistance of "objective" measures of offender risks and needs, which allow staff to assess the improvement or lack thereof of each offender as they progress toward release in the community.

However, as the reality of correctional overcrowding remains, the federal government has merged the risk prediction ideology with the reintegration model. The Correctional Service of Canada now operates under the Corrections and Conditional Release Act (1992), which states that the purpose of the federal correctional system is to contribute to the maintenance of federal corrections by (1) carrying out sentences imposed by the courts through the safe and humane custody and supervision of offenders, and (2) assisting the rehabilitation of offenders and their reintegration into law-abiding citizens through the provision of programs in penitentiaries and in the community.

Section 10 of the act further specifies that the Correctional Service of Canada "use the least restrictive measures consistent with the protection of the public, staff members and offenders." Further facilitating the reintegration ideology as official federal policy were the policy changes recommended by the Task Force on Reintegration of Offenders (1997), specifically that (1) low-risk offenders will receive more of their programming in the community, and (2) program referrals are being monitored more closely to make sure that only offenders who require specific programs are referred.

SUMMARY

Canada developed its penitentiary system within the broader context of prison reform that was sweeping the Western world in the late eighteenth and early nineteenth centuries. At issue, however, was the type of facility in which inmates should be confined. Two such models existed: the Pennsylvania (separate) system and the Auburn (congregate) system. The Auburn system proved to be the model selected by most jurisdictions, including the Ontario provincial government. Therefore, it was the congregate model that became the model for the first prison in Canada, the Kingston Provincial Penitentiary, as well as for all other prisons built in the nineteenth and early twentieth centuries in Canada.

While the model for correctional facilities remained the same for more than a century, the dominant correctional ideology changed a number of times. The dominant ideology of the 1990s is reintegration, but both rehabilitation and deterrence models have been dominant at other times. The history of the Canadian federal system of corrections includes a number of major directional shifts, usually as the result of a government inquiry into the conditions in the correctional institutions themselves. This led to a number of changes in the governing legislation directing the focus of the correctional enterprise. The Corrections and Conditional Release Act (1992) supports the reintegration ideology. However, public concern about safety has led to the retention of a significant amount of the deterrence model, so that those inmates considered to be high-risk offenders now spend a longer period of time incarcerated in the federal system.

DISCUSSION QUESTIONS

1. What other alternatives to imprisonment do you think existed at the end of the eighteenth century? Why do you think they were not used very often?

2. What benefits did the penitentiary bring to society?

3. Do you think that early penitentiaries were too brutal in their treatment of inmates? Do you think the protection of the legal rights of inmates has gone too far in comparison to the treatment of offenders 50 to 100 years ago in Canada?

4. What are the reasons for the rise of the reintegration model of corrections in Canada? Do you think this model should be changed? If so, how should it be changed? Do you think that we can successfully predict the risk of reoffending by offenders? What difficulties do you think are associated with this approach?

5. Do you think Canada should change to a more deterrence-based approach in the area of corrections?

REFERENCES

Allen, Harry E. And Clifford E. Simonsen (1998). *Corrections in America: An Introduction,* Eighth Edition. Upper Saddle River, NJ: Prentice-Hall.

Annual Report of the Commissioner of Penitentiaries, 1949 (1950). Ottawa: King's Printer.

Austin, James and Barry Krisberg (1982). "The Unmet Promise of Alternatives to Incarceration." *Crime & Delinquency*, Volume 28, 374-409.

Baehre, Rainer (1977). "Origins of the Penitentiary in Upper Canada." *Ontario History*, Volume 59, 447-478.

Barnes, Henry Elmer and Negley K. Teeters (1959). *New Horizons in Criminology,* Third Edition. Englewood Cliffs, NJ: Prentice-Hall.

Beattie, J.M. (1977). *Attitudes Toward Crime and Punishment in Canada, 1830-1850: A Documentary Study.* Toronto: Centre of Criminology, University of Toronto.

Beaumont G.D. and A. de Tocqueville (1964). *On the Penitentiary System in the United States and Its Application in France.* Carbondale, IL: Southern Illinois Press.

Beccaria, Cesare (1765). Translated by Richard Davies and Virginia Cox. In *On Crimes and Punishments and Other Writings*, Richard Bellamy (ed.). Cambridge, England: Cambridge University Press, 1995.

Beirne, Piers (1987). "Between Classicism and Positivism: Crime and Penality in the Writings of Gabriel Tarde." *Criminology*, Volume 25, 785-819.

Beirne, Piers and James Messerschmidt (1995). *Criminology,* Second Edition. Fort Worth, TX: Harcourt Brace.

Blumstein, Alfred (1997). "Interaction of Criminological Research and Public Policy." *Journal of Quantitative Criminology*, Volume 12, 349-361.

Carrigan, D. Owen (1991). *Crime and Punishment in Canada: A History.* Toronto: McClelland and Stewart.

Clear, Todd (1994). *Harm in American Penology: Offenders, Victims, and Their Communities.* Albany, NY: State University of New York Press.

Clear, Todd and Vincent O'Leary (1981). *Controlling the Offender in the Community: Reforming the Community Supervision Function.* Lexington, MA: Lexington.

Cohen, Stanley (1985). *Visions of Social Control.* Cambridge, England: Polity Press.

Conley, John A. (1980) "Prisons, Products, and Profit: Reconsidering the Importance of Prison Industries." *Journal of Social History*, Volume 14, 257-275.

Dobash, Richard P. (1983). "Labour and Discipline in Scottish and English Prisons: Moral Correction, Punishment and Useful Toil." *Sociology*, Volume 17, 1-25.

Edmison, J.A. (1970). "Perspectives in Corrections." *Canadian Journal of Corrections*, Volume 12, 534-548.

Ekstedt, John W. and Curt T. Griffiths (1988). *Corrections in Canada: Policy and Practice*, Second Edition. Toronto: Butterworths.

Fogel, David (1975). *"We are Living Proof:" The Justice Model for Corrections*. Cincinnati: Anderson.

Foucault, Michel (1977). *Discipline and Punishment: The Birth of the Prison*. New York: Panthon.

Frankel, Marvin (1973). *Criminal Sentences: Law Without Order*. New York: Hill and Wang.

Gosselin, Luc (1982). *Prisons in Canada*. Montreal: Black Rose Books.

Hudson, Barbara (1987). *Justice Through Punishment: A Critique of the "Justice" Model of Corrections*. New York: St. Martin's Press.

Ignatieff, Michael (1978). *A Justice Measure of Pain: The Penitentiary in the Industrial Revolution, 1750-1850*. New York: Pantheon.

Jackson, George (1970). *Soledad Brother*. New York: Random House

Jackson, Michael (1983). *Prisoners of Isolation: Solitary Confinement in Canada*. Toronto: University of Toronto Press.

Jaffray, Stuart K. (1963). *Sentencing of Adults in Canada*. Toronto: University of Toronto Press.

Johnson, Robert (1996). *Hard Time: Understanding and Reforming the Prison*, Second Edition. Belmont, CA: Wadsworth.

Kittrie, Nicholas M. (1971). *The Right to Be Different: Deviance and Enforced Therapy*. Baltimore: Johns Hopkins University Press.

Law Reform Commission of Canada (1976). *Our Criminal Law*. Ottawa: Information Canada.

Martinson, Robert (1974). "What Works—Questions and Answers About Prison Reform." *The Public Interest*, Volume 35, 22-54

Mathiesen, Thomas (1974). *The Politics of Abolition*. Oslo: Universitetsforlaget.

Melossi, Dario and Massimo Pavarini (1981). *The Prison and the Factory: Origins of the Penitentiary System*. Totowa, NJ: Barnes and Noble.

Mitford, Jessica (1975). *Kind and Usual Punishment: The Prison Business*. New York: Knopf.

Motiuk, Larry and Ralph Serin (1998). "Situating Risk Assessment in the Reintegration Potential Framework." *Forum on Corrections Research*, Volume 10, 19-22.

O'Leary, V. and D. Duffee (1971). "Correctional Policy: A Classification of Goals Designed for Change." *Crime & Delinquency*, Volume 17, 373-386.

Ouimet, R. (1969). *Report of the Canadian Committee on Corrections—Toward Unity: Criminal Justice and Corrections*. Ottawa: Information Canada.

Outerbridge, W.R. (1972). *Report of the Task Force on Community-Based Residential Centres*. Ottawa: Information Canada.

Rothman, David (1971). *The Discovery of the Asylum: Social Order and Disorder in the New Republic*. Boston: Little, Brown.

Schwartz, Martin D. and Lawerence F. Travis (1997). *Corrections: An Issues Approach*, Fourth Edition. Cincinnati: Anderson.

Scull, Andrew (1977). *Decarceration: Community Treatment and the Deviant—A Radical View*. Englewood Cliffs, NJ: Prentice-Hall.

Shoom, Sydney (1972-73). "The Upper Canada Reformatory Penetanguishene: The Dawn of Prison Reform in Canada." *Canadian Journal of Criminology*, Volume 14/15, 260-267.

Splane, Richard (1966). *Social Welfare in Ontario 1791-1893*. Toronto: University of Toronto Press.

Stojkovic, Stan and Rick Lovell (1997). *Corrections: An Introduction*, Second Edition. Cincinnati: Anderson.

Subcommittee on the Penitentiary System in Canada (1977). *Report to Parliament by the Subcommittee on the Penitentiary System in Canada*. Ottawa: Supply and Services Canada.

Taft, Donald R. (1956). *Criminology*, Third Edition. New York: Macmillan.

von Hirsch (1976). *Doing Justice: The Choice of Punishments*. New York: Hill and Wang.

Zedlewski, Edwin H. (1995). "Risky Business." *American Probation and Parole Association Perspectives*, Volume 19, 2.

CHAPTER 4

Conditional Release Programs:
Parole, Temporary Absences and Statutory Release

Conditional Release Programs

The gradual release of inmates back into the community through a variety of conditional release programs is considered a priority of Canadian contemporary federal correctional programming. On any given day in 1994-95, there were more than 9,000 offenders on full federal and provincial parole; 1,506 federal and provincial offenders on day parole; and 2,365 federal offenders in the community under statutory release provisions (Reed and Roberts, 1996). As will be discussed later in this chapter, some form of conditional release into the community is currently viewed as an essential factor in the successful reintegration of an offender.

The authority to grant parole is found in the Corrections and Conditional Release Act (1992) and relevant provincial legislation for the two provinces (Ontario and Quebec) that still maintain a provincial parole board. In the summer of 1997, British Columbia announced it will no longer operate a provincial parole board. The National Parole Board has jurisdiction over all those offenders sentenced to federal institutions and those offenders sentenced to provincial/territorial institutions where there is no provincial parole board. Provincial parole boards operate their own parole boards, and they have jurisdiction for all provincial offenders serving a sentence in a provincial institution. It is

KEY TERMS		
accelerated review	Goldenberg Report	risk assessment
clemency	good time	SIR Scale
Daubney Committee	Hugessen Report	statutory release
day parole	intensive supervision parole	statutory remission
earned remission	mandatory supervision	technical violation
"faint hope" clause	remission	temporary absence
full parole		ticket-of-leave

important to remember that all types of conditional release programs are a privilege, not a right, and the authorities have legal powers to keep any inmate locked up until the end of his or her sentence if he or she is deemed a risk to society. The Corrections and Conditional Release Act lists six principles that apply specifically to the granting of parole, with the first stating that the protection of society is the central concern in the granting of parole to any offender. The Correctional Service of Canada, as part of its mission statement, works to protect society, and the release of any inmate has to be balanced with considerations of public safety. Due to shifting political, public and "scientific" notions of treatment, definitions of conditional release programs have changed over the years to reflect better knowledge of risk factors by correctional specialists as well as concerns about such programs by the public.

At the present time, the Solicitor General of Canada (1997) maintains five conditional release programs in Canada:

(1) **Full parole**—Most offenders (except those serving life sentences for murder) are eligible to apply for full parole after serving either a minimum of one-third of their sentence or seven years, whichever comes first. Offenders serving a life sentence for first-degree murder are eligible to apply for full parole after serving 25 years of their sentence. Offenders who have been convicted of second-degree murder have their eligibility dates for full parole set between 10 and 25 years. All offenders released on full parole are placed under the supervision of a parole or probation officer and are required to follow general and specific conditions developed to reduce the risk of reoffending and to enhance reintegration into the community. Full parole can be granted by both federal and provincial parole boards.

(2) **Day parole**—Offenders serving sentences of three years or more are eligible to apply for day parole six months prior to their date of full parole eligibility. Offenders serving sentences of between two and three years are eligible for day parole after serving six months of their sentence. If an offender is serving a life sentence, he or she can apply for day parole three years before his or her full parole eligibility date. In most cases in which an offender is granted day parole, he or she lives in a correctional facility or community residence. Day parole is oftentimes granted to prepare an inmate for full parole and statutory release. The National Parole Board has the authority to grant day parole to offenders (both federal and provincial) under its jurisdiction.

(3) **Temporary absence**—This allows offenders to leave a correctional facility for a specific program purpose. Offenders may be released on either an escorted or unescorted temporary absence. Reasons for such release include family visits, medical services, rehabilitation programs, humanitarian reasons, etc. Both the Correctional Service of Canada and the National Parole Board have the authority to grant temporary absences. In the provinces and territories, the release of an offender on temporary absence falls under the responsibility of the superintendent (warden) of the institution.

(4) **Statutory release**—By law, most federal offenders are automatically released after serving two-thirds of their sentence if they have not already been released on parole. This allows them to serve the final one-third of their sentence in the community under supervision and conditions similar to those given to offenders released on full parole. The National Parole Board is the only agency that has the authority to place offenders on statutory release.

(5) **Accelerated review**—The Corrections and Conditional Release Act stipulates that some offenders who are serving their first term of imprisonment in a federal institution (regardless of the number of times they have been sentenced to a provincial correctional facility) be released on full parole after they have served one-third of their sentence. These offenders must be released on full parole unless the National Parole Board finds reasonable grounds to believe the offender is likely to commit an offence before the end of his or her sentence. Accelerated review applies only when (1) the offender is serving the sentence for a nonviolent offence; or (2) the offender is serving the sentence for a serious drug charge for which the judge did not set parole eligibility at one-half of the sentence. An offender who is serving a sentence for murder, an offence involving violence, or a serious drug offence for which the judge set eligibility at one-half of the sentence is not eligible for accelerated review (National Parole Board, 1994:7).

The Use of Conditional Release Programs

The majority of federal and provincial offenders serving time in a correctional facility will be placed on a conditional release program prior to the termination of their sentence. The most commonly used conditional release programs in Canada during 1996-97 were escorted and unescorted temporary absences, with 46,666 federal inmates granted either type of temporary absence (these figures do not include work releases). The success rate for both escorted and unescorted temporary absences is almost perfect. At the federal level of jurisdiction in 1996-97, 99.7 percent of all federally sentenced men released on an escorted temporary absence successfully completed their release; in comparison, 98.8 percent of all men successfully completed their unescorted temporary absence. The corresponding rates of success for federally sentenced women released on an escorted temporary absence were 99.6 percent and 99.5 percent for an unescorted temporary absence.

The use of parole by both federal and provincial boards of parole has been increasing throughout the 1990s. In 1994-95 there was a total of 9,227 offenders on full parole, an increase from 7,522 (or almost 23 percent) compared to 1990-91. The use of full parole increased most in Quebec (up 109 percent from 916 to 1,981 offenders between 1990-91 and 1994-94), the National Parole Board for federally sentenced offenders (up 14 percent from 4,467 to 5,224 offenders) and Ontario (up 9 percent from 1,273 to 1,405 offenders). Decreases were registered in British Columbia (down 10 percent from 355 to 290 offenders) and the National Parole Board for provincially sentenced offenders (down 36 percent from 511 to 327 offenders). The number of offenders released into the community on statutory release by the National Parole Board increased by 8 percent, while the use of escorted temporary absences granted by the Correctional Service of Canada and the National Parole Board increased by 11 percent. In the same year, provincial authorities granted 214,799 temporary absences, up from 151,508 (or 42 percent) during the previous year (Reed and Roberts, 1996).

All other conditional release programs experienced decline during 1994-95. The number of escorted temporary absences granted by the National Parole Board decreased by 17 percent, while the rate for those offenders released on the unescorted temporary absence by the Corrections Service of Canada declined by 2 percent. Day parole declined by 9 percent during 1994-95 in comparison to 1993-94 (Reed and Roberts, 1996).

History of Federal Conditional Release Programs

The Antecedents of Conditional Release Programs

Canada has used a variety of conditional release programs for approximately 130 years. Most of the programs practised today had their antecedents introduced during the past 40 years, as the importance of community reintegration has grown. The most significant of these programs have been earned remission, first used in 1868; ticket-of-leave (1899), which is the forerunner of our parole system (1959); and mandatory supervision, now referred to as statutory release (1970). In addition, the policy of temporary absence was formally recognized in 1961, while day parole was first introduced in 1969.

Box 4.1 Offenders on Day Parole

Demographic Characteristics (at the time of their offence) of Offenders on Day Parole

	Male Offenders	Female Offenders	Native Male Offenders
Age*			
17-25 years old	22.0%	29.5%	25.0%
26-40 years old	59.0%	52.3%	60.5%
Older than 40	19.0%	18.2%	14.5%
Marital status			
Single	35.7%	35.0%	29.6%
Married or common-law relationship	49.6%	52.5%	56.3%
Separated, divorced or widowed	14.7%	12.5%	14.1%
Employment status			
Unemployed	50.3%	57.1%	60.0%
Employed	45.8%	40.5%	29.2%
Student, retired or incarcerated	3.9%	2.4%	10.8%
Education level			
8th grade or less	30.8%	27.9%	56.8%
Grade 9-13	59.1%	65.1%	41.9%
Post-secondary	10.1%	7.0%	1.3%
Number+	929	44	77

*This is the only category not measured at the time of the offence; it was measured at the time of the study.

+The total numbers of the various categories may not equal the total samples because of missing values.

Source: Linda Lefebvre (1994). "The Demographic Characteristics of Offenders in Day Parole." *Forum on Correctional Research*, Volume 6, Number 3, page 8.

According to Walker (1980:92-98), conditional release programs have been in existence almost as long as prisons. They achieve a number of goals beyond the mere incarceration of offenders. These include giving discretionary powers to criminal justice authorities to individualize punishments, to relieve problems of overcrowding, supervising and controlling of offenders in the community, as well as to encourage incarcerated offenders to practice good behaviour in the hope they will be granted early release.

While the creation of the first contemporary conditional release system in North America is usually credited to the state of Michigan for its introduction of a parole system in the 1850s, the antecedents for this system were already well-established in various jurisdictions. Carter, McGee and Nelson (1975) point out that the first operational system of conditional release existed in Spain. Spain had a policy whereby up to one-third of a sentence could be reduced by good behaviour and the demonstration of good behaviour. However, the foundation for conditional release programs is generally credited to the creation of the "mark system" by Captain Alexander Maconochie in 1840 and the formation of the "Irish System" by Sir William Crofton in 1853. Maconochie took command of the British penal colony on Norfolk Island in 1840 and introduced what is known today as the indeterminate sentence. The core of this approach was a system that allowed an inmate to earn a "mark" for work and good behaviour, thereby allowing him (or her) to achieve an early, though conditional, release. In essence, Maconochie changed the existing system by placing the burden of release upon the inmate instead of the correctional authorities. His system consisted of five principles:

1. Release should not be based on the completing of a sentence for a set period of time, but on the completion of a determined and specified quantity of labor.

2. The quantity of labor a prisoner must perform should be expressed in a number of "marks" that he must earn . . .

3. While in prison he should earn everything he receives.

4. . . . he should work in association with a small number of other prisoners, . . . and the whole group should be answerable for the conduct and labor of each member.

5. In the final stage, a prisoner . . . should be subject to less rigorous discipline (Barnes and Teeters, 1959:419)

However, when Maconochie's efforts came to the attention of his supervisors, they terminated the program. Nevertheless, his ideas so impressed reformers and other correctional administrators that England passed legislation in 1853 allowing inmates to be granted early release on a "ticket-of-leave" to reenter the community while under the supervision of the police.

Sir William Crofton, the head of the Irish prison system subsequently implemented this new early release program, but on the basis of a system of four levels or stages:

(1) The first stage involved solitary confinement for nine months. During the first three months the inmate was on reduced rations and was allowed no labor whatsoever.

(2) In the second stage, the convict was placed in a special prison to work with other inmates, during which time he could earn marks to qualify for a transfer to the third stage.

(3) Stage three involved transportation to an open institution, where the convict, by evidencing signs of reformation, could earn release on a Ticket of Leave.

(4) Ticket of Leave men were conditionally released . . . (Abadinsky, 1987:145).

The Irish System became internationally recognized as a progressive system, later becoming the basis of the parole system in the United States. In 1870, Crofton addressed the American Prison Association held in Cincinnati, Ohio. At the conclusion of these meetings, a parole system, in principle, was adopted by those in attendance. It was not until six years later, however, that the first parole system was established at the Elmira Reformatory located in New York. The superintendent between 1877 and 1900 was Zebulon Brockway. He instituted a "mark" system as well as the indeterminate sentence allowing for the individualization of punishment. According to Barnes and Teeters (1959) and Abadinsky (1987), Brockway introduced his system of early release in order to allow inmates to benefit from good behaviour. All early releases were granted by a special committee composed of the institutional board of managers, and parole was granted for a maximum of six months. During their time on conditional release, all parolees had to report to an assigned official.

The First Century of Parole in Canada (1868–1958)

Canada's first release program—known as **remission**—was part of the first Penitentiary Act (1868). It used a point system similar to those already in existence. This program allowed an offender to receive early release at the maximum rate of six days per month for good behaviour. Merit and demerit points were awarded for cooperative behaviour and attitude as well as for industrious work habits. The policy governing remission was later amended to permit an inmate up to 10 days remission once 72 days had been earned at the original rate. This formula, which could potentially allow inmates to be released after serving three-quarters of their sentence, remained in practice until 1961.

Toward the end of the nineteenth century, Canadian authorities became interested in the system of parole then practised by numerous jurisdictions in the United States. During discussions about parole in the House of Commons, Prime Minister Wilfred Laurier remarked that inmates should be divided into two categories: the "dangerous" and the "hopeless," both of whom were to be confined for the protection of the public. Both were to be placed in a category separate from those deemed as "the victims of accidents rather than of criminal instincts, whom prison can only make worse but for whom conditional release is designed to give them a chance to redeem their characters" (Mandel, 1975:527). This philosophy of separating high-risk inmates from society while allowing low-risk inmates to be released back into the community "in the shortest possible time" continues today.

The first major legislation concerning parole passed in Canada occurred in 1899. The Ticket-of-Leave Act specified that inmates could gain a particular form of early release—clemency—that was independent of earned remission Clemency, under the Ticket-of-Leave Act, gave the Governor-General the power to grant a license to an inmate in a federal or provincial facility to be released early under certain conditions. This system was based on considerations such as the age and criminal background of the offender, the nature of the offence, and similar personal factors that would be used to assess the character of inmates as well as the probability of their "relapse." Importantly, this form of release allowed for administrative discretion and the reduction of the term of imprisonment to a much greater extent than what was permitted under the policy of remission. The Ticket-of-Leave Act established both clemency and "parole" (or "earned remission," as it was known then). Parole was rarely granted in the early years; most inmates were given clemency. This changed gradually when various public and private agencies became involved in the early release of inmates, particularly in the 1910s and later. Most reviews of this piece of legislation indicate that most inmates who applied for release received some form of either remission or **ticket-of-leave**.

At first, the supervision of parolees was the responsibility of the local police, and those granted early release were required to report on a monthly basis. It was soon realized that closer surveillance of offenders was necessary. As a result, voluntary organizations, in particular the Salvation Army, gradually took over this role. In 1905, the first parole officer (known as the Dominion Parole Officer) was appointed. This individual, who was an officer of the Salvation Army, had the responsibility of visiting federal correctional facilities to evaluate inmates to see if they were "fit" for parole release. In 1913, the Remission Service was created (and placed under the control of the federal Department of Justice).

Other staff were soon hired to investigate the increasing numbers of individuals applying for ticket-of-leave. The significance of these developments was that they created "a more systematic approach to conditional release" (Canada, 1992:122).

From the early 1900s until 1958, the ticket-of-leave system gradually changed to resemble the modern parole process. To gain a conditional release, remission officers concentrated on the selection of inmates who could be safely released into the community. Once released, very little assistance was given to those reentering the community (Miller, 1965).

The Contemporary Era (1959–Present)

A significant change in the development of conditional release programs in Canada occurred in 1956, when the Fauteux Committee was established by the federal government to investigate the Ticket-of-Leave-Act. The Committee (Fauteux Report, 1956:55) criticized the existing system, reporting that it was "astonished" that "such antiquated legislation" could lead to "such satisfactory results." However, the Committee recognized the importance of a system of early release, in particular parole, which they viewed as "a well recognized procedure . . . designed to be a logical step in the reformation and rehabilitation of a person who has been convicted of an offence and as a result is undergoing imprisonment" (Fauteux Report, 1956:51). They also recognized that treatment was to be the primary focus of parole rather than simply punishment. To this end, they recommended the establishment of a separate parole authority, independent from the penal service (Fauteux Report, 1956:87). Part of this treatment approach was to facilitate the growth of aftercare agencies in the community. To ensure that inmates granted conditional release would obey the law and reintegrate into society, it was recommended that such programs be started far in advance of any conditional release into the community. In summary, the Fauteux Committee placed its support behind the rehabilitation of offenders, a concept of which early release into the community was an essential component.

In 1959, the Ticket-of-Leave-Act was repealed and replaced by the Parole Act. The Parole Act gave the National Parole Board the exclusive jurisdiction and absolute discretion to grant, deny, terminate or revoke all varieties of conditional release programs for offenders under its control. Section 10 of the new act stipulated that parole be granted when the inmate had derived maximum benefit from imprisonment, that parole will assist in the rehabilitation of the offender and that releasing the offender into the community would not constitute an undue risk to society. This act also created the National Parole Board, largely as a result of a recommendation of the Fauteux Committee. The National Parole Board was given powers that allowed its members to develop statutory and regulatory powers over the granting of parole as well as to set conditions for the inmate while on parole. The National Parole Service was also created, and they were given the authority to investigate and prepare cases for the National Parole Board as well as to arrange or provide for appropriate supervision. Parole was essentially seen as a component of treatment given to the inmate, and "a transitional step" between incarceration and total release. It was assumed that the treatment received by confined inmates "could be formed into a sequence of increasingly greater benefits for the individual prisoner, until a point of 'maximum benefit,' or 'optimum time' occurred" (Nuffield, 1982:2). Ideally, when the inmate reached this point, it would be recognized by the National Parole Board and its staff, who would then place the offender on a conditional release program. The assumption about parole was that it was "treatment-oriented" as opposed to being a sentence-correcting measure.

Due to their commitment to rehabilitation, one of the more serious concerns raised by the Fauteux Committee was the traditional use of **good time** systems or remission to promote good institutional behaviour among federal inmates. Inmates automatically received remission on their placement into custody, which could then be lost only by misconduct. Because offenders who gained remission through good behaviour had not necessarily been rehabilitated, the Fauteux Commission recommended a statutory period of parole supervision in the community for all those individuals released, corresponding to the amount of time earned by way of remission (Solicitor General of Canada, 1981a). In addition, the new act introduced temporary absences, allowing inmates to be granted short releases (with or without escorts) for humanitarian, rehabilitative or medical reasons. Over time, temporary absences were sometimes granted "back-to-back," allowing certain inmates to participate in a variety of activities requiring more time than that allowed by a single pass (Canada, 1992). A variety of temporary absence programs emerged, notably

(a) *Short Parole*: These typically lasted for less than 30 days in order to enable an inmate to participate in rehabilitation by obtaining full employment,

(b) *Parole with Gradual Release*: In these cases, permission would be granted to inmates to leave a correctional facility, with or without escort, for short periods of time just prior to final release date in order to assist in their reintegration into society,

(c) *Temporary Parole*: This program was developed in order to release inmates when full parole was not possible.

The concerns of the Fauteux Committee were soon borne out when in 1961 the Penitentiary Act was revised to differentiate between two types of remission: statutory and earned. **Statutory remission** allowed for 25 percent of a sentence to be credited to inmates when they were sentenced, but it had the power to eliminate or reduce this benefit as a punishment for problematic behaviour. **Earned remission** referred to the three days of remission that could be earned each month for good conduct, and could not be lost once earned. An inmate taking maximum benefit of these programs could reduce his or her sentence by almost one-third. The problem of this policy was that both forms of remission specified prisoners to be released into the community without supervision (as compared to parole, by which inmates were required to be supervised). Between 1959 and 1968, most inmates refused to apply for parole, choosing instead to earn remission so that when they were released, they would not be under the supervision of a parole officer. During this 10-year period, the percentage of applicants granted parole varied between 29 percent in 1963 and 49 percent in 1968. Overall, an average of 40 percent of the eligible inmates refused to apply for parole (Jobson, 1972). This issue led the to creation of mandatory supervision in 1970 (to be discussed later).

Problems soon surrounded the purpose, role and operation of the growing number of various conditional release programs. For example, the National Parole Board argued that the temporary absences issued by the Canadian Penitentiary Service were too lengthy and/or too commonly granted, making it difficult for the members of the Board to make independent judgments about the appropriateness of release. For its part, the Canadian Penitentiary Service argued that it would not cooperate with the National Parole Board, because the Board "refused to endorse a case plan in advance for fear of prejudicing its ability to take a completely unbiased release decision at a later date" (Canada, 1992:10).

Since the National Parole Board was firmly committed to the benefits of treatment, it tried to introduce new programs that would encourage inmates to become involved in treatment. In 1964, a new category of conditional release known as "minimum parole" was introduced by the National Parole Board. This

Willie Gibbs, chair of the National Parole Board, appears before the Commons justice committee in Ottawa to discuss amendments to the Criminal Code and the Corrections and Conditional Release Act. *Canapress Photo Service (Tom Hanson).*

release program was, in essence, a second chance for inmates who were refused release under parole. They could apply for minimum parole prior to their release due to remission (as long as they were allowed). Minimum parole could be granted on the basis of one month for each year served in custody, up to a maximum of six months in addition to statutory remission. Virtually everyone who applied for this form of release received it.

Because there was much confusion about the potential benefits and drawbacks of these myriad conditional release programs, the federal government appointed another commission, the Ouimet Committee, to give advice on reforming the entire criminal justice system. This new committee viewed the main purpose of parole "to assist the offender's reintegration into the community. They continued to support the view that parole was to be treatment-oriented rather than sentence-reducing." The distinction between low-risk and high-risk offenders continued, as the committee advocated the development of "dangerous offender" legislation because they believed that "improved methods of identifying the dangerous offender would promote a wider acceptance of community-based treatment for non-dangerous offenders . . ." (Ouimet, 1969:24). Overall, it was recommended that both probation and parole be used more often as alternatives to imprisonment.

The impact of the Ouimet Report had significant implications for conditional release programs. The Parole Act was amended in 1969 in order to create day parole. Day parole consolidated the various other short terms of parole and the longer rehabilitative types of temporary absences. Day parole could be granted after most inmates served one-sixth of their parole eligibility. Minimum parole was formally discontinued in the early 1970s.

In order to deal with the continuing debate over remission, the Parole Act was revised in 1970 to allow all inmates being released as a result of earned or statutory remission of 60 days or more to be placed under the authority of the National Parole Board. This new program was termed **mandatory supervision**. It meant that an additional 70 percent of all inmates released would now be subject to the authority and supervision of the National Parole Board until sentence expiry. The official goals of mandatory supervision were

(1) to reduce reoffending by giving some amount of control and/or assistance to the offender in the community;

(2) to be humane (by assisting offenders with anxieties, practical problems involved in leaving prison);

(3) to increase the rate at which inmates apply for parole;

(4) to reassure the public that virtually all penitentiary releases are supervised; and

(5) to assist the police to know the whereabouts and movements of mandatory releases (Solicitor General of Canada, 1981b:9-11).

The actual source of this policy was a recommendation made 14 years earlier by the Fauteux Committee. It had questioned the effectiveness of traditional remission policies in the promotion of good behaviour, feeling that automatic release did not necessarily lead to adjustment to community life. Instead, they proposed a statutory period of supervision in the community for everyone released, corresponding to the time earned by way of remission. The key point of this program was the supervision of the offender in the community.

Despite these amendments and new legislation, concerns continued to be raised concerning the low numbers of inmates applying for and released on parole. Between 1973 and 1980, for example, only 25 to 33 percent of all federal offenders who could apply for parole actually did. In comparison, up to 67 percent were released on mandatory supervision (Solicitor General of Canada, 1981a). As a response to these low numbers of parolees, two new federal government committees were created during the early 1970s to investigate the nature and operation of parole and how it could be improved so that more inmates would apply to be placed on parole.

The **Hugessen Report** (1973) and the **Goldenberg Report** (1974) were similar in that both advocated changes to the parole system. They recommended that parole should be fully integrated into the criminal justice system (Hugessen Report, 1973:57) and divest itself of the image of "the benevolent state giving clemency-type freedom to the deserving few" (Goldenberg Report, 1974:5). The Hugessen Committee viewed parole as a mechanism to reduce the "social and human costs" of prisons, pointing out that the criteria used to assess inmates for parole were too vague, so that "neither inmates nor members of the board are able to articulate with any certainty or precision what positive and negative factors enter into the parole decision" (Hugessen Report, 1973:32). The following year, the report of the Goldenberg Committee (1974:43) recommended that "parole should be fully extended to the greatest number of possible offenders." It emphasized that the objective of parole be amended to include "the protection of all members of society from seriously harmful and dangerous conduct" as well as to assist in social reintegration.

Both reports concurred that procedural safeguards should be introduced to the parole decision-making process, thereby making the National Parole Board a quasi-judicial body. The Hugessen Report, for example, included the recommendation that the reasons for rejecting parole be written down and given to the parole applicant. As a result of these recommendations, additional procedural protections were introduced by the end of the decade, including the requirement that reasons for denying parole be documented. These themes were reiterated by the Law Reform Commission of Canada (1977), which pointed out that these problems would potentially lead to problems of disparity, account-ability and evaluation. Notable was the fact that in all these reports there was "an absence of any explicit endorsement of the rehabilitative ideal" (Nuffield, 1982:4). It was recommended by many critics that the National Parole Board adopt parole guidelines in which the assessment of risk would be the central issue in parole release decisions.

In 1978, the Penitentiary Act removed the statutory crediting of remission, replacing it with an amendment that specified that up to 15 days remission could be earned for each month served (up to one-third of the sentence). In addition, inmates were provided with the option of refusing mandatory supervision if they chose to remain incarcerated until the termination of the sentence. Despite these changes, however, the number of parole applicants continued to be relatively small. Bottomley (1990) interprets these events as being indicative of the inmates' concern about the lack of due process protections for inmates, such as the right to a fair hearing and knowledge about complaints against oneself. These concerns about the parole process led to the belief among many inmates that the "pains of parole," with its policy of supervision in the commu-nity, were worse than the "pains of imprisonment."

In 1981, the Solicitor General's Study of Conditional Release (1981a) was completed, and the problems of due process and fairness in parole were once again highlighted but not solved. An important rec-ommendation was directed toward the National Parole Board, which was informed that it "must resolve questions of objections before it, and must provide more specific criteria in law to guide its decisions and pro-vide notice of its policies" (Solicitor General of Canada, 1981a:64). This report also pointed out the obvious: many inmates placed on mandato-ry supervision resented the fact that they were subject to compulsory supervision. In response to this issue, the members of the Solicitor Gen-eral's Study on Conditional Release warned that removing the mandato-ry supervision of some inmates convicted of violent crimes could lead to serious public concerns.

At the same time, a special committee was formed by the federal gov-ernment to investigate the issue of mandatory supervision. This commit-tee produced the report *Mandatory Supervision* (Solicitor General of Canada, 1981b), which endorsed the continuation of this program of conditional release. It reported that mandatory supervision was largely a successful program (the recidivism rate for mandatory supervision was around 30 percent, which was comparable to the rate for those released on parole). To alleviate public concerns, it suggested that authorities give more attention to identifying high-risk offenders who should not be released back into the community until later in their sentence. Moreover, if an offender was to commit a technical or criminal violation while on mandatory supervision, he or she was to be returned to a federal insti-tution to serve the remainder of his or her sentence. All offenders were therefore to be given "one chance to prove themselves on the street and have the opportunity for access to some assistance in reestablishing themselves" (Solicitor General of Canada, 1981b). In 1986, amendments were made to mandatory supervision, allowing the National Parole Board to gate offenders, that is, "to keep in custody certain dangerous or violent offenders for the whole duration of the sentence, without either parole or earned remission" (Bottomley, 1990:361).

In 1986, the National Parole Board adopted its first mission statement, specifically that it has "as its primary objective the protection of society" (Harman and Hann, 1986). In order to achieve this, risk assessment of inmates became "the critical issue in the decision-making process" (National Parole Board, 1987:9). In 1988, it released the document, *National Parole Board Pre-Release Decision Policies*, which attempted to make the decision-making process of the National Parole Board both "more open and understandable" Policies on release were now guided by three basic policies:

(1) risk to society is the fundamental consideration in any conditional release program;

(2) the limits on the freedom of the offender in the community must be limited to those that are necessary and reasonable for the protection of society and for facilitating the safe reintegration of the offender; and

(3) supervised release increases the likelihood of reintegration and contributes to the long-term protection of society (National Parole Board, 1988:4).

Since this time, debate about conditional release programs and the National Parole Board has taken on many dimensions in Canada. Inmates have contested the powers of the National Parole Board under the Charter of Rights and Freedoms with the result that some of the policies devised by the Board were found to be unconstitutional. The basis of conditional release and the powers of the National Parole Board were questioned by the Canadian Sentencing Commission (1987). While the Commission recommended the end of the system of full parole (this issue is discussed later in the chapter), it did state that a system of earned remission be retained on the belief that "if remission is abolished, harsher measures will have to be systematically used to ensure prison discipline, . . . making prisons an even more punitive environment than they already are" (Canadian Sentencing Commission, 1987:247). The following year, however, another investigation into conditional release by the **Daubney Committee** recommended that "conditional release in its various forms be retained and improved upon," stating that "public protection will be enhanced by preparing inmates for release into the society while they are still incarcerated and then providing them with the requisite degree of supervision and assistance once they are released into the community" (Daubney Committee, 1988:187-188). In contrast to the Canadian Sentencing Commission, they recommended that earned remission be abolished and most inmates be released on a statutory release program, which would replace mandatory supervision.

James Kelleher, then the Solicitor General of Canada, announced in 1990 that "the overriding criteria has to be, will releasing him constitute undue risk to the public? That is now going to be the guiding principle" (Marshall and Barrett, 1990:22). As a result of these concerns about the fairness of parole hearings and the protection of the public, the federal government enacted the Corrections and Conditional Release Act in 1992. It contains six principles that apply directly to parole boards:

(1) protection of society is the paramount consideration in any conditional release decision;

(2) all available, relevant information must be considered;

(3) parole boards enhance their effectiveness through the timely exchange of relevant information among criminal justice components and by providing information about policies and programs to offenders, victims, and the general public;

(4) parole boards will make the least restrictive decision consistent with the protection of society;

(5) parole boards will adopt and be guided by appropriate policies and board members will be given appropriate training; and

(6) offenders must be given relevant information, reasons for decisions, and access to the review of decisions to ensure a fair and understandable conditional release process (National Parole Board, 1994:3-4).

To say the least, the contemporary history of conditional release programs appears to be in a state of constant change in Canada, as the public's concerns influence policymakers and as the knowledge about offenders improves.

THE CONDITIONAL RELEASE SELECTION PROCESS

Many groups and individuals have criticized parole boards for their discretionary powers and judgments. In particular, the degree of subjectivity and lack of fairness of parole board decisions has been a source of great controversy for decades. Another concern is that the parole board operates in relative secrecy and is not accountable to the community.

The National Parole Board, however, is not a totally independent institution. It is an agency of the Solicitor General of Canada as well as being an administrative tribunal with the authority to grant or deny parole and statutory release.

Decision-making Powers

In Canada, all federal and provincial inmates (with the exception of provincial offenders in Ontario and Quebec whose applications are heard by their respective provincial parole boards) have to apply to the National Parole Board in order to be released on day parole and full parole. The members of the National Parole Board are not employees of the Correctional Service of Canada but are order-in-council appointees who are serving for a specific amount of time. Depending upon the parole application, a parole hearing involves one to five parole board members. All parole applications, whether for day or full parole, are heard by the National Parole Board. While they do not have the authority to grant statutory release because it is automatic, specific conditions concerning the release of an inmate may be added.

Most parole decisions are made after a hearing is held in the correctional facility where the offender is incarcerated, but the board makes decisions about accelerated review based purely on a file review. At the parole hearing, the inmate is interviewed by the parole board and then asked to leave while a decision is reached. Inmates are allowed to select someone to be present as an "assistant." These individuals may advise the offender and/or make a presentation on behalf of the offender. The assistant could be a friend, a relation, a lawyer, a member of the clergy, an elder, a prospective employer or a member of the penitentiary staff. In addition, relevant documentation may be included in any decision made by the National Parole Board. For example, the victims are now able to attend a parole board hearing. They are also allowed to submit letters, as can police officers and crown prosecutors.

In order to protect society, National Parole Board members are now required to review all available information about the inmate in order to make a preliminary assessment of risk. Relevant criteria can be classified as general (i.e., they apply to all parole applicants) or specific (i.e., they apply directly to an individual offender). Some of the general criteria used include whether (1) the offender will not, by committing another offence, present an undue risk to society before the end of the sentence, and (2) the release of the offender will contribute to the protection of society by facilitating return to the community as a law-abiding citizen (National Parole Board, 1994). The National Parole Board requires its members to look at a number of factors when conducting a preliminary **risk assessment**, including:

(1) the offence;

(2) criminal history;

(3) social problems, such as alcohol or drug use and family violence;

(4) performance on earlier releases, if any;

(5) mental status, especially if it affects the likelihood of future crime;

(6) information about the offender's relationships and employment;

(7) psychological or psychiatric reports;

(8) opinions from professionals and others such as aboriginal elders, judges, police, and other information that indicates whether release would present an undue risk or society; and

(9) information from victims (National Parole Board, 1994:10-11).

Beyond risk assessment, the National Parole Board is also required to make a decision about the statistical probability of reoffence by an offender. In this situation, they attempt to assess the rate of offences committed by a group of offenders with characteristics and histories similar to those of the person under review. Members of the National Parole Board try to predict future criminal behaviour by looking at certain specific factors such as:

(1) appropriate treatment for any disorder diagnosed by a professional;

(2) programs that help offenders become law-abiding citizens, such as substance abuse counselling, native spiritual guidance and elder counselling, literacy training, employment, and cultural programs, and programs that help offenders deal with family violence issues;

(3) the offender's understanding of the offence; and

(4) the offender's release plan.

If the National Parole Board approves of a parole application, the offender receives a date of release. However, if a request is turned down, the offender can apply to the Appeal Division of the National Parole Board for a reexamination of the decision. In 1996-97, the National Parole Board granted 2,693 applications for day parole for federally sentenced offenders while denying 1,362 applications. For provincial offenders, 280 applications were granted and 325 were rejected. In addition, 1,737 applications from federal inmates for full parole were granted, while 2,564 were denied. The grant rate for provincial offenders was 461, while 424 were denied (Solicitor General of Canada, 1997:56-57).

One important issue concerning the granting of conditional release revolves around the fairness of the release decision. Concerns were raised during the 1980s about the release rate of members of minority groups on parole. In 1988, the National Parole Board published their final report on aboriginal peoples in the federal correctional system and noted that only 9.5 percent of aboriginal offenders were released on parole in comparison to 24 percent of nonaboriginal offenders. It was also noted that aboriginal offenders were waiving their right to a parole hearing much more frequently than nonaboriginal offenders. Harman and Hann (1986) also discovered that aboriginals who were granted parole were more likely to have their parole terminated or revoked. Three years later, in their assessment of the applicability of the Nuffield scoring system for aboriginals, Harman and Hann (1986:9) reported that basing "parole release decisions for aboriginals solely on Nuffield scores would have resulted in a significant increase in the parole release rate for natives—from 12 percent to 41 percent." Other studies have indicated that certain parole criteria are biased against aboriginal offenders. For example, the Royal Commission investigating the wrongful conviction of Donald Marshall concluded that using employment prospects as a criterion for release actually leads to less aboriginals being released (Law Reform Commission of Canada, 1991:81).

The Mimico Correctional Centre, a medium-security prison facility near Toronto, Ontario. *Canapress Photo Service (Veronica Henri).*

Concerns have also been made about the lack of inadequate support for aboriginals once they are released (National Parole Board, 1988:31). Aftercare services to assist in the reintegration of aboriginal offenders have traditionally been limited, and where they existed, underfunded (Law Reform Commission of Canada, 1991:82). The Law Reform Commission of Canada (1991) recommended that culturally specific community programs for aboriginals be instituted as part of their conditional release programs. Finkler (1992) describes the efforts that have led to increased indigenisation of community programs in the Northwest Territories and some of the broader issues yet to be resolved. Some of the questions raised about the decisions made by the National Parole Board in terms of potential discrimination against members of minority groups were tested empirically. Two studies conducted by the federal government (Grant and Belcourt, 1992; Pepino et al., 1992) attempted to assess the treatment of aboriginals in temporary release programs. Grant and Porporino (1992) studied whether there was any discrimination against aboriginal peoples in the granting of temporary absences (TAs) over a five-year period (1986-87 to 1990-91). They reported that aboriginal offenders received more favourable treatment in terms of compassionate and family and community contact temporary absences. In their conclusion, they noted that "as far as early considerations for a graduated release program, native offenders are not discriminated against by correctional decision makers" (Grant and Porporino, 1992:530). This held constant across types of violence and criminality, meaning that "there is no systematic attempt to treat native offenders differently from non-native offenders" (Grant and Porporino, 1992:531).

In comparison to the concerns at the federal level, the "Report of the Commission on Systemic Racism in the Ontario Criminal Justice System" (1995) noted that while black applicants and white applicants for temporary absences in the provincial correctional system "were equally successful in obtaining TAs," black men were "under-represented among applicants relative to their representation to the prison population" (Commission on Systemic Racism, 1995:317). These differences were largely attributed to the proactive policies of the female institution and the reactive policies of the male facility studied. The women's facility had a case management system in operation, which meant that offenders were better informed and prepared for the TA process. At the men's facility, the onus was completely placed upon the inmate himself, with the result that many inmates were implicitly favoured. In the institution for men, correctional officers on shift staffed an "ad hoc" committee that reviewed applications and made recommendations without any direct inmate input such as an interview. All recommendations were then forwarded to the senior assistant warden for a final decision. The problem was identified as residing within the access to a TA program. According to the report (1995:321), the study found no "evidence of direct or indirect racial bias in the decision-making stages of the TA process . . . but the under-representation of black prisoners in the application process suggests that systemic barriers may impede their access to TA programs."

Release or Detention

In addition, members of the National Parole Board must consider the statistical probability of an offender committing another offence in the near future. In order to determine this probability, they must base their decision largely on how many similar offenders committed new offences when they were released on a conditional release program.

However, predictions concerning the future behaviour of people are never going to be completely accurate. Difficulties and inaccuracies associated with these predictions have been identified.

> . . . the degree of inaccuracy which should be tolerated in predictions . . . hinges on the ratio of two types of errors. The first error involves persons predicted as good risks, but who later prove to commit [a criminal act]. In prediction jargon, they are termed false negatives. The second type of error is false positive. These individuals are predicted as dangerous but do not commit a [criminal] act, that is, would not offend if released. There [are] two types of accurate predictions, true positive [predicted as criminal and is] and true negative [predicted as not criminal and is] (Hawkins and Albert, 1989:120-124).

Other problems exist in this area. Stanley (1976:56) points out that predictions are based on aggregate data, that is, from the actions of a large group of individuals such as parolees. He illustrates the difficulty involved in stating that of "100 offenders with a certain set of characteristics," perhaps 75 will succeed and 25 will fail. The question for the parole board is to figure out whether the applicant before them belongs to the 75 group or to the 25 group. If the National Parole Board decides that an offender poses an undue threat, they will deny full parole—but this simply means that an offender denied parole can be released on statutory release after serving two-thirds of his or her sentence. However, due to a series of cases during the 1980s that saw offenders automatically released into the community on statutory release, the government decided to pass legislation that would authorize detention until the end of their sentences for inmates likely to commit a new violent offence or serious drug offence.

As a result of these concerns, when the Corrections and Conditional Release Act was passed, it contained detailed procedures outlining those procedures that need to be followed when an offender is about to be released on statutory release but is considered a threat to public safety. Inmates who committed a violent or drug offence are now automatically reviewed to assess if they should be granted statutory release or detained. Correctional staff members also can report any concerns they have about an offender who they feel is likely to commit a violent or drug offence when released. The National Parole Board must consider all these issues, and if they decide to detain an inmate, an annual review has to be held to review whether the inmate is to be held in detention any longer. Since the passing of the Corrections and Conditional Release Act in 1992, more than 1,000 inmates have been detained for some extra period of time.

Due to a series of violent offences and murders committed by a few offenders released on either parole or mandatory supervision (the forerunner of statutory release) in the late 1970s and mid-1980s, the federal government decided to change the nature of early release programs. Legislation was passed in 1986 giving the authorities more power to detain those offenders predicted to commit a future violent offence when released. The length of detention varied, with an inmate serving an average of an extra one to two years beyond their statutory release date. In addition, the number of inmates detained has increased dramatically. Initial estimates made in 1986 predicted that approximately 100 inmates were to be detained per year, but that number now exceeds 400, meaning that in excess of 250 inmates who have never been supervised in the community are released each year. This has led to an intense debate about whether it was beneficial to detain those inmates who were predicted to commit a future offence or to release them under supervision in the community prior to the end of their sentence to assist them in their reintegration efforts. The question revolved around the issue of whether it would keep those detained from committing crimes and thus lead to a safer society.

In order to determine whether this was in fact true, Grant (1997) studied the success of this policy of detaining an offender until the end of his or her sentence. Almost one-half of the inmates referred to the National Parole Board were detained until the end of his or her sentence. This meant that, for all those detained under the new legislation for any amount of time, an average of 415 extra days were served. However, Grant discovered that 37 percent of those inmates released on full parole or statutory release at the scheduled time actually reoffended within two years. In contrast, however, only 16 percent of those detained for at least another year reoffended during the two years from their release date. Once released, Grant found those detained for an extra period of time committed less violent crimes as compared to those released early. As Grant points out, his findings defy much of the logic of the policy of detaining certain inmates on the basis of future criminal activity. "If referred offenders were truly the most serious offenders, it would be expected that they would return at a higher rate than those released at the statutory release date. The recidivism results seem to support the observation that the offenders who are detained are not the higher risk (Makin, 1997:A3)." The implications of these results include the possibility that incorrect criteria are being used to select which inmates are to be detained, that the detainees were not high-risk cases for reoffending in the first place, and that the parole authorities board is not interested in trying to educate the public that it is better to release an inmate into the community under supervision (Makin, 1997). Other research concurs with these results. For example, Grant and Gillis (1996:21), in their study of 555 day parolees who completed this program in 1990-91, report that "3 percent of those offenders who successfully completed day parole committed a violent offence before the end of their sentence while approximately 8 percent of offenders who failed on day parole committed a violent offence later in their sentence." This indicates that day parole is an effective mechanism to identify and prepare offenders for later conditional release programs.

CONDITIONS OF PAROLE, PAROLE SUSPENSION AND REVOCATION

Conditional releases (in particular full parole and statutory release) are, in essence, a contract between the state and the offender. If the offender is able to abide by the conditions as set out by the Parole Board for the duration of their conditional release program, they remain in the community until the expiry of their sentence. If release on one of these two programs is granted, the National Parole Board has the power to add conditions to those already required by law. Conditions required by law include remaining in a designated geographical area, refraining from breaking the law, not possessing a firearm, not associating with persons who have a criminal record and staying in contact with a parole or probation officer. Additional conditions can also be given to parolees if they are based on the risk assessment and any reasons why they committed their prior offences. Specific conditions can also be established, such as not being in the company of children or participating in treatment programs. The Corrections and Conditional Release Act (§ 55) now permits a parole officer to require offenders who are released on a conditional release program to submit to regular urinalysis.

If an offender released on full parole violates any condition, he or she may have his or her release suspended. While an offender may not have broken the criminal code or any other legal statute, he or she may be "guilty" of what is referred to as a **technical violation**. In these cases, a suspension warrant is issued and the parolee is placed in custody. A parole board hearing has to convene within 45 days to assess the case. If the parole board decides the parolee did in fact violate the conditions of parole, it may decide to issue a warrant and return the offender to a correctional facility for the remainder of the sentence. However, if the board decides the offender is not a risk to society (even if he or she did violate the conditions of his or her parole), it may decide to cancel the suspension and return the offender to the community. In such cases, the board may decide to add more conditions. However, if an individual has had his or her parole suspended twice previously for technical violations, the parole board has the power to extend the suspension warrant for another 30 days before it allows the offender to return to the community. If a parolee is sent back to a correctional facility due to a reason beyond his or her control, the parole is classified as "terminated." For all other reasons (such as a conviction for a criminal code violation), parole is "revoked" and the offender is returned to a correctional facility.

RELEASE, RISK PREDICTION AND RECIDIVISM RATES

One of the most commonly asked questions about any conditional release program is the program's rate of recidivism, that is, the rate at which offenders reoffend. The answer is usually taken as some indicator as to the "health" of the correctional system. If there is a high rate of recidivism, then the system has somehow failed to accomplish a significant goal. It appears that some members of the public are suspicious of the kinds of treatment offenders receive in a federal correctional facility, generally preferring to support deterrence and detention (i.e., longer sentences and long-term incarceration) over treatment, conditional release programs and reintegration into the community. In large part, their fears are based on incidents during the late 1960s, the 1970s and the early 1980s, when some parolees committed high-profile crimes. At the core of their concerns was the seemingly arbitrary decisions made by the National Parole Board, decisions that sometimes led to offenders being released who then committed violent offences in the community. While these crimes were not common incidents, they led to great fear in the community and, subsequently, to demands that the parole board restrict the number of inmates released on conditional release programs.

What exactly is the rate of recidivism in Canada today? In 1997-98, the success rate of the 2,279 male offenders who completed their full parole supervision was 89.2 percent (or 2,032 offenders). Of the 247 cases of parole revocation, 205 were for a nonviolent offence, while the remaining 42 were revoked for a violent offence. The success rate for women offenders was 92.7 percent, or 115 of the 124 offenders released on full parole. Of the nine cases revoked for the commission of a new offence, all nine were for a nonviolent offence.

For day parole, the success rate for the 3,004 male offenders who completed their day parole was 96.4 percent (2,896). Of the 108 cases in which day parole was revoked, 82 were for a nonviolent offence, while the remaining 26 were for a violent crime. In comparison, 98.6 percent (137 of 139 offenders) of women granted day parole successfully completed the program. Both of the two revoked cases involved nonviolent offences.

The lowest success rates for both men and women offenders were for those on statutory release. The rate of success for men was 87.9 percent, or 4,401 cases out of a total of 5,008. Of the 608 cases revoked, 501 (82.4 percent) were for a nonviolent offence, while the remaining cases involved a violent crime. Of the 96 women offenders placed on statutory release, 85.4 percent (or 82 of the 96) successfully completed their statutory release supervision period. Of the 14 cases that were revoked, 12 were for a nonviolent offence and two were for a violent crime (Solicitor General of Canada, 1997:57-60).

These high rates of success are largely the result of two changes introduced by the federal government during the past 15 years. First was the decision to detain larger number of offenders to the end of their sentence in a correctional facility. Just as important were efforts to increase the information about the risk posed by offenders prior to their release. With regard to the latter point, the Solicitor General of Canada decided to construct empirical predictors of recidivism that could assist decisionmakers in determining the risk of releasing an offender. Joan Nuffield (1982) was responsible for developing a risk prediction scale that is, in essence, an actuarial risk assessment instrument. To identify major risk factors, she selected a random sample of 2,745 offenders released during 1970, 1971 and 1972 who entered a federal correctional facility as the result of a new offence (revocations and provincial transfers were excluded). She gathered data concerning the current offence, previous criminal history and social/demographic information from the Inmate Records System. Records of arrest and reconviction were provided by the Canadian Police Information Centre. Nuffield then examined the relationship between the criminal variables and the social/demographic variables and recidivism. She then produced the General Statistical Information on Release Scale (usually referred to as the **SIR Scale**), which combines 15 factors related to criminal activity and social functioning. This scale was able to discriminate between high-risk cases and low-risk cases and, as a result, was formally introduced by the National Parole Board and Correctional Service of Canada (Cormier, 1997:3-4). Over the next decade, a series of studies (Hann and Harman, 1986; Serin, 1996) have validated the scale in terms of released inmates as well as assessing the impact of cognitive skills training on post-release recidivism (Robinson, 1995).

Because the SIR Scale was developed to predict risk and general recidivism among male offenders, questions were raised about its applicability as a tool for predicting recidivism among violent and sexual offenders. Concerns were also expressed about its use for federally sentenced aboriginals and women. These questions were raised because Nuffield was unable to develop separate scales to predict, for example, violent reoffending due to the low numbers of violent reoffending in her sample (Cormier, 1997).

Most of the initial studies that attempted to see if the SIR Scale could, in fact, predict reoffending were inconclusive. This conclusion was largely attributable to the small sample sizes used by the researchers. For example, Serin (1996) studied a sample of 81 male offenders released from Ontario federal correctional facilities over a 30-month period. The reported recidivism rate was 10 percent but no correlation was found between the SIR Scale and violent recidivism. Inconclusive evidence concerning women offenders was found by Hann and Harman (1986) and Blanchette (1996). All of these studies, however, used small sample sizes, ranging from 59 to 81. Bonta and Hanson (1995) concluded that the SIR Scale failed to predict recidivism among sexual offenders. Criticisms of the SIR Scale and its ability to predict recidivism among aboriginals argued that more culturally specific classification and assessment instruments were needed (LaPrairie, 1996; Waldrum, 1992) As Bonta et al. (1997:130) point out, in the correctional system "aboriginal offenders tend to be treated as an homogenous group despite the diversity of the aboriginal experience in Canada." The first studies found little or no difference when they compared aboriginal and nonaboriginal offenders (Hann and Harman, 1986). However, when studying a sample of three different groups of aboriginals with nonaboriginal probationers in Manitoba, Bonta et al. (1997) discovered differences among the aboriginal groups, although, as a group, the aboriginals and nonaboriginals were similar. As Cormier (1997:5) points out, these few studies should be interpreted with caution "considering the gaps in our knowledge of cross-cultural assessment."

These research studies indicate that while the SIR Scale can be used as a basis for a general prediction of risk, certain changes may have to be made to it in order to reflect cultural, gender and specific-offender needs. However, other instruments are in use (such as the Risk/Needs Scale) that may be used for comparative purposes. In addition, an annual assessment may be needed because, as more and better research is produced, certain items may be found to be poor predictors of general recidivism.

PAROLE ELIGIBILITY: THE "FAINT HOPE" CLAUSE

In July 1976, Bill C-84, which abolished capital punishment, was passed by Parliament. This bill introduced mandatory life sentences, with parole restrictions of 25 years for those convicted of first-degree murder and 10 to 25 years for those convicted of second-degree murder. Provisions in Bill C-84 included the possibility of early release for those offenders convicted of these sentences. Part of the new law allowed for the

Judicial Review of Parole Eligibility, creating an exception to these long periods of incarceration before parole eligibility. These provisions were prescribed in Section 745 of the Criminal Code of Canada. This was essentially a compromise between the opponents and supporters of capital punishment. When capital punishment was abolished, the period of ineligibility was raised to 25 years for first-degree murder and 10 to 25 years for second-degree murder. Those opposing such measures fought successfully to have the 15-year reviews included as part of the new bill. Legal experts have termed Section 745 a clemency-based amelioration of the most severe penalty known to our law.

Essentially, Section 745, which is known as the **"faint hope" clause**, allows offenders serving at least 15 years of a sentence to apply for a reduction in the amount of time they have to wait before their parole eligibility date, as specified by the sentencing judge in their cases. An application for a Judicial Review of Parole Eligibility is made to the Chief Justice in the province or territory where the original conviction occurred. The chief justice has to agree that the offender is eligible to apply and, if so, informs the provincial justice minister of the decision. In most provinces, a two-stage process is invoked: (1) a preliminary hearing, and (2) the actual hearing itself. The preliminary hearing (also referred to as a prehearing conference) allows the court to prepare for certain factors, such as transportation and housing, as well as to determine what evidence will be heard at the hearing. The evidence usually includes testimony from character and expert witnesses as well as relevant reports and statements of fact agreed upon by the offender and the provincial justice minister. In the hearing, a jury decides whether the application has merit. The hearing is adversarial in nature and usually takes from four to eight days to complete. Juries have three options in reaching their decision:

(1) make no change or reduction to the period of parole eligibility;

(2) reduce the number of years of imprisonment without eligibility for parole; or

(3) terminate the ineligibility for parole, making the applicant eligible to apply immediately. This does not mean that the offender will automatically be released on parole, but that the offender may now apply to the National Parole Board for release (Brown, 1992:16).

If the jury decides on the third option, the National Parole Board reviews the relevant information about the offender just as they would do in any parole hearing.

One of the major controversies about this section is that no clear principles direct juries in reaching their verdicts. According to Section 745, juries can consider "the character of the applicant, his conduct while serv-

A teenager holds a (misspelled) sign protesting convicted murder-er Clifford Olson's bid for early parole. Olson's parole eligibility was a result of Canada's "faint hope" clause. *Reuters/Jeff Vinnick/Archive Photos.*

ing his sentence, the nature of the offence for which he was convicted and such other matters as the judge deems relevant in the circumstances." If the jury decides to reject the application, the offender can appeal the decision to the Supreme Court of Canada (although Section 745 makes no provisions for such appeals), which can then order a second hearing. Another issue is whether multiple murderers should have the right to apply for parole review. In December 1996, Parliament revised Section 745 to eliminate multiple murderers from applying at all. Other revisions included the requirement that all applications for reviews be assessed by the federal Minister of Justice and that a jury has to be unanimous (which differs from the original legislation, which stipulated that only two-thirds of the jurors had to be in agreement).

How many successful applications have been made for early parole in Canada? Despite the common impression that most inmates apply for early review and those who do so actually receive it, this is not the case. By the end of 1996, fewer than one-third of all inmates who could apply for early parole actually had done so. It is speculated that the low number of applications can be attributed to the fact that the rate of success for immediate release, as opposed to release at a later date, is extremely low. For example, some individuals receive jury approval to apply for early release only to have the National Parole Board establish their date of release at a much later date. One such case involved an offender receiving a jury's decision to apply for early release in December 1993, but the reality was that this "successful" individual was still serving his sentence in a correctional facility three years later.

According to Correctional Service of Canada statistics, from February 1, 1991 (when the first offenders were legally allowed to apply) to October 1, 1996, 66 of the 222 had undergone a review. Of these, 52 (or 80 percent) achieved some success, as a jury granted them immediate eligibility to apply for parole or to apply for a second early review at a later date. Of the 52 successful applicants, 22 were still serving their sentence in a correctional facility because the parole board set their release date at a future point in time. Of the remaining 30 successful cases, 17 were on full parole, seven were on day parole and one had died, while the parole of two others had been revoked and three others had had their parole suspended for noncriminal violations.

INTENSIVE SUPERVISION PAROLE

Intensive supervision parole programs are community-based criminal sanctions that emphasize the close monitoring of offenders while they are in the community. There is no standard type of program, but all appear to share certain features, such as some combination of close contact with a supervising parole officer, drug testing, strict enforcement of parole conditions, and requirements to attend work and/or community programs. Those who support these types of programs forward two ideas that they believe establishes their worthiness. The first is that these programs can alleviate overcrowding in prisons and assist in the reintegration of offenders back into the community. The second argument is that offenders who return to the community remain under the close scrutiny of the authorities.

These arguments were largely borne out in some of the earliest evaluations of intensive evaluation programs. In Georgia, it was discovered that participants on the intensive supervision program had reincarceration rates of 16 percent and that there was a 10 percent reduction in the number of felons sentenced to incarceration (Erwin, 1987). However, other researchers pointed out critical methodological problems with the Georgia program that made the results somewhat ambiguous (Byrne et al., 1989). One criticism of the progam was that it included large numbers of low-risk, easily manageable offenders who were unlikely to be rearrested or violate the technical conditions of their parole orders (Petersilia and Turner, 1993). Another well publicized program, this time located in New Jersey, was reported to have reduced the rate of incarceration. However, upon further analysis, when rearrest and revocations for technical violations were combined, 40 percent of the program participants recidivated, as compared to 32 percent of the control group. This means that the close supervision of offenders released on an intensive supervision program plays a significant factor in the higher number of individuals sent back to correctional facilities.

Thus, despite the interest in these programs, early indications were that the benefits of these programs were overstated. In order to further evaluate these programs, the U.S. Department of Justice funded the RAND Corporation to investigate whether participation in intensive supervision programs influenced the behaviour of more than 2,000 offenders in 14 programs that were operated in nine states between 1986

Box 4.2 Intensive Supervision

The Intensive Supervision Program in Quebec and Ontario

Target Clientele

The clientele of its Intensive Supervision Program includes the following:

- high-risk statutory release cases;
- one-chance statutory release cases [An offender whose case has been referred with a view to continued detention may be granted statutory release by the National Parole Board (NPB). If, for one reason or another, statutory release is revoked, the offender cannot be released again until his sentence has expired.] (these are normally referred automatically to the Program);
- cases involving alternatives to incarceration—the offender has at one time or another committed an offence under Schedule I of the Corrections and Conditional Release Act, [Schedule I of the Corrections and Conditional Release Act lists serious offences involving violence] or has shown violent tendencies in an institutional setting or in the community;
- offenders who were previously in the Program and who are coming again on statutory release;
- exceptional cases referred to the team.

Program Goals

The Program aims to:

- improve public safety by carrying out intensive supervision, exceeding currently prescribed standards, of clients with a high risk of recidivism;
- provide parolees with the wherewithal to meet specific needs (food and housing) and deal with their problems (drugs, alcohol, psychological and psychiatric problems, etc.);
- manage risk and prevent recidivism.

Program Components

The Program usually last six months. It can be shorter if the offender's warrant is due to expire, or longer if the offender is experiencing difficulties or is unstable. If progress is not made, the offender may have to repeat an earlier phase of the program and the amount of supervision and support increased.

During Phase I of the Program, emphasis is placed on control and contacts with the offender and community resources (at least two client contacts a week). Officers work out a correctional plan with the subject and give the local police force a small file on him. A curfew from midnight to 8:00 a.m. is imposed and checked regularly. The curfew is lifted during Phase II. In Phase III supervision drops to one contact a week and an assessment of the situation is made with a view to switching to regular supervision.

Special Features

Offenders convicted of sex crimes undergo a special assessment to determine the risk of recidivism and, if appropriate, set up a specific therapy program in the community.

Box 4.2—*continued*

Program officers discuss cases once a week and carry out supervision mainly in the community.

Telephone contact with offenders and with third parties is made as often as necessary.

A liaison officer with the Montreal Urban Community police co-ordinates all program activities involving the various Montreal police forces. A liaison officer in each police station is responsible for following up on offenders in his or her area.

The Community Projects Program

Day parole for community projects enables the parolee to reintegrate society by doing volunteer work in the community. Community projects are relatively restrictive forms of release. Yet for many it is the first step toward other types of release, including regular day parole [Day parole gives the offender an opportunity to participate in community activities on a continuing bases. In general he lives in a correctional institution or community residential facility. He is granted day parole in order to prepare for full parole or statutory release.] and full parole. [Full parole is a form of conditional release granted at the NPB's discretion. It enables the offender to serve a part of his sentence in the community. In every case the offender is under supervision and must meet the conditions that have been set in order to reduce the risk of refunding and promote his reintegration into the community. He is not required to return to the institution every night, but he must report regularly to a parole officer and, in some instances, to the police.]

Two years ago the Ville-Marie Office added a new dimension to the community projects formula by including a day-parole volunteer work program combined with residency at a halfway house. This allows inmates serving long sentences or with long criminal records to make a gradual return to the community. Offenders' movements are controlled and supervised strictly, to meet their needs more effectively while at the same time minimizing the risk. Access to the community is more limited than with other forms of release, but contacts with society are nonetheless real. All aspects of every day life are developed with the community projects parolees.

In November 1996 the Greater Montreal District introduced another element to the community projects approach, offering certain inmates the opportunity to do unpaid work with residency at a halfway house. Inmates join the existing community projects day parole program, do volunteer work every day, take part in the halfway house program, and may be granted absences within the limits prescribed by the Act.

Experience shows that the supervision and support given the inmate or parolee under the community projects program helped the offender to take control of his/her life, improves self-esteem and enhances employability. There are few failures, and many who are getting their first or their last chance at parole will eventually gain access to other forms of release. In addition, the work done by parolees and inmates allows community organizations to provide services that they could not have offered otherwise, the offenders' involvement helps to break down prejudices against them, and they do earn a reward through the social benefits the program affords them.

Source: Correctional Service of Canada, Ottawa, "The Ottawa Supervision Program in Quebec and Ontario," 1997. Reproduced with the permission of the Minister of Public Works and Government Services, Canada, 1998.

and 1991. This evaluation introduced great methodological rigor and, as such, its results are considered to be the best in terms of the success or failure of these programs. Their conclusions went against many of the assumed benefits of these programs, finding higher-than-expected costs, an increase in the size of the prison population in some areas, and that the programs were no more effective than regular programs in terms of reducing recidivism.

Great interest was directed toward the impact of intensive supervision programs upon recidivism. However, it must be noted that "intensive" in terms of the number of contacts between a parole officer and an offender has varied considerably according to the state under study. In some states, "intensive" meant four contacts per month over a year, while in others it meant five contacts in a six-week period. In addition, two recidivism measures were used: arrests and technical violations. The RAND researchers found that arrests for those individuals placed on an intensive supervision program were actually higher than those placed on the regular programs. Specifically, they report that after one year, arrests were higher among the intensive supervision offenders (37 percent) than among the control group (33 percent). In terms of technical violations, the results were found to be even less promising. The average intensive supervision program violation rate was 65 percent, compared to 38 percent for the control group—a significant difference. In addition, the RAND investigators found that those individuals who participated in treatment programs and an intensive supervision program experienced a 10 percent to 20 percent decrease in recidivism (Petersilia and Turner, 1993).

SHOULD PAROLE BE ABOLISHED?

In recent decades an increasing number of jurisdictions in the United States have eliminated parole. By 1984, 12 states had abolished parole, although one state—Colorado—reintroduced a parole system in 1985. The policy to abolish parole was typically introduced in conjunction with a determinate sentencing structure. The reason parole was abolished was because of the discretionary release decisions made by parole authorities. Reforms usually intended to pass that power to the sentencing judge. The results of parole abolition are now well known. In most states, prison populations have increased to the point of overcrowding. Maine, for example, had to open four new prisons; other states introduced accelerated release programs for certain categories of offenders during periods of prison overcrowding (Bottomley, 1990:342).

Concerns about recidivism while on parole led the Canadian Sentencing Commission to study the impact of conditional release programs, especially parole, upon sentencing. In their report they quoted the work of Waller (1974), who some 15 years previously had found that release on a conditional release program did not prevent subsequent offending but rather simply postponed it until the offender had successfully completed parole.

This issue came to the forefront during the second half of the 1980s, when the Canadian Sentencing Commission (1987:244) concluded that "there did not seem to be any positive benefits of discretionary parole release which could possibly justify its continued existence within the integrated set of reforms advocated by this Commission . . . The length of time an offender will spend in custody should be fixed, as much as possible, at the time of sentencing." The Commission recommended the abolition of full parole (except in cases of life imprisonment) for three reasons: (1) parole systems operate in conflict with the principle of proportionality (i.e., a direct relationship between the length of punishment and the seriousness of the crime) in punishment; (2) discretionary release introduces a great deal of uncertainty into the sentencing process, and (3) parole release transfers sentencing decisions from the judge to the parole board (Canadian Sentencing Commission, 1987:244).

The Canadian Sentencing Commission (1987:247) did recommend the retention of some form of earned remission, because "if remission is abolished, harsher measures will have to be systematically used to ensure prison discipline, . . . making prisons an even more punitive environment than they already are." They also estimated out that if parole were to be abolished, the prison population would double in size. Earned remission was suggested as an alternative to parole because "good time credits" that would reduce a sentence by up to 25 percent could be earned by most inmates. The Sentencing Commission also made a number of other recommendations concerning conditional release programs. They agreed that mandatory supervision should be abolished "unless the judge, upon imposing a sentence of incarceration, specifies that the offender should be released on conditions" (Canadian Sentencing Commission, 1987:251). They also proposed that a decision by a judge could be modified or eliminated under certain circumstances. Day parole programs were to be retained and, for most offenders, this program was to be accessible after two-thirds of their sentence had been served. Programming for inmates was not to be abolished; however, it was to be offered purely on a voluntary assistance basis. These were to be available to all offenders both prior to and once they were released into the community in order to assist them with reintegration (Canadian Sentencing Commission, 1987:253). Greater powers were to be granted to the judiciary. They would, for example, decide if (and what types of) conditions should be granted to offenders. In addition, they proposed the elimination of the parole board, which would in turn be replaced by a Sentence Administration Board whose members would have the power to withhold remission release according to the criteria specified in the Parole Act and the Penitentiary Act. Despite government interest in this approach, it was never introduced. Instead, the Daubney Committee's proposal (see the previous section in this chapter on the history of parole) that conditional release programs be retained with revisions seems to have been the preferred approach. As Brodeur (1990:506) correctly surmises, there was at this time a subtle shift in the focus of parole, largely as the result of the attacks on parole from crime control advocates. This led to a shift from an emphasis upon rehabilitation to a policy of controlling offenders. This resulted in the creation of a new direction for conditional release programs in Canada, one that led directly to the current overcrowding crisis found within Canadian correctional facilities and an undermining of the importance of rehabilitation.

Box 4.3 The Role of the Victim in the Parole Process

Can a victim's information be considered in conditional release decisions?

The Corrections and Conditional Release Act recognizes that victims have certain rights. The Board considers information from victims, especially that which can help to assess whether an offender's release may pose a risk to society. The Board is interested in information that will assist in assessing the offender's understanding of the effect of the offence and whether that person is likely to reoffend. In cases of statutory release, where the Board must decide whether to detain an offender, information about the harm suffered by victims is critical for the Correctional Service of Canada and the National Parole Board.

Information from victims is also important when it is directly relevant to assessing conditions necessary to manage a particular risk that the offender might present, and to the offender's release plans, especially if the offender will be near the victim or is a member of the victim's family. Victims are encouraged to provide this information as soon as possible after sentencing or before an offender becomes eligible for parole.

Will information from victims be kept confidential?

The National Parole Board and the Correctional Service of Canada are required by law to share with the offender any information that will be considered during the decision-making process. Information cannot be used if it is not shared with the offender. Exceptions to this rule are rare; they include extraordinary situations, such as the safety of a person, the security of a correctional institution, or the possible jeopardy of an ongoing investigation.

Who is a victim?

The Corrections and Conditional Release Act defines a victim as someone to whom harm was done or who suffered physical or emotional damage as the result of a crime. The law considers that relatives are victims when the victim has been killed or is unable to be responsible for some reason such as age or illness.

Box 4.3—*continued*

Victims may authorize someone to act for them should they prefer. The Board will recognize someone as an agent for a victim if the victim makes a written statement designating someone to that effect.

How does someone request information about an offender?

Victims may write to request information from either the National Parole Board or the Correctional Service of Canada. If asked, the National Parole Board or the Correctional Service of Canada must release certain information to victims and may release certain other information.

Because the release of certain information about offenders is limited to victims as defined in the law, the request should clearly identify the offender and the crime committed. If guidance is needed, victims are invited to contact any of the offices of the National Parole Board or the Correctional Service of Canada.

A victim, or in some cases a victim's family, can request and will receive basic information about an offender, including;

- when the sentence began and the length of the sentence; and
- the eligibility and review dates of the offender for unescorted temporary absences and parole.

More information may be released if the Chairperson of the National Parole Board or the Commissioner of the Correctional Service of Canada determines that the interest of the victim outweighs any invasion of the offender's privacy that could result from the disclosure.

Such information may include:

- the location of the penitentiary in which the sentence is being served;
- the date, if any, on which the offender is to be released on unescorted or escorted temporary absence, work release, parole, or statutory release;
- the date of any hearing for the purposes of a review for possible detention;
- any of the conditions attached to the offender's unescorted temporary absence, work release, parole, or statutory release;
- the designation of the offender when released on any temporary absence, work release, parole, or statutory release, and whether the offender will be in the vicinity of the victim while travelling to that destination;
- whether the offender is in custody and, if not, why; and
- whether or not the offender has appealed a decision of the Board, and the outcome of that appeal.

In addition, when an offender has been transferred from a penitentiary to a provincial correctional facility, the name of the province in which the provincial facility is located may be disclosed.

Is a victim or the family of a victim informed when a person convicted of a crime is granted conditional release?

No, not automatically. This information will be given only upon written request. Some victims prefer to have no further knowledge of the offender. A victim or a victim's family must ask for information.

Box 4.3—*continued*

Can victims receive ongoing information?

Yes. Victims must make the request in writing and ensure that the National Parole Board or the Correctional Service of Canada has their current address and telephone number. They may then be informed of changes such as a move from one institution to another or the grant of a conditional release.

Can information be given to anyone other than victims?

The same information that can be released to victims can also be given to certain other people. However, they must satisfy the Chairperson of the National Parole Board or the Commissioner of the Correctional Service of Canada that they suffered harm or physical or emotional damage because of an offender's act, whether or not the offender was prosecuted or convicted for that act. If they have made a complaint to the police or the Crown attorney, or an information was laid under the Criminal Code, then the person will be formally recognized as a victim and given the same information that would be given had the offender been convicted of the offence.

Source: National Parole Board of Canada, Ottawa, "Parole: Balancing Public Safety and Criminal Responsibility," 1996. Reproduced with the permission of the National Parole Board.

SUMMARY

Conditional release programs remain a significant component of the federal and provincial/territorial correctional systems. These programs include a variety of parole polices as well as temporary absences and statutory releases. In addition, the federal government introduced an accelerated release program for first-time, low-risk offenders. The success rates of these programs have been high, largely due to advances in knowledge concerning the risk of reoffending among offenders. Detention, another revised policy, also contributes significantly to the success of conditional release programs. This is because those individuals thought to be at high risk now have the potential to be locked up until the termination of their sentence.

The process of selecting offenders to be placed on a conditional release program currently lies with the National Parole Board and the Ontario and Quebec Provincial Parole Boards. The selection of inmates for parole was found to be fraught with selective bias in the past, so much so that the National Parole Board now requires its members to take courses that assist them in the areas of psychology and risk assessment. Recidivism rates for parolees have decreased in recent years, largely as a result of the heightened awareness concerning risk prediction. The "faint hope" clause, which allows long-term offenders to apply for a sentence reduction, highlights a variety of issues relevant to the early release of individuals sentenced to long periods of incarceration. Recent program developments, in particular intensive supervision parole (ISP), indicate the importance placed by authorities on parole as a successful part of the reintegration of offenders in Canadian society.

DISCUSSION QUESTIONS

1. In recent years the federal government has made it more difficult to be given full parole. Do you agree with this policy?

2. What are the major problems associated with conditional release programs? Do you think we can ever overcome these problems or would it be better to reduce the amount of conditional release programs we offer?

3. Do you think the process of conditional release can be unfair to certain groups?

4. Do you think there should be more community participation on the National Parole Board and their decisions?

5. Do you think the "faint-hope clause" should be eliminated? Why do you think it was implemented in the first place?

REFERENCES

Abadinsky, Harold (1987). *Probation and Parole: Theory and Practice,* Fourth Edition. Englewood Cliffs, NJ: Prentice-Hall

Barnes, Henry Elmer and Negley K. Teeters (1959). *New Horizons in Criminology,* Third Edition. Englewood Cliffs, NJ: Prentice-Hall.

Blanchette, Kelley (1996). "Classifying Female Offenders for Correctional Interventions." *Forum on Corrections Research*, Volume 9, 36-41.

Bonta, James (1996). "Do We Need Theory for Offender Risk Assessment?" *Forum on Corrections Research*, Volume 9, 42-45.

Bonta, James, and R.K. Hanson (1995). "Violent Recidivism of Men Released from Prison." Paper presented at the Annual Convention of the American Psychological Association, New York, NY.

Bonta, James, Carol LaPrairie and Suzanne Wallace-Capretta (1997). "Risk Prediction and Re-Offending: Aboriginal and Non-Aboriginal Offenders." *Canadian Journal of Criminology*, Volume 39, 127-144.

Bottomley A. Keith (1990). "Rethinking Parole." In Michael Tonry and Norval Morris (eds.), *Crime and Justice: A Review of Research*, Volume 12. Chicago: University of Chicago Press.

Brown, Glen (1992). "Judicial Review: How Does It Work and How Does It Affect Federal Corrections?" *Forum on Corrections Research*, Volume 4, 14-16.

Brodeur, Jean-Paul (1990). "The Attrition of Parole." *Canadian Journal of Criminology*, Volume 32, 503-510.

Byrne, James M., Arthur J. Lurigio and Christopher Baird (1989). "The Effectiveness of New Intensive Supervision Programs." *Research in Corrections*, Volume 2, 1-48.

Byrne, James M., Arthur J. Lurigio and Joan Petersilia (1992). *Smart Sentencing*. Newbury Park, CA: Sage.

Canada (1992). *Predicting General Release Risk for Canadian Penitentiary Inmates*. Ottawa: Solicitor General of Canada.

Canadian Sentencing Commission (1987). *Sentencing Reform: A Canadian Approach*. Ottawa: Canadian Government Publishing Centre.

Carter, R.M., R.A. McGee and K.E. Nelson (1975). *Corrections in America*. Philadelphia: Lippincott.

Commission on Systemic Racism in the Ontario Criminal Justice System (1995). *Report of the Commission on Systemic Racism in the Ontario Criminal Justice System*. Toronto: Queen's Printer for Ontario.

Cormier, Robert B. (1997). "Yes SIR! A Stable Risk Prediction Tool." *Forum on Corrections Research*, Volume 9, 3-7.

Daubney Committee (1988). *Taking Responsibility*. Ottawa: Queen's Printer.

Erwin, Billie (1987). *Evaluation of Intensive Probation Supervision in Georgia*. Washington, DC: National Institute of Justice.

Fauteux Report (1956). *Report of a Committee to Inquire into the Principles and Procedures Followed in the Remission Service of the Department of Justice of Canada*. Ottawa: Queen's Printer.

Finkler, H. (1992). "Community Participation in Socio-Legal Control: The Northern Context." *Canadian Journal of Criminology*, Volume 34, 503-512.

Goldenberg Report (1974). *Parole in Canada: Report of the Standing Committee on Legal and Constitutional Affairs*. Ottawa: Queen's Printer.

Grant, Brian A. (1997). "Detention: Is It Meeting It's Goal?" *Forum on Corrections Research*, Volume 9, 19-24.

Grant, Brian A. and Ray L. Belcourt (1992). *An Analysis of Temporary Absences with the People Who Receive Them*. Ottawa: Correctional Services of Canada.

Grant Brian and Christa A. Gillis (1996). "Gradual Release Programs: Day Parole Performance and Subsequent Release Outcome." *Forum on Corrections Research*, Volume 8, 19-21.

Grant, Brian A. and Frank J. Porporino (1992). "Are Native Offenders Treated Differently in the Granting of Temporary Absences from Federal Correctional Institutions?" *Canadian Journal of Criminology*, Volume 34, 525-532.

Harman, William G. and Robert G. Hann (1986). *Release Risk Assessment: An Historical Descriptive Analysis*. Ottawa: Solicitor General of Canada.

Hawkins R.A. and G. Albert (1989). *American Prison Systems: Punishment and Justice*. Englewood Cliffs, NJ: Prentice-Hall.

Hugessen Report (1973). *Report of the Task Force on the Release of Inmates*. Ottawa: Information Canada.

Jobson, Keith (1972). "Fair Procedure in Parole." *University of Toronto Law Journal*, Volume 22, 267-303.

LaPrairie, Carol (1996). *Examining Aboriginal Corrections in Canada*. Ottawa: Aboriginal Corrections, Ministry of the Solicitor General.

Law Reform Commission of Canada (1991). *Report on Aboriginal Peoples and Criminal Justice*. Ottawa: Ministry of Supply and Services.

Law Reform Commission of Canada (1977). *The Parole Process: A Study of the National Parole Board*. Ottawa: Ministry of Supply and Services.

Makin, Kirk (1997). "Conditional Release Law a Failure, Study Says." *Globe and Mail*, October 14, 1997, A3.

Mandel, Michael (1975). "Rethinking Parole." *Osgoode Hall Law Journal*, Volume 13, 501-546.

Marshall, W.K. and Sylvia Barrett (1990). *Criminal Neglect: Why Sex Offenders Go Free*. Toronto: Doubleday.

Miller, Frank P. (1965). "Parole." In W.T. McGrath (ed), *Crime and Its Treatment in Canada*. Toronto: Macmillan.

National Parole Board (1994). *Parole: Balancing Public Safety and Personal Responsibility*. Ottawa: Ministry of Supply and Services.

National Parole Board (1988). *National Parole Board Pre-Release Decision Policies*. Ottawa: Minister of Supply and Services.

National Parole Board (1987). *Chairman's Presentation to the Standing Committee on Justice and Solicitor General*. Ottawa: National Parole Board.

Nuffield, Joan (1982). *Parole Decision-Making in Canada: Research Towards Decision Guidelines*. Ottawa: Ministry of Supply and Services.

Ouimet, R. (1969). *Report of the Canadian Committee on Corrections—Toward Unity: Criminal Justice and Corrections*. Ottawa: Information Canada.

Pepino, N. Jane, Lucie Pepin and Robert J. Stewart (1992). *Report of the Panel Appointed to Review the Temporary Absence Program for Penitentiary Inmates*. Ottawa: Solicitor General of Canada.

Petersilia, Joan and Susan Turner (1993). "Intensive Probation and Parole." In Michael Tonry (ed.), *Crime and Justice: A Review of Research,* Volume 17. Chicago: University of Chicago Press.

Reed Michelle and Julian Roberts (1996). *Adult Community Corrections in Canada: 1994-95*. Ottawa: Statistics Canada.

Robinson, David (1995). "Federal Offender Family Violence: Estimates From a National File Study." *Forum on Corrections Research*, Volume 7, 15-18.

Serin, Ralph (1996). "Psychological Intake Assessment: Contributing to Contemporary Offender Classification." *Forum on Corrections Research*, Volume 9, 51-54.

Solicitor General of Canada (1997). *Basic Facts About Corrections in Canada*. Ottawa: Solicitor General of Canada.

Solicitor General of Canada (1981a). *Solicitor General's Study of Correctional Release*. Ottawa: Ministry of Supply and Services.

Solicitor General of Canada (1981b). *Mandatory Supervision*. Ottawa: Ministry of Supply and Services.

Stanley, D. (1976). *Prisoners Among Us: The Problem of Parole*. Washington, DC: The Brookings Institution.

Waldrum, J. (1992). "Cultural Profiling and the Forensic Treatment of Aboriginal Offenders in Canada." Paper presented at the American Society of Criminology, New Orleans, LA.

Walker, Samuel (1980). *Popular Justice: A History of American Criminal Justice*. New York: Oxford University Press.

Waller, Irwin (1974). *Men Released From Prison*. Toronto: University of Toronto Press.

CHAPTER 5

Probation

PROBATION

Probation is defined as "a court-ordered dispositional alternative through which an adjudicated offender is placed under the control, supervision and care of a probation staff member in lieu of imprisonment, so long as the probationer meets certain standards of conduct" (American Correctional Association, 1995). It is the most common form of criminal sentencing in Canada and therefore represents the largest group of offenders who are placed into the arena of community sanctions. Of the 154,000 individuals under the supervision of both federal and provincial correctional systems during 1995-96, 100,799 (or 67 percent) were on probation (Reed and Morrison, 1997). Despite its popularity among judges and prosecutors, probation suffers from intense public criticism. It has been given a "soft on crime" image and therefore is constantly under attack as a sentence that allows dangerous criminals to be released back into the community when they should be incarcerated. Probation has certain advantages that will keep it as a primary policy in the decades to come, including lower costs, increased opportunities for rehabilitation, flexibility of programming and the reduction of the risk of criminal socialization, among others. In recent years, however, supporters of probation have been calling for the "restructuring" of probation. In this chapter, the history, operation and current status of probation will be reviewed as well as some issues and future possibilities.

Probation services are operated at the provincial level of jurisdiction in Canada. The maximum probation sentence is three years. A period of probation cannot be imposed as a separate sanction but instead must be given in conjunction with a suspended sentence, a fine or a term of incarceration not exceeding two years. If multiple probation sanctions are given to an offender, they must be served concurrently. Probation differs

<table>
<tr><th colspan="3">KEY TERMS</th></tr>
<tr><td>benefit of clergy</td><td>judicial reprieve</td><td>prison release ISP</td></tr>
<tr><td>case management ISP</td><td>postsentence report</td><td>probation</td></tr>
<tr><td></td><td>presentence report</td><td>specific conditions</td></tr>
<tr><td>general conditions</td><td>prison diversion</td><td>split sentence</td></tr>
<tr><td>intensive supervision probation (ISP)</td><td></td><td></td></tr>
</table>

from parole in a number of ways. Every probation sanction is attached with a condition to keep the peace, be of good behaviour, and appear before the court as specified by an agent of the court. While an offender "earns" his or her early release into a conditional release program, probation is a sentence given to an offender by the sentencing judge. In its original form, probation was designed for first-time offenders who would typically be convicted of a property crime and for whom individualized programming could make a difference in their lives. This reality has changed over the years.

Since 1990-91, the intake rates of probationers (i.e., the number of individuals starting a term of probation) in Canada increased relative to other dispositions such as incarceration. Between 1990-91 and 1994-95, the national rate of probation intakes went up by 42 percent, or from 804 per 10,000 adults charged to 1,139 per 10,000 adults charged. This increase in rates was evident in all provincial jurisdictions except Prince Edward Island, where the rate declined by 24 percent.

Probation is a judicial function, that is, a judge has the legal authority to grant probation to an offender as well as to revoke the grant of probation. However, provincial correctional authorities have the responsibility to ensure that probationers fulfill all general and specific conditions and their actions can influence some of the decisions made by the judiciary.

As a sentencing option, probation is generally used in the following situations: (1) accompanying a suspended sentence; (2) in connection with a conditional discharge; or (3) in addition to a fine or sentence (provided that the sentence does not exceed two years), or an intermittent sentence (Griffiths and Verdun-Jones, 1994:359). In suspending the execution of a sentence of incarceration, the judge suspends the actual process of sentencing itself. If offenders successfully complete the term on probation, in most cases they avoid the period of incarceration. If they are not successful in completing their terms of probation, the imposed period of incarceration remaining will be served in a correctional facility.

Probation is commonly used with other types of sentences. For example, an offender may be sentenced to a brief or relatively short period of time of incarceration to be followed by a period of time on probation (referred to as a **split sentence**) or it can be imposed in conjunction with a fine, community service or restitution, usually in order to ensure compliance with the court order. In most cases, judges have a significant amount of discretion in deciding when to use probation as a sentencing option.

Probation involves the conditional release of an offender into the community. This means that those individuals given a term of probation are obliged to observe a number of general conditions (a series of requirements that all probationers in a particular jurisdiction must agree to fulfill) and, possibly, a set of specific conditions (requirements specific to the individual offender that are imposed at the time of sentencing by the judge).

The nature of these general conditions can vary tremendously between and within jurisdictions. The amount of discretion available to a judge (per Section 737(2) of the Criminal Code), as well as to probation officers in adhering to these conditions, has become a source of controversy, and will be discussed later in this chapter.

Another aspect of probation involves supervision. All individuals placed on probation are to be supervised directly or indirectly in order to make sure they are complying with the conditions of probation. Supervision involves concerns about the protection of society as per Section 737(2) of the Criminal Code (i.e., ". . . that the accused shall keep the peace and be of good behaviour . . ."), as well as providing some form of assistance to the probationer. In reality, there is a continuum of supervision, from minimal to extensive, and the means of actually supervising the probationer can be extremely varied.

A PROFILE OF PROBATIONERS: AGE, RACE AND GENDER

It is a common belief that probation is usually granted to young adults, because most young people have no criminal record. While this is still true, in Canada, the average age of probationers has been increasing since 1990-91. In 1990-91, the average age was 27 and it increased to 30 in 1993-94 before decreasing to 29 in 1994-95. Nationally, 17 percent of all offenders sentenced to probation were women in 1994-95. These national rates, however, hide great variability at the provincial level. During 1994-95, the rate of women sentenced to probation was higher than for males for all provinces and territories except for Quebec, Manitoba and the Northwest Territories. The percent distribution of women probationers varies considerably across Canada, from a high of 22 percent in Alberta to 12 percent in Quebec. In 1995-96, Ontario accounted for almost 50 percent of probationers. In most jurisdictions, men sentenced to probation have been traditionally convicted of a crime of violence, while women were likely to receive probation after having committed crimes against property (Reed and Roberts, 1996:8). However, Birkenmayer and Besserer (1997) discovered in their study of sentencing in nine adult provincial courts during 1993-94 that women were more likely to be placed on probation as their most serious sanction for multiple-charge cases (see Table 5.1).

Table 5.1
Comparison of Gender and Types of Most Serious Sanction

| Offence Category | Most Serious Sanction (% of Cases) | | | | | | Total (%) | |
| | Prison | | Probation | | Fines | | | |
	Males	Females	Males	Females	Males	Females	Males	Females
Against Person	38	18	46	60	14	16	98	94
Property	40	16	36	48	22	28	97	92
Motor Vehicle	27	14	9	12	63	74	100	100
Morals	7	32	26	25	43	34	76	90
Administration of Justice	50	40	14	23	32	31	97	94
Other Criminal Code	24	14	32	35	40	42	95	91
Drugs	31	29	16	25	48	39	94	93
Other Federal Statutes	5	3	4	4	88	86	96	93
Total %	34	20	24	35	39	40	97	94
Number of Cases	153,620	14,726	108,859	26,239	178,368	29,784	440,847	70,749

Note: Restitution and "other" sanctions are not shown because the values are too small. As a result, the totals may not add to 100%.

Source: Statistics Canada, "Comparison of Gender and Types of Most Serious Sanction," from "Sentencing in Adult Provincial Courts: A Study of Nine Provincial Jurisdictions," Catalogue 85-513, page 26.

Aboriginal offenders accounted for 14 percent of all probation intakes during 1994-95, a figure that has remained almost constant since 1990-91 (Reed and Roberts, 1996).

The decision to grant probation is a highly discretionary act made within certain legal parameters. Practises vary considerably across Canada. The reasons for this variability in Canada can only be speculated on, but in the United States variations have been attributed to the type of sentencing structure used in a particular jurisdiction (Cunniff and Shilton, 1991) as well as the perception of judges regarding the ability of the probation department to provide an officer who can monitor the probationer closely and provide at least some quality assistance to him or her (Frank et al., 1987).

THE PREVALENCE OF PROBATION SENTENCES

In Canada during 1994-95, 39 percent of all probationers sentenced for a criminal code violation were convicted for a violent crime, 37 percent for a property crime and 6 percent for impaired driving. As Reed and Roberts qualify (1996:8), these figures do not mean

> that 39 percent of offenders received only probation for a crime of violence. A significant number of these offenders would have received another sentence in addition to the pro-

bation term. Previous research has shown that over one-quarter of probation terms imposed by provincial courts were accompanied by a period of imprisonment.

Birkenmayer and Besserer (1997) report that in their study of nine jurisdictions across Canada during 1993-94, probation was used most frequently as the most serious sanction in 25 percent of single-charge cases. They found that the highest rate of probation occurred for offences against the person (53 percent), followed by property offences (40 percent). This high rate for probation in the category of violent crime is attributed to the high probation rate for the offence of assault (level 1). This one particular offence accounted for more than 60 percent of all offences placed in the category of violent crime.

Table 5.2
Offences with Probation as the Most Serious Sanction in at Least 50% of Cases, Single-Charge Cases

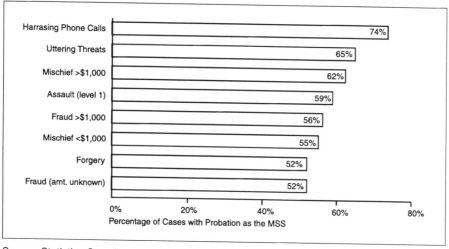

Source: Statistics Canada, "Offences with Probation as the MSS in at Least 50% of Cases, Single Charge Cases," from "Sentencing in Adult Provincial Courts: A Study of Nine Jurisdictions," Catalogue No. 85-513, page 17.

For single-charge cases with probation as the most serious sanction, probation terms ranged from one day to three years, with the average term being 405 days, or 14 months. The median probation term was 12 months. The length of probation terms was similar for all offence categories, with only a small departure being found in the offence categories of property and motor vehicle offences.

Because probation cannot be imposed as a separate sentence, it has to be imposed as an additional or an "add-on" sentence to another sentence, such as a suspended sentence, a fine or a period of incarceration not exceeding two years. Table 5.4 reveals that when probation was used as the most serious sanction, 82 percent of all probation orders were

Table 5.3
Length of Probation Terms, Single Charge Cases with Probation as the Most Serious Sanction

Offence Category	Number of cases 100%=	Distribution of Probation Terms (%)								Average Probation (Days)
		<6 mos	6 mos	>6mos <1yr	1yr	>1yr <2yr	2yr	>2yr <3yr	3yr	
Against Person	35,542	2	11	4	50	14	15	-	3	436
Property	43,684	5	18	5	43	10	15	-	4	409
Motor Vehicle	10,116	6	41	6	34	5	6	-	2	313
Morals	2,399	8	21	5	43	10	11	-	3	372
Administration of Justice	10,670	8	21	4	40	9	14	-	4	397
Other Criminal Code	2,718	6	20	5	47	7	12	-	3	376
Drugs	4,830	6	21	4	44	8	15	-	2	389
Other Federal Statutes	1,074	9	18	3	46	6	14	-	4	393
Total	111,033	5	18	5	44	11	14	-	3	405

Source: Statistics Canada, "Length of Probation Terms, Single Charge Cases with Probation as the MSS," from "Sentencing in Adult Provincial Courts: A Study of Nine Jurisdictions," Catalogue No. 85-513, page 18.

accompanied by some "other" sanction. For example, fines were imposed as an addition to probation in 31 percent of all offence categories, with the exception of motor vehicle offences, where 92 percent of all sanctions were attached with a probation order.

In their study, Birkenmayer and Besserer report that probation was used as the most serious sanction in almost 30,000 multiple-charge cases. The rate for multiple-charge cases (26 percent) was the same as that for single-charge cases. As Table 5.5 reveals, the highest probation rate was around 35 percent and it occurred in four offence categories: (1) offences against the person, (2) property offences, (3) morals offences, and (4) "other criminal code" offences. However, the average length of probation terms was slightly longer for multiple-charge cases (17 months). The median length was the same at 12 months.

Table 5.4
Sanctions Associated with Probation Single-Charge Cases, with Probation as the Most Serious Sanction

Offence Category	Number of cases 100%=	Sanctions Associated with Probation					
		Fine		Restitution		Other	
		N	%	N	%	N	%
Against Person	35,542	8,154	23	1,117	3	30,010	84
Property	43,684	10,425	35	11,421	26	35,767	82
Motor Vehicle	10,116	9,344	92	187	2	2,020	84
Morals	2,339	595	25	45	2	2,020	84
Administration of Justice	10,670	2,746	26	842	8	8,952	84
Other Criminal Code	2,718	767	28	202	7	2,224	82
Drugs	4,830	1,901	39	92	2	3,554	74
Other Federal Statutes	1,074	447	42	88	8	686	64
Total %	111,033	34,379	31	13,994	13	91,405	82

Source: Statistics Canada, "Sanctions Associated with Probation Single Charge Cases with Probation as the MSS," from "Sentencing in Adult Provincial Courts: A Study of Nine Jurisdictions," Catalogue No. 85-513, page 19.

Table 5.5
Type of Most Serious Sanction, Multiple-Charge Cases

Offence Category	Number of cases 100%=	Most Serious Sanction Imposed per Case					
		Prison		Probation		Fine	
		N	%	N	%	N	%
Against Person	24,679	14,060	57	8,484	34	1,970	8
Property	41,855	22,682	54	14,307	34	4,516	11
Motor Vehicle	21,053	11,091	53	2,063	10	7,871	37
Morals	1,125	404	36	358	32	342	30
Administration of Justice	14,100	7,811	55	5,509	18	3,565	26
Other Criminal Code	1,577	754	48	550	35	263	17
Drugs	4,973	2,774	56	954	19	1,207	24
Other Federal Statutes	4,453	404	9	452	10	3,573	80
Total	113,833	59,980	53	29,677	26	23,397	21

Source: Statistics Canada, "Type of Most Serious Sanctions, Multiple Charge Cases," from "Sentencing in Adult Provincial Courts: A Study of Nine Provincial Jurisdictions," Catalogue No. 85-513, page 22.

While the conclusions provided by Birkenmayer and Besserer are the result of the aggregation of data from the nine different jurisdictions across Canada, it is fair to assume that great variability is found across these jurisdictions in terms of the use of probation. The main reason for this is that there are no national guidelines for directing prosecutors and judges regarding when probation should be used as a sanction. The so-called "test" for probation in Canada, as in most other Western jurisdictions, is that probation should be granted when the offender does not pose a risk to society or need correctional supervision. As a result, these determinants have been defined with great flexibility. It should be noted, however, that 40 percent of those convicted of multiple charges also received probation (see Table 5.6).

Table 5.6
Sanctions Associated with Prison, Multiple-Charge Cases

Offence Category	Number of cases 100%=	Prison Only		Sanctions Associated with Prison							
		N	%	Probation		Fine		Restitution		Other	
				N	%	N	%	N	%	N	%
Against Person	14,060	5,865	42	7,237	51	82	1	187	1	2,449	17
Property	22,682	12,004	56	9,204	41	87	-	1,459	6	2,906	13
Motor Vehicle	11,091	2,047	18	3,937	35	197	2	62	1	7,778	70
Morals	404	279	69	116	29	-	-	-	-	20	5
Administration of Justice	7,811	4,809	62	1,774	23	40	1	98	1	1,598	20
Other Criminal Code	754	298	40	346	46	6	1	19	3	194	26
Drugs	2,774	1,353	49	1,229	44	45	2	10	-	427	15
Other Federal Statutes	404	238	59	138	34	29	7	35	9	22	5
Total	59,980	26,893	45	23,981	40	487	1	1,870	3	15,394	26

Source: Statistics Canada, "Sanctions Associated with Prison, Multiple Charge Cases," from "Sentencing in Adult Provincial Courts: A Study of Nine Provincial Jurisdictions," Catalogue No. 85-513, page 24.

The History of Probation

The idea of releasing offenders into the community under certain conditions and supervising them has existed for centuries. According to Walker (1980:27), the history of probation can be traced to the **benefit of clergy,** a practise of the Middle Ages that exempted clergy members from many civil punishments. Over time, this "benefit" was extended to common citizens who were able to demonstrate their religiosity by either reading or reciting from memory a passage from the Bible. Another form of probation, practised as early as the fourteenth century, was **judicial reprieve,** which "permitted judges to temporarily delay the imposition of sentence and to continue to delay upon evidence of good behavior" (Walker, 1980:88). Reprieves were usually reserved for children and first-time offenders. This was usually accomplished "by the appointment of a surety, who had power to enforce conditions and a duty to return the offender for sentence if he failed in the conditions or committed further crimes." However, this practice was not commonly used and was not a part of any statute until 1861.

The value of probation was first demonstrated by an English magistrate, Matthew Davenport Hill, who started keeping records of those offenders sentenced to probation. Of the 484 individuals he placed on probation, 78 (or 16 percent) failed and were returned to court for sentencing. That same year, an American, John Augustus, started what many historians point to as the origin of contemporary probation systems. As a private citizen and court volunteer, Augustus began to supervise offenders released to his custody by a Boston judge in 1841. For the next 18 years, he supervised approximately 2,000 probationers (typically those with alcohol-related problems and the indigent) and assisted them in securing jobs and establishing themselves in the community. His probationers were generally successful and few of them became involved in crime during their period of probation (Senna and Siegel, 1995:428).

Another important figure in the development of probation was Edward Savage, a member of the Boston police who, in 1858, started to conduct what is referred to today as presentence investigations or reports. The successes in this area led the state of Massachusetts to create the first probation department. An experiment with children was initiated in 1869; in 1878, Massachusetts became the first state to formally adopt a probation law for juveniles. However, it was not until 1901 that New York passed the first statute authorizing probation for adult offenders (Latessa and Allen, 1997).

In 1870, the National Congress of Penitentiary Reform and Reformatory Discipline endorsed the system of probation by supporting the individualization of correctional practice. At the beginning, probation officers were volunteers who simply needed to have "a good heart." As the idea gained acceptance, however, having state employees conduct probation functions was deemed essential, with the result that probation became a formalized part of the administration of justice. These first formal probation officers were usually retired or former law enforcement officers, and they worked directly for a judge as opposed to correctional administrators. Over time, the concept of the probation officer evolved to what it is today. In 1891, Massachusetts developed and put into practice a statewide probation system and "transferred power of appointment (to probation officers) from municipal officials to the courts" (Walker, 1980:88-89). By 1920, almost every state in the United States had a formal probation system in operation. In 1925, England required probation officers for all jurisdictions.

In Canada, provinces are responsible for probation services. The date of when probation services first started varies by provincial jurisdiction, with Ontario having created the first adult probation service in 1922, when the Ontario Probation Act was passed. While all other provinces created publicly funded probation departments over the next four decades, it should be pointed out that private agencies oftentimes provided for the same services. Today, every province has a probation service, although the exact nature of their organization and duties differs.

THE ROLE OF PROBATION

There are a number of advantages to having probation as part of the correctional system. It allows for large numbers of offenders to be supervised but at the same time remain in the community. As a result, they do not suffer the psychological or physical hardships of incarceration. Just as important, they are able to maintain their employment, family ties, friendship networks, and hopefully remain a productive citizen. Remaining in the community also allows them to more easily meet any specific conditions (e.g., therapy) of their probation order, pay fines and/or make restitution to victims, and to avoid the stigma of imprisonment. Probation usually includes a large number of first-time offenders who have committed a minor crime and are considered to be stable and/or in greater need for assistance available in the community rather than in correctional facilities.

A significant attraction of probation is the fact that it is economically less expensive than incarceration. The average cost of incarcerating an offender in a federal institute was approximately $46,250 in 1995-96 (or $39,470 at the provincial level). In addition, probation services employ a significant number of individuals across Canada. At the same time, there are a significant number of individuals who criticize the concept and/or use of probation. Some point out that probation is, at best, an amorphous concept, and there is no specific theoretical base that provides for its foundation. In reality, the critics are partially correct: "probation" is not a singular correctional approach, but rather a term that refers to a collection of tactics that attempt to achieve the goals of both the criminal code and provincial probation legislation. Probation, therefore, is not a specific approach or practice.

Why is this a problem for probation? As Stojkovic and Lovell (1997) point out, it is difficult for some people to determine whether probation is punishment, reintegration, rehabilitation or a combination of some or all of these, as well as whether there are specific aims and/or anticipated outcomes for probationers. In fact, in many cases, probation represents the exercise of a large amount of discretion by judges. While judges operate under certain parameters concerning when to use conditions of probation, they are not provided specifics for the determination of expected outcomes. For example, individuals convicted of heroin possession generally do not receive probation unless it involves therapy and/or treatment programs. However, in the case of *R. v. Richards* (1979), an Ontario Court decided to grant the condition of playing a free concert for charity to a famous rock musician (Keith Richards of the Rolling Stones) who was convicted for possession of heroin. Other similar conditions may be applied: for example, an individual convicted of a minor assault may be granted probation providing he or she meets the conditions of attendance and involvement in a drug treatment program.

Different actors in the criminal justice system may see the advantage of using a probation order differently according to their view of the defendant. Judges may decide to use probation when a correctional facility is full, when under normal circumstances the defendant would be incarcerated. A Crown prosecutor may decide to use probation as part of a plea bargain, particularly when discussing the sentence. A probation office, or a probation officer, may decide to treat any case with an individualized approach, granting some people access to treatment, intensively surveilling others, or using any other approach that is believed to be appropriate.

Some argue that the use of discretion in probation may lead to sentencing disparity or that it depreciates the seriousness of the offence, especially when a relatively lengthy period of incarceration could have been imposed. These arguments are based on the issue of equity in sentencing, both in the imposition of sentence and in the actual sentence served. There are also questions concerning the cultural bias involved in probation decisions. As the Law Reform Commission of Canada (1991:73) notes, "the terms and conditions typically included in probation orders are not always appropriate to the Aboriginal person." For aboriginals living in remote areas, it may be impossible to report to a parole officer. Problems may occur because treatment conditions are not culturally specific or sensitive to the needs of aboriginals, and "some non-association orders can be difficult to comply with in small communities and may almost amount to banishment." These arguments extend to plea bargaining, as it may distort due process, "where the imposition of probation has more connection to the negotiation than to the process established for making subsequent decisions concerning the offender" (Stojkovic and Lovell, 1997:426).

Several issues surround the use of probation for offenders who have committed serious violent crimes. High rates of probation are granted to offenders convicted of assault level 1 (43 percent), sexual touching of a child under the age of 14 (28 percent), assault level 2 (26 percent), assault of a police officer (26 percent) and sexual assault (21 percent). Questions abound about the deterrent effect of placing such offenders on probation and whether releasing the offender immediately into the community simply allows them to reoffend. Critics of probation point to studies conducted in the United States that have found high rates of recidivism of such offenders (Petersilia, 1985). Supporters of probation for violent offenders point to other studies, such as Vito (1983), which found much lower rates of recidivism.

Despite the controversy, probation remains a part of Canada's correctional system. No matter what happens in the immediate future, it appears that politicians and criminal justice authorities will continue to pursue less costly alternatives to incarceration, and as a result, will utilize probation as a viable approach. However, the possibility always exists that probation will change in the near future.

Keith Richards of the Rolling Stones plays guitar at a 1979 concert in Toronto, Ontario. Richards was required to perform a concert for charity as part of his sentence for illegal drug possession. *Neal Preston/Corbis.*

PROBATION SERVICES

Each province in Canada has its own probation service. Its members are readily identifiable as key figures in the correctional system. They supervise offenders, conduct presentence reports and provide various services to probationers. In addition, private agencies across Canada are involved with the delivery of services to probationers as well as the supervision of these individuals. These agencies may have a focus group of a certain type of offender (such as women) and receive funds from their respective provincial governments to supervise and counsel offenders for the duration of their term of probation. Whether it is conducted by private or public agencies, probation involves similar styles of operation, which are reviewed below. It should be noted that in some jurisdictions, probation officers may be responsible for providing services for both probationers and parolees.

The probation officer is involved in the decisionmaking about an offender long before sentencing. In some United States jurisdictions, it is the probation officer who determines if an individual charged with a serious offence will be released on bail. Probation officers conduct investigations into the offender's background and prepare a report. What is provided in the report generally becomes an important source of information for court personnel. If the court orders a term of probation, the probation officer has considerable discretion about which court orders will be enforced. If an offender is incarcerated, the presentence report conducted by the probation officer becomes an essential item in the determination of the appropriate security classification in many jurisdictions. In addition, if an offender is released from a period of incarceration on probation, the probation officer will conduct the appropriate community supervision.

The Presentence Report

Probation officers are often responsible for preparing sentencing reports, whether they are conducted at the presentence or postsentence stage. Such reports investigate the background of offenders and the circumstances surrounding the offence. The **presentence report** is used to help the court in determining the appropriate sentence in the case. These reports should be conducted after a conviction has been made. As Latessa and Allen (1997) point out, reports are conducted after adjudication because if the report is completed before the finding of guilt, (1) the accused may be acquitted or questions about the invasion of privacy may arise; (2) information collected for the report is not admissible at trial, but the possibly exists that some of this information may inadvertently be used during the trial; and (3) there are questions about the cost of conducting a report when it may never be used.

A **postsentence report** is used to give information for further decisionmaking that involves the offender. This can include: (1) serving as the basis for a probation order and plan; (2) assisting correctional personnel in classification and program decisions, and (3) giving a parole board useful information concerning consideration of parole.

Generally, a presentence report is written by a probation officer and involves interviews about the offender and the review of records (e.g., prior record of the offender) and relevant family information that form the basis of the evaluation and recommendations that will appear in the report. Sometimes, depending upon the offender and the offence, the investigation can be extensive and detailed. In such cases, the workload of a probation officer increases dramatically. In most cases, the probation officer provides the judge with the necessary information and an evaluation or summary. These reports usually are significant, as most offenders plead guilty, with the result that the only contact a judge has with the offender is during sentencing. The judge can then use the information and summary to assist in determining the appropriate sentence. While it is not known how often judges follow every presentence or postsentence report recommendation, Latessa (1993), in his study of 285 cases in Cuyahoga County, Ohio (which includes part of the city of Cleveland), reported that judges followed recommendations in 85 percent of the cases that recommended a probation order, and in 66 percent of the cases that recommended incarceration. This research verifies earlier research by Hagan (1975) and Walsh (1985) that reported a high correlation between a recommendation made by a probation officer and the judge's sentencing decision.

Of particular concern today are issues concerning the protection of the community and the nature of the offence. Section 732(2) of the criminal code specifies that, for all probation orders, the accused must "keep the peace and be of good behaviour." Judges must therefore decide if placing the offender on probation poses a threat to the safety of the community and/or specific individuals. Other considerations include whether probation will act as a sufficient deterrent and, if necessary, what community resources are available. Of course, an important consideration is the nature of the offence and the offender. Is the defendant a first-time or persistent offender? Was the offence in question a violent offence or a property offence, was a weapon used, and/or was there a motive involved? Furthermore, certain aspects of the offender himself or herself should be assessed. For example, does the potential probationer have a job and a supportive family?

A few studies in Canada have attempted to identify those factors that are important when a judge decides to incarcerate an offender or to place him or her on probation. Hagan (1975) discovered a strong positive relationship between probation officer recommendations and the sentence imposed by the judge. In his Alberta study, Hagan reports that judges agreed with the recommendations of probation officers in 80 percent of the cases. Boldt et al. (1983) found a rate of 85 percent in their study in the Yukon, but judges were found to impose harsher sentences than those recommended by probation officers. Both of these studies evaluated aboriginal and nonaboriginal offenders in an attempt to assess whether the relationship between probation officers' recommendations and judges' sentences led to differential rates of incarceration. According to Hagan (1975), probation officers viewed aboriginal offenders as less cooperative and/or less remorseful, leading to less positive evaluations and thus recommendations for harsher sentences. Boldt et al. (1983), however, reported no differences between aboriginals and nonaboriginals in terms of the recommendations given by probation officers. A number of studies conducted in the United States have verified these studies.

For more than 30 years, studies have attempted to investigate what variables a judge considers when granting parole to an offender. These include the offender's employment history, educational background, occupation, residence, stability and participation in church activities. Welch and Spohn (1986) reported that the prior record of the offender is the best predictor of the decision to incarcerate. Rosencrance (1988) concluded that "the present offence and prior criminal record are the factors that determine the probation officer's final sentencing recommendation." Latessa (1993) looked at which factors most strongly influenced the recommendation of probation officers as well as the sentencing decision of the judge. He reports that offenders were more likely to be recommended for imprisonment by a probation officer if: (1) they were repeat offenders, (2) they committed more serious offences, (3) a victim was involved, and/or (4) they had a prior juvenile record. The factors that influenced the sentencing decision included: (1) the recommendation of the probation order, (2) drug histories, (3) mental health history, (4) seriousness of the offence, and (5) a prior record involving incarceration. Certain sociodemographic variables, such as race, sex and age, did not influence the recommendations made by either the probation officers or judges.

Probation Supervision

Supervision, while an essential component of probation, can involve a variety of purposes, including community protection, rule enforcement and offender assistance. Exactly how much supervision an offender receives can vary from offender to offender, probation officer to probation officer, and jurisdiction to jurisdiction. Conditions always accompany probation, and there are a number of different categories of conditions. There are general and specific conditions given to each probationer. **General conditions** are imposed on all probationers and include such things as reporting changes in residence and not leaving a particular jurisdiction without permission. **Specific conditions** relate to the needs of a particular individual. For example, the individual in question may be given treatment conditions whereby the probationer has to attend counselling sessions to deal with a significant personal problem, such as substance abuse and/or family counselling. At the same time, punitive conditions can be applied; these are usually attached to a probation order in order to indicate the seriousness of the offence as well as to increase the intrusiveness of probation. Examples of punitive sanctions include fines, community service and drug testing.

One of the main issues that arises with regard to supervision is size of caseload. Caseloads may vary according to a number of factors. Caseloads may be generalized (i.e., the probation officer supervises a variety of categories of offenders and offence types) or they may be specialized (i.e., the probation-officer supervises offenders assigned on the basis of certain characteristics of the offender and offence type). Whatever the type, most probation officers have large caseloads, usually from 75 to 100 probationers. Given that probation officers have such large caseloads and are required to conduct presentence or postsentence reports, critics argue that little supervision occurs during the term of probation. Many probationers may therefore be subject to only a minimum level of supervision while sentenced to probation. As a result, they say, probationers fail to change their questionable behaviour because of lack of supervision and treatment.

Probation officers use a variety of risk and needs classification systems in order to identify those offenders who require more intensive supervision and services. While it is not known how many offenders on probation are in each category in Canada, in the United States it has been estimated that 95 percent of all probationers are on regular caseloads and the other 5 percent are on intensive supervision.

Regardless of the type of supervision, probation officers utilize a number of different ways of supervising offenders. Direct supervision involves discussing the probationer with employees, family and friends. In addition, probation officers utilize a number of indirect techniques, including checking local police arrest sheets and remand lists. Whatever the technique used, the progress of the offender has to be constantly monitored—as a result, significant amounts of paperwork have to be submitted. However, a relatively large percentage of probationers do not report to their probation officers or do so only by monthly telephone calls. These individuals are usually classified as exceptionally good risks and pose no threat to society.

In recent years, a new type of supervision has become popular—intensive supervision probation—which allows the probation officer to supervise small numbers (e.g., six to 12) of probationers. Intensive supervision probation is discussed in more detail later in this chapter.

DOES PROBATION WORK?

There are many questions about probation, but perhaps the most common question focuses on the issue of the recidivism rates of probationers. Yet, no national information has been provided about the recidivism of probationers in Canada. In the United States, the Bureau of Justice Statistics (1995) reported that of all probationers, 67 percent successfully completed their term of probation. The highest levels of success were for those individuals sentenced to probation for misdemeanours, or relatively nonserious offences. This figure is low, according to Clear and Braga (1995), who report that adult probation is very successful, with about 80 percent of all probationers successfully completing their sentences. However, these high rates are generally attributed to the large numbers of offenders placed on probation who have committed nonserious offences. For those who have committed serious crimes, the rates of failure are much higher. For example, Petersilia et al. (1985) studied 1,675 probationers who were convicted of serious offences in Los Angeles and Alameda Counties (in California). After a three-year period, they found that 65 percent of probationers were rearrested, 51 percent were reconvicted and 34 percent were reincarcerated. In a follow-up study, Geerken and Hayes (1993) summarized the results of 17 studies investigating the success or failure rates of probationers. They reported that felony rearrest rates varied from 12 to 65 percent. This variation was attributed to the flexibility in the granting of probation and the enforcement of court-ordered conditions.

Studies have explored the issue of whether probationer recidivism can be accomplished with any reasonable degree of accuracy. Suffering from the same issues confronting parole and its recidivism rates (e.g., public pressure to tighten up the availability of such programs), several studies have attempted to examine probationers' backgrounds and criminal records in an attempt to identify those factors associated with recidivism. These studies have recently been analysed by Morgan (1993) and summarized into five different categories. The first category, the kind of crime conviction and extent of prior record, found that burglars and those offenders with greater amounts of prior convictions showed higher rates of recidivism. The second category includes those studies that looked at "income at arrest," which found that higher unemployment and/or lower income are associated with higher recidivism rates. The third category, household composition, found that individuals living with their spouses, children or both have lower recidivism rates. In the fourth category of age, younger offenders have higher recidivism rates; and in the fifth category of drug use, probationers who used heroin had higher recidivism rates than all other drug users.

Petersilia and Turner (1986), however, report that while these characteristics were correlated with recidivism, they were not able to predict with any great accuracy just who would recidivate. They did discover that accurate predictions would have occurred approximately 70 percent of the time, but, they reported that certain other factors, such as environmental considerations, family support and employment, were able to predict recidivism as much as or more than the factors summarized by Morgan.

INTENSIVE SUPERVISION PROBATION

Between 1950 and the early 1970s, probation and parole departments experimented with the size of the probation officers' caseloads in an attempt to assess whether smaller caseloads led to the offering of higher-quality services to the clientele and, consequently, lower recidivism rates. These early studies reported that there were no differences in the recidivism rates of program participants who had been matched with a group of offenders who were incarcerated and matched by caseload size (Banks et al., 1977; Carter et al., 1967).

During the late 1980s, **intensive supervision probation (ISP)** programs flourished in the United States and began to appear with regularity in all jursidictions. Generally speaking, the positive aspects of ISP programs have been attributed to smaller caseloads, although this still may mean probation officers have to supervise 40 or more clients. Theoretically, this figure should be much lower, ideally at a ratio of 1:10. In addition, it was believed that greater frequency of contacts would lead to closer surveillance of probationers, which would improve public safety by making it more likely that infractions would be noticed and subsequently reported, thereby bringing about a higher standard of public safety.

There is no one single type of ISP. Three different types have been identified. One type has been termed **prison diversion** because convicted offenders are sent to the ISP program by judges according to certain standards established for them by probation officials. For example, the state of Georgia operates one of the longest-running of these programs. This program specifies that judges send to an ISP program those offenders who otherwise would have been sent to prison. Erwin (1987) evaluated this program and by comparing the ISP clientele with a matched group of incarcerated offenders reported that the ISP program reduced the number of offenders being sent to prison. However, subsequent analyses of the Georgia program revealed that the matched group was actually not comparable and the low rates of recidivism by the ISP group could not be attributed to the program but rather to the low-risk category of the offenders.

The second type is referred to as the **prison release ISP**. It operates on the basis of low-risk prison inmates being released to the ISP program after a careful evaluation by officials. If accepted onto the ISP program, they are placed into small caseloads with intensive contacts and frequent drug testing and other enforcement activities. Pearson (1987) conducted an early evaluation of one of these programs that was being operated in New Jersey, reporting positive results. However, later analyses found that the two groups were not comparable on the basis of risk. In addition, it was found that almost 50 percent of all participants were reincarcerated after they were found to be in violation of a technical aspect of the ISP orders.

A young man models the uniform worn by inmates sentenced to Ontario boot camps. Military-style camps are part of the trend toward intermediate sanctions. *Canapress Photo Service (Ron Bull).*

The third type of ISP is known as **case management ISP**. This type operates on the basis of potential ISP program participants being classified according to their risk of reoffending as determined by a risk classification instrument. Byrne and Kelly (1989) conducted an evaluation and reported significant problems associated with the implementation of the program. They concluded that the offenders were no more likely to have lower recidivism rates than comparable offenders who were not placed on the program.

The continued existence of these programs in the face of higher-than-predicted recidivism rates of program participants is largely attributed to ISP's surveillance capabilities and punitive properties. In addition, it answers the public demand that sanctions place a significant burden upon offenders. The fact that recidivism rates of ISP participants are no higher than those who are not on the program gains the favor of policymakers who note that such innovative programs save them large sums of money. Supporters of rehabilitation view ISP programs as progressive because they enable probation programs to involve participants in effective counselling sessions while serving in the community.

SUMMARY

While probation is viewed as a key policy in the administration of correctional policy, very little is known about its various dimensions in Canada as compared to conditional release programs operated by the federal government. However, the use of probation continues to be practised as the most common form of community sanction. As a result, a variety of different types of probation have been introduced during the past 20 years in an attempt to maintain offender populations as well as to placate community concerns about the safety of its residents. While there are many problems and concerns associated with probation, it appears that its use will continue to grow. The impact and benefits of such programs need to be more carefully evaluated and assessed. This chapter has reviewed much contemporary information about probation, but it also reveals the diversity and flexibility of such a program. There is no doubt that probation will continue to increase in its importance in the future due to the federal government's concern with community corrections

DISCUSSION QUESTIONS

1. Do you think that the probation process is unfair to some offenders? If so, how can we change it to make it more fair?

2. Do you believe that probation is overused in Canada? What other policies should be substituted in its place?

3. Is probation a successful program? Explain.

4. Do you believe that it is too easy to get probation in Canada today?

5. Do you feel that intensive probation supervision programs should become more common in Canada? What are the benefits and drawbacks of your decision?

REFERENCES

American Correctional Association (1995). *Probation and Parole Directory, 1997-1997*. Lanham, MD: American Correctional Association.

Banks, J., A.L. Porter, R.L. Hardin, T.R. Silver and V.E. Unger (1977). *Phase I Evaluation of Intensive Special Probation Projects*. Washington, DC: Law Enforcment Assistance Administration.

Birkenmayer, Andy and Sandra Besserer (1997). *Sentencing in Adult Provincial Courts: A Study of Nine Jurisdictions: 1993 and 1994.* Ottawa: Statistics Canada, Canadian Centre for Justice Statistics.

Boldt, Edward, L. Hursh, S. Johnson and W. Taylor (1983). "Presentence Reports and the Incarceration of Natives." *Canandian Journal of Criminology,* Volume 25, 269-276.

Bureau of Justice Statistics (1995). *Correctional Populations in the United States, 1992.* Washington, DC: U.S. Government Printing Office.

Byrne, James M. and Linda Kelly (1989). *Restructuring Probation as an Intermediate Sanction: An Evaluation of the Implementation and Impact of the Massachusetts Intensive Supervision Program: Final Report.* Washington, DC: National Institute of Justice.

Carter, R.M., J. Robinson and L.T. Wilkins (1967). *The San Francisco Project: A Study of Federal Probation and Parole.* Berkeley, CA: University of California Press.

Clear, Todd and Anthony A. Braga (1995). "Community Corrections." In James Q. Wilson and Joan Petesilia (eds.), *Crime.* San Francisco: Institute for Contemporary Studies.

Cunniff, Mark and Mary Shilton (1991). *Variations on Felony Probation: Persons Under Supervision in 32 Urban and Suburban Counties.* Washington, DC: U.S. Department of Justice.

Erwin, Billie (1987). *Evaluation of Intensive Supervision in Georgia.* Washington, DC: National Institute of Justice.

Frank, J., F. Cullen and J. Cullen (1987). "Sources of Judicial Attitudes Toward Criminal Sanctioning." *American Journal of Justice,* Volume 11, 17-36.

Geerken, Michael and Hennessey D. Hayes (1993). "Probation and Parole: Public Risk and the Future of Incarceration Alternatives." *Criminology,* Volume 31, 549-564.

Griffiths, Curt T. and Simon N. Verdun-Jones (1994). *Canadian Criminal Justice,* Second Edition. Toronto: Harcourt, Brace and Company.

Hagan, John (1975). "The Social and Legal Construction of Criminal Justice: A Study of the Presentence Report." *Social Problems,* Volume 22, 620-637.

Latessa, Edward J. (1993). *An Analysis of Pre-Sentencing Investigation Recommendations and Judicial Outcome in the Cuyahoga County Adult Probation Department.* Cincinnati: Department of Criminal Justice, University of Cincinnati.

Latessa, Edward J. and Harry E. Allen (1997). *Corrections in the Community.* Cincinnati: Anderson.

Law Reform Commission of Canada (1991). *Aboriginal Peoples and Criminal Justice.* Ottawa: Law Reform Commission of Canada.

Morgan, Kathryn (1993). "Factors Influencing Probation Outcome: A Review of the Literature." *Federal Probation,* Volume 57, 23-29.

Pearson, Frank (1987). *Final Report of Research on New Jersey's Intensive Supervision Program.* New Brunswick, NJ: Rutgers University, Department of Sociology, Institute for Criminological Research.

Petersilia, Joan (1985). "Probation and Felony Offenders." *Federal Probation,* Volume 49, 4-9.

Petersilia, Joan and Susan Turner (1986). *Prison Versus Probation in California: Implications for Crime and Offender Recidivism.* Santa Monica, CA: RAND.

Petersilia, Joan, Susan Turner, J. Kahan and J. Peterson (1985). *Granting Felons Probation: Public Risks and Alternatives.* Santa Monica, CA: RAND.

Reed, Micheline and Peter Morrison (1997). *Adult Correctional Services in Canada, 1995-96.* Ottawa: Canadian Centre for Justice Statistics.

Reed, Micheline and Julian V. Roberts (1996). "Adult Community Corrections in Canada: 1994-95." Ottawa: Statistics Canada, Canadian Centre of Justice Statistics.

Rosencrance, John (1988). "Maintaining the Myth of Individualized Justice: Probation Presentence Reports." *Justice Quarterly,* Volume 5, 235-256.

Senna, Joseph and Larry Siegel (1995). *Essentials of Criminal Justice.* St. Paul, MN: West.

Stojkovic, Stan and Rick Lovell (1997). *Corrections: An Introduction,* Second Edition. Cincinnati: Anderson.

Vito, Gennaro (1983). "Reducing the Use of Imprisonment." In Lawrence F. Travis III, Martin Schwartz and Todd Clear (eds.), *Corrections: An Issues Approach,* Second Edition. Cincinnati: Anderson.

Walker, Samuel (1980). *Popular Justice: A History of American Criminal Justice.* New York: Oxford University Press.

Walsh, Anthony (1985). "The Role of the Probation Officer in the Sentencing Process." *Criminal Justice and Behavior,* Volume 12, 289-303.

Welch, S. and C. Spohn (1986). "Evaluating the Impact of Prior Record on Judges' Sentencing Decisions: A Seven-City Comparison." *Justice Quarterly,* Volume 3, 389-407.

CHAPTER 6

Women and Corrections

WOMEN OFFENDERS

This chapter reviews a number of issues facing imprisoned women offenders in Canada today. Like their male counterparts, women are institutionalized in both provincial and federal correctional facilities; unlike men, however, women are placed in institutions that operate under the ideology of a "traditional" role model of women, which has led to policies emphasizing their domestic rather than social roles. This has created a situation that has promoted women's emotional and physical isolation, destroyed families and other intimate relationships and engendered a sense of injustice among women offenders as well as their supporters. Women's prisons have historically been ignored in the history of Western corrections; the first studies documenting in detail the unique experiences and histories of women did not appear until the late 1960s. This inattention was fostered for three reasons:

KEY TERMS

Clarke Report	Mercer Reformatory	R. v. Daniels
co-correctional facilities	Nickle Commission	R. v. Gayle Horii
Exchange of Service Agreements	mother-child program	Skills and Needs Inventory
Macdonnell Commission	pains of imprisonment	substantive equality
	Prison for Women	

(1) Women have constituted a small proportion of the total correctional population thereby giving rise to the comment that they are "too few too count";

(2) Women are typically incarcerated for less dangerous and serious crimes than men;

(3) Women are less likely to create disturbances, litigate their concerns in court, and make demands for reform (Barry, 1991; Mann, 1984; Wheeler et al., 1989).

This inattention began to change during the 1970s when a substantial literature emerged that continues today. However, progressive changes have been slow in Canada. It was not until the early 1990s that the federal government began to study some of these issues in earnest and to try to introduce new policies that would improve the conditions of incarcerated women. This chapter documents the current reality of federally sentenced women as well as some of the unique issues facing them.

A Profile of Women Offenders in Canada Today

As mentioned in Chapter 1, on March 31, 1997, 2.5 percent of all incarcerated inmates in the federal correctional system were women. This meant that 357 women were serving a sentence of two years or more at some institution in Canada on that day. Most information collected on federally sentenced women has been demographic and descriptive in its orientation. According to the latest information produced by the Solicitor General of Canada (1997), federally sentenced women in 1997 shared the following common characteristics: they were between 20 and 34 years of age, single, Caucasian, with most only receiving a high school education at best, serving their first federal sentence for a period of less than six years in length, and most having more than one child, with many of the women being the primary caregiver.

Most federally sentenced women (205, or 57.4 percent) identified themselves as caucasian, 66 (or 18.5 percent) were aboriginal, 35 (or 10.1 percent) were black, nine (or 2.5 percent) were Asiatic, while the remaining 41 stated they belonged to another race (eight individuals, or 2.2 percent); 33 (or 9.2 percent) did not identify their race. The highest percentage of federally sentenced aboriginal women offenders (48.1 percent) were located in the Prairie Region of the Correctional Service of Canada, while the largest numbers of black women sentenced to a federal term of incarceration were located in Ontario (16.8 percent) and the Atlantic Region (13.9 percent).

Most women (74.8 percent) were serving their first period of federal incarceration. Seventy-one (or 19.9 percent) of all federally sentenced women in 1997 were serving a life sentence for murder. The most common sentence for women was between three and six years (35.3 percent) followed by between two and three years (22.7 percent), life (19.9 percent), six to 10 years (17.4 percent), 10 years or more (4.2 percent) and an indeterminate sentence (.5 percent).

In Canada, women represent a small percentage of offenders sentenced to a period of incarceration in either a provincial/territorial or federal correctional facility. According to the Canadian Centre for Justice Statistics (1997:9), women accounted for 3 percent of all admissions to federal facilities and 9 percent of all admissions to provincial/territorial facilities during 1995-96. In 1991, very few women (a total of 141) were sentenced to a federal facility. Currently, the total population of federally sentenced women is approximately 350, in comparison to about 12,000 men. This means that women represent about 2.8 percent of the federal offender population, a ratio that has remained relatively stable since 1975. The rate of incarceration of women per 100,000 population remained stable between 1975 and 1985 (between 0.9 and 1.2), while for men it increased from 37.4 to 47.0 per 100,000 population (Johnson, 1986).

At the federal level, the number of women incarcerated has increased by about 50 percent since 1975, while the number of men has also increased by approximately 50 percent. However, these percentages are misleading because they are founded on such small base figures. The increase amounts to an approximate increase of 175 women, compared with an increase of 3,500 men.

At the provincial level of custody, a slight increase of the percentage of women admitted to custody occurred in the decade between 1978-79 and 1989-90. The number of women increased by a little more than 100 percent while the percentage for men was approximately 20 percent. Once again, however, the actual numbers for women were much lower than for men. During 1989-90, the number of women admitted to a provincial custody facility was 9,209, in comparison to 105,905 men.

These much smaller numbers of women serving a sentence indicate women's lower incidence of offending overall, as well as the less serious nature of their offences. Women tend to receive shorter sentences than men, a statistic related to the less serious nature of their crimes and the fact that they have been convicted for fewer previous criminal offences. Shaw (1991a:6) points out that in 1989, 87 percent of federally sentenced women were serving their first federal prison term, more than 50 percent had never been previously incarcerated in a provincial/territorial facility and 36 percent had never before been convicted of a criminal code offence. Less than 10 percent of women sentenced to a provincial/territorial facility were convicted of a violent offence, and of these, most involved charges for minor assaults. More than 25 percent of women sentenced to a provincial facility were sentenced for property offences, most typically for shoplifting and fraud offences. Almost 20 percent were sentenced for public-order offences, drinking offences, traffic offences or drug offences (Johnson and Rodgers, 1993). Thirty percent of all women were admitted for failing to pay a fine, while others were admitted for violations of court orders or the conditions of their probation orders. Most women sentenced to a provincial facility were first-time offenders. About 25 percent of them were repeat offenders, usually for committing such offences as drinking, prostitution, theft or fraud (Shaw, 1994:15-16). Federally sentenced women have most typically been convicted of more serious offences than those in provincial/territorial facilities, including crimes such as murder, manslaughter and attempted murder. Property offenders include those convicted of repeat offences, such as robbery, drugs, theft or fraud.

Research on women offenders has traditionally focused on gender differences in crime rates, demographic profiles of women offenders, and the processing of women through the court system (MacKenzie et al., 1989; Morris, 1987). Studies that have attempted to isolate the factors most associated with women offenders have tended to focus on one or two specific groups of women offenders, most notably prostitutes. As a result, and in stark comparison to the proliferation of studies on male offenders, very little research has been directed toward understanding the factors associated with either the origin or maintenance of women's criminal behaviour. Recent studies have revealed that many federally sentenced women and men come from disadvantaged backgrounds. Lefebvre (1994), in her study of 973 offenders who successfully completed day parole during 1990-91, found the majority of women and men offenders to have a similar marital status, employment status and educational level at the time of their offence. Loucks and Zamble (1994) compared 100 women offenders incarcerated at the federal Prison for Women to federally sentenced male offenders. They too discovered significant similarities between women and men. A significant number of both groups had spent their preteen years raised by adults other than their parents. For the first five years of their lives, about 20 percent of the women lived with adoptive or foster parents, compared to 10 percent for men. Between the ages of six and 11, this number increased to 25 percent for women and 20 percent for men. Both women and men offenders dropped out of school at an early age (usually around the age of 16) and, as a result, had poor employment skills. At the time of their most recent arrest, approximately 50 percent were unemployed or were employed in unskilled positions, while another 30 percent were employed in semiskilled jobs. About 33 percent of the men were unemployed or held unskilled positions, and approximately 50 percent were employed in semiskilled occupations. While incarcerated women share similar backgrounds to the men in our correctional system, the impact of these factors typically have a much greater impact on women. Women are more susceptible to the effects of substance abuse and experience more physical health difficulties as well as extensive amounts of physical and sexual abuse. In addition, women have fewer possibilities, diminished job opportunities and greater responsibilities for their children than do men (Shaw, 1994).

Major differences between federally sentenced women and men offenders were found in the area of emotional maladjustment, from suicide attempts to substance abuse (Loucks and Zamble, 1994:24-25). Women were approximately four times more likely to attempt suicide (48 percent vs. 13 percent), 2.5 times more likely to suffer from moderate depression (31 percent vs. 12 percent) and more than twice as likely to report moderate drug abuse (54 percent vs. 22 percent). Women were also less likely to report hopelessness (7 percent vs. 12 percent) and moderate alcohol abuse (26 percent vs. 55 percent).

Perhaps the most significant difference between federally sentenced women and men is the realization that women are much more likely to have suffered sexual and/or physical abuse during all stages of their lives. According to Shaw (1994), the majority of

Maximum-security inmates at Kingston's Prison for Women. In 1988, the Daubney Committee recommended closing the Prison for Women in order to provide appropriate community and institutional accommodation and programming. *Canapress Photo Service/Maclean's (Chris Schwarz).*

provincial and federally sentenced women report some form of abuse. Almost 70 percent of federally sentenced women in 1989 indicated they had suffered from physical abuse, while 53 percent revealed they had experienced some form of sexual abuse. For aboriginal women, these figures were higher, with 90 percent reporting physical abuse and 61 percent reporting sexual abuse; in addition, they reported both types of abuse as often prolonged and extensive. Comparable levels of abuse have been reported by provincially sentenced women as well (Shaw, 1994:17). Prior sexual abuse has been found to be a major reason for slashing and other forms of self-injurious behavior among federally sentenced women (Heney, 1990).

Another issue that impacts on women offenders is the care of children. At least 65 percent of incarcerated women are mothers, and 67 percent of them are single mothers. When they are sentenced to a period of incarceration, many have to make special arrangements for child care. Some have to place their children in care, with the possibility that they will have problems regaining custody of their children when they are released. Separation from their children and the inability to do anything for them are major problems facing women in Canada's correctional facilities (MacLeod, 1992; Shaw, 1991a).

Women in Canadian federal institutions have specific risks and needs that are very different from those of their male counterparts, yet these needs have traditionally been ignored. Women's correctional facilities provide less services of a general or specific nature, poorer facilities for rehabilitation and job training, and fewer programs than provided by male facilities. As a result, critics (e.g., Heidensohn, 1985) have argued that the **pains of imprisonment** are much greater for women than they are for men. It is precisely this issue of needs that became so important for those involved in the federal government's study of female offenders in the late 1980s.

THE HISTORY OF CORRECTIONAL FACILITIES FOR WOMEN

To understand the historical development of women's correctional facilities and treatment in Canada, it is first necessary to explore the beliefs held about women in general, and women offenders in particular, in early England. These beliefs formed the foundation of how women offenders were to be treated in Canada, and despite recent changes, continue in may ways to do so.

Many of these differences are rooted in certain ideas about the presumed differences in the social status of women in English society. Women were generally viewed as chattels of men, an ideology that meant that if they were to cause hardship for their husbands, it was entirely possible for them to be sent to a workhouse, poorhouse or monastery. Wherever she ended up, the woman generally had to look after herself, which often meant committing crimes in order to subsist (Pollock-Byrne, 1990).

If they were institutionalized for their offences, women were viewed "as morally bankrupt and deserving of very severe punishments" (Stojkovic and Lovell, 1997:551). Harsh and brutal punishments were handed out in the hope they would make the woman offender obedient and subservient to the demands of her husband (Dobash et al., 1986:23). When women were placed into a correctional facility, they suffered abuse from male inmates, as rarely were there any separate facilities available. Even when women offenders were separated from men, the abuse usually continued at the hands of male staff. Women offenders also were neglected because they were not considered to be significant enough to warrant any extra efforts to assist their return to society.

During the first decades of the 1700s in England, the policy of transportation allowed women offenders to be sent with men convicts to the American colonies and Australia to serve their sentences. Women accounted for a little more than 10 percent of those transported. They were typically young and usually transported for their first offence (the most common of which was petty theft). This policy typically led women into being forced into prostitution at their destination (Dobash et al., 1986).

When correctional facilities became more common, women prisoners were usually placed in male facilities to serve their sentences. It was very typical for women inmates to suffer from neglect in these facilities due to their small numbers. This environment led to a variety of reform efforts aimed at alleviating some of the hardships affiliated with their living conditions. Generally, reformers tried to assist women prisoners by attempting to improve their prison conditions and to build separate correctional facilities. The first significant reformer to focus exclusively on women was Elizabeth Fry, a Quaker who established the Ladies Society for Promoting the Reformation of Female Prisoners in England. Starting in 1816, Fry attempted to persuade officials that women and men had different needs. For example, women required special training in "useful labor" (e.g., needlework) and religious instruction, which required the hiring of "decidedly religious women guards" (Dobash et al., 1986:52). Fry argued that women inmates were not dangerous criminals but rather "fallen women" who needed to be resocialized into appropriate women's roles. She played an important role in the betterment of women prisoners in England, the creation of separate correctional facilities, the hiring of women to supervise women inmates and the reduction of the amount of hard labor demanded of them (Morris, 1987).

Following Fry's successes, reform movements concerned with the plight of incarcerated women appeared intermittently in Canada, England and the United States throughout the remainder of the nineteenth century. A focal point of these reform movements was the recommendation that women be removed from any type of custodial facility that was designed for men and be placed into buildings specifically designed for women. Another important aspect of these reform movements was an attempt to get funds so that women inmates could be trained into "appropriate" gender roles, focusing on skills such as cooking and sewing. Despite limited success, conditions for women continued to remain largely the same.

Slowly over time, progressive moves concerning women's correctional facilities disappeared. By the 1930s, when Canada's first separate federal facility for women opened in Kingston, gender stratification in terms of programs and services had become institutionalized. Changes for the better occurred during the next few decades, but they were relatively minor in nature. In terms of ideology, however, these decades saw the focus on women inmates changing from turning women prisoners from good housemaids into good housewives (Carlen, 1983; Morris, 1987). It was not until the late 1960s and early 1970s that these gender stereotypes were challenged with fervor. This occurred due to three reasons: (1) the rise of modern feminism and the subsequent reevaluation of women's role in society as criminals and victims; (2) concern over the issue of women's crime rates and whether they were increasing faster than those of men; and (3) a recommendation introduced in England that suggested that women offenders be treated differently than men due to their specific physical and psychological concerns (Heidensohn, 1985). This ultimately led to a major federal review of women offenders, which culminated in a series of major investigations and reports.

Box 6.1 Major Developments for Female Offenders

Outline of Major Developments and Reports Relating to the Imprisonment of Federal Female Offenders

1848 **Brown Commission**: recommended the separation of women in a new unit at Kingston Penitentiary.

1913 New prison built for women inside penitentiary walls.

1914 **Macdonnell Commission**: suggested women be moved closer to their homes under provincial authority.

1921 **Nickle Commission**: suggested building a new central facility outside walls of penitentiary.

1934 New Prison for Women completed.

1938 **Archambault Commission**: recommended women be returned to home provinces under provincial authority. Provinces favourable.

1946 Minister of Justice sought views of provinces on transfer of all women at Kingston. Only one province now felt able to take on federal offenders.

1956 **Fauteux Committee**: recommended more intensive treatment programs in the new central facility being planned.

1956 Plans to build a new prison for women at Kingston shelved. Public outcry against a central facility.

1965 Ministry of Justice proposed new federal prison at Cornwall. Plans abandoned.

1968 Plans to build new federal prison in Ottawa area abandoned.

1968 **Canadian Correctional Association**: provinces should assume responsibility for all federal female offenders.

1969 **Ouimet Committee**: developed a unified service for women in each province with purchase of services from larger provinces, and establishment of regional federal services in small provinces. The latter to purchase services for short-term offenders.

1970 **Royal Commission on Status of Women**: recommended closure of Prison for Women.

1977 **Clark Report**: National Advisory Committee on the Female Offender: recommended closure within three years. Outlined two alternative plans: the retention of federal responsibility but development of small regional secure facilities and purchase of services from provinces or transfer of all federal female offenders to provincial authority.

Box 6.1—*continued*

1977   **MacGuigan Report**: recommended immediate phasing out of Prison for Women and development of small cottage-type institutions in at least three regions.

1978   **Needham Report**: National Planning Committee on the Female Offender: Closure of Prison for Women; at least one community-based residential centre in East and one in West on basis of feasibility study.

1978   **Chinnery Report**: Joint Committee to Study Alternatives for the Housing of the Federal Female Offender: develop two main facilities (Vanier or a rebuilt Prison for Women plus co-correctional Mission BC) and expand use of ESAs

1978   **Berezins and Dunn**: Progress Report on the Federal Female Offender Programme. Primarily the detailed findings of Working Group to Chinnery committee.

1978   Solicitor General announced plans to phase out Prison for Women.

1980   **Advisory Council on Status of Women**: close Prison for Women; develop ESAs

1981   **Canadian Human Rights Commission**: upheld nine charges of unequal treatment of federal women by CSC brought by **Women for Justice**. Case sent to conciliation.

1981   **CAEFS**: recommendations on upgrading programmes at Prison for Women, and establishment of a sixth CSC region for women.

1982   Establishment of PNACFFO: **Permanent National Advisory Committee on Federal Female Offenders**, with representation from national and regional offices of the Correctional Service Canada and the voluntary sector. Mandate to advise the Commissioner on all current and long-term policy, program and planning issues.

1988   **Canadian Bar Association**: Justice Behind the Walls: legislate to compel closure of Prison for Women.

1988   **Daubney Committee**: close Prison for Women within five years: set up task force to propose plan for community and institutional accommodation and programming.

Source: *Creating Choices: Report of the Task Force on Federally Sentenced Women* (1990). Ottawa: Correctional Service of Canada.

THE CANADIAN EXPERIENCE

Two issues have been the central focus of federally sentenced women in Canada over the past 170 years: (1) the appropriate location(s) for women's correctional facilities, and (2) the proper type and method of treatment for women offenders. In terms of the first issue, Canada is somewhat unique among Western nations in its inability to resolve the issue of location. In the United States, New York opened the first separate women's prison in 1839, and by the time the federal authorities opened a separate facility in 1934, more than 20 states had already opened separate facilities for women. The federal government mirrored the then-current thinking about appropriate treatment programs for women, following the ideology of viewing women as "wayward" individuals in need of moral assistance.

In Canada, the earliest institution for women offenders was the Kingston Provincial Penitentiary (called the Kingston Penitentiary after 1867, when federal authorities took it over). While the original plans for the penitentiary called for separate facilities to be built for women inmates within the walls, the first two women inmates were placed in the infirmary. This action marked a decision to care for women and men differently: while men were locked in separate cells at night, women were confined together in a single room above the dining hall. Men laboured together in silence under the close supervision of guards who punished them harshly for any rule infractions. No provisions were granted to the women for privacy or exercise, and their labour consisted mainly of sewing for the institution. They were not supervised on a constant basis, but were for the most part left unattended. Women were considered an "inconvenience" to the overall operation and administration of the facility (Faith, 1993). In an attempt to control the slowly increasing number of women, a woman matron was hired in 1836 to ensure that the women worked hard and obeyed institutional rules. These conditions existed for the next 25 years, with women being "confined wherever and in whatever manner best served the administration of the larger male population" (Cooper, 1993:5). By 1859, 68 women were serving a sentence in the Kingston Provincial Penitentiary, resulting in severely overcrowded conditions. The next year, larger quarters for women were made available, but they were still located within the walls.

The general move to place women in larger, separate facilities was largely for the convenience of administrators and to make the inmates produce more items. The benefits of these new conditions were identified by the prison model presented in the 1868 report of the Director of Penitentiaries. Noting the drawbacks of the present situation, which involved placing women "in a dark cell on bread and water, where they can sleep all day and in the night, sing and hammer so as to disturb the whole establishment," a new larger, separate facility would "tend much more to subduing and reforming them" (Cooper, 1993:36). This move to separate facilities was the result of a changing conception of the female criminal/inmate. Law-abiding women were considered a moral force, but once they violated the law, they were seen as threatening the social order. Representing this line of thought was the belief "that the injury done to society by a criminal woman is in most cases much greater than that suffered from a male criminal" (Lieber, 1969:207). As a result, the conditions under which women inmates suffered were much greater than their male counterparts because they were viewed as less deserving of any progressive care.

At this time, social reformers were starting great opposition to the treatment of women offenders in penitentiaries. The needs of women placed in male custodial facilities were neglected. Reformers demanded sweeping changes: separate facilities for women and appropriate programs for treatment and skill development. Their arguments were largely based on the work of Elizabeth Fry, who had pronounced some 50 years earlier that not only should separate facilities be provided for women offenders, they should be run by women administrators and should serve as a place where the inmates would receive moral and domestic training.

The advantages of such a system, according to Fry, include that it would (1) prevent sexual abuse of women inmates at the hands of male guards, (2) give "moral" examples of proper women for the inmates, and (3) better provide for the needs of incarcerated women (Pollock-Byrne, 1990:41). The reformists' zeal led to the creation of separate correctional facilities, but it was provincial authorities who decided to implement a new approach to the treatment of women offenders. After the federal government took control of the Kingston Penitentiary, Ontario was left with no separate institution for women serving intermediate sentences of two months to two years. In 1880, however, this circumstance changed with the opening of the **Mercer Reformatory** in Toronto. One of the notable features of this reformatory was the appointment of Mary Jane O'Reilly as superintendent. It was through her efforts that social support and gender-specific programs were created, a significant change and alternative to existing approaches.

These changes did not mean that women were given the same programs and treatment as male inmates at either the provincial or federal level of jurisdiction. Rather, the approaches used were based on an image that "maternal care" programs were necessary to reintegrate women inmates, particularly those that would correct poor work habits, lack of self-control, drunkenness, violent behaviour and "a general weakness in controlling one's passions" (Wetherell, 1979:248). They were essentially the victims of a poor upbringing and home life. As O'Reilly noted in her annual report in 1887, a large number of women inmates under her charge "have drifted into criminal way through not having been trained to habits of industry in their own homes" (Wetherell, 1988:249). Through O'Reilly's efforts, the Mercer Reformatory was a success story of the times, as "there were no scandals, riots, charges of brutality or other incidents characteristic of punitive prisons everywhere" (Oliver, 1994:551). This "success," however, was relatively short-lived, as later superintendents were men who "lacked the insight and capacity to fully comprehend and appreciate Mercer's accomplishments under Mary Jane O'Reilly, and their relevance to a general penal strategy relating to women offenders" (Boritch, 1997:177).

Despite the reverence given to early reformers and administrators like Mary Jane O'Reilly, reform efforts failed significantly on the ideological level. Although women inmates were now separated from men and provided with some beneficial gender-specific programs, a tradition of treating women inmates very different from male inmates was established. This policy toward women offenders began a system of differential treatment that "is the source of many of the problems which plague the women's prison system today" (Rafter, 1983:148). The problem lay in the fact that the programs were based on "the principle of inmate sexual difference, not sexual equality."

Despite the fact that changes were largely for the worse for the women inmates housed in the Mercer Reformatory, they were somewhat better than the conditions experienced by federally sentenced women. It was not until 1914 that the federal **Prison for Women** was built. These were separate quarters that were built for women, but they were still located within the confines of the Kingston Penitentiary. A lack of progress in the treatment of women and the continued refusal to appoint a woman administrator and female staff led the Royal Commission on Penitentiaries (usually referred to as the **Macdonnell Commission**) in 1914 to recommend that federally sentenced women be sent to their provinces of origin and supervised by the provincial authorities. This was not done, however; the Prison for Women continued to operate for the next two decades in almost the same way as it had in the past. One notable event in the history of the Prison for Women was the investigation by the **Nickle Commission** into allegations of sexual misconduct in the women's facility. As Shaw (1991b:14) points out, the formation of this commission was notable because it was the first inquiry specifically appointed to investigate issues concerning federally sentenced women. While the allegations were not founded, the conditions the commissioners found during their investigation appalled them, leading them to recommend that a new prison be built outside the existing facility, and that improvements be made in pay, type of work and working conditions. Notably, the commission recommended that, if the new facility was constructed, it should not be enclosed by walls.

Construction of a new federal facility for women was started in 1925, and finally completed nine years later. Despite the recommendations of the Nickle Commission, the new prison was designated as max-imum-security and was surrounded by 16-foot walls topped by 10 feet of wire mesh fencing, which in turn was topped with six strands of barbed wire. The exterior was completely bathed under electric lights spaced every 100 feet—perhaps a substitute for guard towers (of which there were none). The cost for these security measures was almost $85,000, a significant sum for the 41 women who moved in and who were not classified as dangerous threats to society. As Carrigan (1991:462) has noted, these security measures extended into the prison itself. There were no outside windows and all letters were censored, first by a staff member of the women's prison and then by the censor located in the men's prison. Notably, the new facility provided no opportunities for education, and the library consisted of only 100 volumes.

Only three years after its opening, the Archambault Commission rec-ommended that the Prison for Women be closed, with all women inmates returned to their home provinces, where they would serve the remainder of their sentence at provincial institutions. The Commission's main concern was the expense of operating the facility for so few inmates as well as the ability of women to maintain relationships with their families. The commission concluded that the women inmates did not pose a threat to society, and they were characterized as members of the "occasional or accidental offender class, carried away by the over-mastering impulse of the moment, often the outbreak of long pent-up emotion. They are not a custodial problem . . ." (Archambault Report, 1938:315). Their conclusion about the minimal dangerousness of women inmates was an insight that has resurfaced throughout the decades and has continued into the 1990s, most recently with regard to the proper security classification of the new regional centres for federal-ly sentenced women.

At the start of World War II, the Kingston Penitentiary was more than 100 years old. A "report card" on the treatment of women, specif-ically federally sentenced women, has been made by Carrigan (1991:467), who notes that "except for improvements in facilities and food and clothing, there were few significant changes in the treatment of female criminals for almost a century. The criminal justice system arrest-ed women, housed them for various periods, and then turned them loose on their own resources. There was little effort at rehabilitation or help-ing them . . ." Nonetheless, the issue of women offenders was not to become an issue of national importance until the 1960s.

There was one exception to this lack of attention: the Fauteux Com-mittee (1956). This committee's recommendation went against the belief that the Prison for Women should be closed. Instead, they suggested that a central correctional facility had a number of benefits, in particular the fact that it was much easier to develop and improve programs for women in one prison. The perceived benefits, they argued, far outweighed any benefits that could be derived from provincial institutions. Yet, that same year, a proposal to build a new prison for women in Kingston was discarded "following a public outcry against a central facility" (Shaw, 1991b:15).

In 1959, overcrowding became a reality, with the population reaching 116 inmates. This increase was attributable to a large number of drug offenders and members of the Doukhobor community from British Columbia. To alleviate the overcrowding, one wing of the Matsqui Prison in British Columbia had to be opened to house and treat drug offenders, and the Prison for Women had to be expanded by 50 beds. In 1965, the Ministry of Justice recommended that a new prison for women be constructed in Cornwall, Ontario, but this plan was rejected due to a lack of support facilities in the surrounding area. As Belknap (1996) has suggested, the traditional focus of women's correctional facilities resulted in a system of institutionalized sexism. This is because women's prisons are isolated, making continued contact between family and friends difficult and economically problematic. Furthermore, the smaller numbers of women incarcerated make it easy for prison administrators to somehow rationalize the "lack of diverse educational, vocational, and other programs available" as well as the "low levels of specialization in treatment. . . ."

Starting in 1968, numerous reports, studies, investigations and commissions have focused on the Prison for Women. One theme was constant—that the Prison for Women should be closed and that the inmates either be located in their home provinces or in residential centres located across the various regions in Canada. One significant policy that emerged in the early 1970s was the **Exchange of Service Agreements** between the federal government and all provinces except Ontario and Prince Edward Island.

The proposals that emerged throughout the 1970s and the 1980s reflected a significant ideological change. Their attack on the inadequacy of the facility and treatment programs at the Prison for Women reflected the ideology of formal equality, namely that all policies and practices directed toward federally sentenced women be based on gender-neutral standards. A number of different approaches were taken in order to achieve this goal. The **Clark Report** (1976:43) maintained the attack on the location issue by arguing that the federal government's correctional legislation of the day, the Prisons and Reformatories Act, "be revised to eliminate all provisions that discriminate on the basis of sex or religion." Attempts were made through the courts to achieve equal rights between women and men in programming, services, geographical location and facilities, among other things. While many of these court challenges were successful and existing programs were altered and new programs introduced, it is difficult to assess exactly how they were implemented in practice. Other problems associated with this approach included:

(1) that although administrators recognize the problem(s) and agree that change is needed, they may not have the resources to make the necessary provisions and structural alterations; and

(2) the failure to recognize the standard by which equality is measured is based on male standards. As a result, women's programs are brought up to par with men's, instead of being designed at the outset to meet the needs of women (Hannah-Moffat, 1994:8).

Recognizing the limits of the reforms brought about by the ideology of equal rights, a new approach was applied to federally sentenced women: **substantive equality**, which focuses on situational diversity. In essence, this approach recognizes that female offenders and male offenders are different, hence they should have programs, services and facilities designed to meet each group's specific needs. A key component in this ideology is the woman-centered approach to corrections, which argues that policies must be restructured to reflect the variety of realities experienced by women and men.

Elizabeth Fry, 1780-1845. This English Quaker philanthropist was one of the first to lobby for separate facilities for incarcerated women offenders. *Archive Photos (Kean).*

This ideology was reflected in large part in *Creating Choices: Report of the Task Force on Federally Sentenced Women* (1990), which recommended a number of changes in the correctional approach to federally sentenced women inmates. The recommendations reiterated a number of items that had been previously discussed: geographical dislocation, lack of programming, lack of community-based programs and alternatives, the closing of the Prison for Women, and a recognition of the unique needs of aboriginal women (*Creating Choices*, 1990:36-42). Commissions after 1934 recognized these problems, but the authors of *Creating Choices* reflected the feminist belief that a different approach was necessary to classify, treat and reintegrate women offenders into society properly. Specifically, their approach was based "on feminist principles of empowerment, meaningful choices, respect and dignity, supportive environments and shared responsibilities" (*Creating Choices*, 1990:126-135;

Hannah-Moffat, 1994:9). *Creating Choices* stressed the need for women to recover from their past experiences of abuse and to develop programs based on self-esteem and self-sufficiency through a variety of programs and services "designed to respond to women's needs as they define them" (Hannah-Moffat, 1994:9). Their recommended plan of action was based on two key areas: (1) the establishment of five regional women's facilities and a healing lodge for aboriginal women, and (2) a community release strategy, which would offer "a wide variety of programs and services to women who no longer need, or are legally required to be held in, closed custody" (*Creating Choices*, 1990:148). It was proposed that the new regional centres be located on several acres of land, include cottage-style facilities and create self-sufficiency, and use community standards and resources as much as possible. As an alternative to using physical restraints as the main means of maintaining security, the task force recommended an "emphasis on dynamic rather than static security measures . . ." (Shaw 1992:441). Programs would be holistic and culturally sensitive and responsive to the needs of all women (*Creating Choices*, 1990). These recommendations were "ideal articulations of a substantive feminist theory of corrections and are an excellent example of how feminist theory has influenced the policy-making process and, to some degree, correctional practice" (Hannah-Moffat, 1994:9-10).

ISSUES CONCERNING FEDERALLY SENTENCED WOMEN

Many of the problems facing federally sentenced women once they are incarcerated involve the two major concerns of location and treatment, which are addressed in the previous section. Women face different issues while incarcerated in such areas as programming, dislocation and personal relationships. Yet, relative to the number of legal challenges made by men with regard to these and other areas or prison services, women have spent much less time litigating their interests in the courts. It has only been during the past 10 years that women have legally contested various issues concerning the conditions of their confinement. The two areas in which legal challenges by women have contested prison conditions are (1) the issue of dislocation to the Prison for Women at Kingston, Ontario, while men can be sent to an institution in the area in which they live, and (2) the issue of quality and quantity of prison programs and services.

The placement of women offenders in the Prison for Women in Kingston has long been a major issue for women in Canada. While Exchange of Service Agreements between most provinces and the federal government were implemented in 1973, not all federally sentenced women were deemed eligible for placement in a provincial correctional facility due to their criminal history, needs and type of offence. As a result, women from all over Canada were sentenced to the Prison for Women, thereby creating specific hardships for them that the majority of federally sentenced men did not have to confront.

The issue of placement for federally sentenced women became a major issue between 1989 and 1991, when eight women inmates at the Prison for Women committed or attempted to commit suicide. Due to concerns about her safety and the problems associated with the Prison for Women, a federally sentenced aboriginal woman, Carol Maureen Daniels, who was charged with second-degree murder, argued that her rights under the Canadian Charter of Rights and Freedoms would be violated if she served any part of her sentence at the Prison for Women. In *R. v. Daniels* [(1991) 5 W.W.R. 340 Sask., C.A.] on July 15, 1990, the Saskatchewan Court of Queen's Bench ruled that Carol Daniels's rights to life and security as specified by the Charter of Rights and Freedoms would be violated if she had to serve any part of her sentence at an institution in which there was a high risk of inmates committing suicide. The judge noted that two aboriginal women at the Prison for Women had recently committed suicide and another had also committed suicide shortly after release. The judge ruled that any offender who commits a serious offence must be punished, but that imprisoning them where there was a high risk of suicide "is in my opinion unacceptable in a free and democratic society." In addition, the judge also ruled that Daniels's Section 12 Charter right not to be subjected to cruel and unusual punishment would be violated if she were incarcerated in the Prison for Women. The fact that she would be sent to a prison far from her home, family and friends was in violation of her Section 12 rights. This decision was based on a Supreme Court ruling that included under the definition of cruel and unusual punishment "imprisonment at locations far distant from home, family and friends, a condition amounting to virtual exile which is particularly relevant to women, since there is only one federal penitentiary in Canada."

Upon finding Daniels guilty and sentencing her to life imprisonment without eligibility for parole for 10 years, the judge ordered that she not serve any part of her sentence at the Prison for Women in Kingston, Ontario. She was then ordered to spend her period of incarceration at a federal male facility. Following this decision, the Correctional Service of Canada opened a wing in the Saskatchewan Penitentiary. There was also room made to house up to four other aboriginal women, because the lower court ruling also included the statement that no other women of aboriginal ancestry were to be incarcerated at the Prison for Women. The following year, the Saskatchewan Court of Appeal reversed the lower court's decision, largely on the basis that the trial judge's powers ended at sentencing. The *Daniels* decision is largely speculative in terms of its implications over the issue of the location for federally sentenced women because the issue was considered by many to become largely irrelevant with the construction of the new regional facilities for women and a healing lodge for aboriginal women during the 1990s.

Another legal issue for federally sentenced women has been the variety and quality of programming they have received from the federal authorities. This issue was litigated in ***R. v. Gayle Horii*** [(1991) 132 N.R. 48 Fed. C.A.] when Gayle Horii, a resident of British Columbia who was convicted of second-degree murder in 1986 and received a life sentence without parole eligibility for 10 years, chose to serve her sentence at the Prison for Women. Her decision was based upon her desire to enroll in the postsecondary education program offered at that federal correctional institution. However, when she arrived, she discovered she would have to wait two years before she could participate in the program. Her application to transfer back to British Columbia was rejected until 1989, when she was transferred to Matsqui Medium-Security Institution, a federal male medium-security institution well known for its postsecondary program and facilities. Living accomodations were provided for her in the hospital area and she proceeded to take the postsecondary education course offerings. However, when the federal government started to administrate federally sentenced women in British Columbia at the Burnaby Correctional Centre for Women, she was informed that she would be transferred there. This transfer meant that she would lose her involvement with on-site instruction for her postsecondary program. In addition, she would have fewer visiting privileges and be placed in a higher-security institution. Horii applied to have the transfer denied on the basis that her right to equal protection and equal benefit of the law without discrimination on the basis of sex would be violated. Her application was successfully argued to the Federal Court of Appeal and she was allowed to remain at Matsqui.

Programs and Services for Federally Sentenced Women

Until the 1990s, programs available for federally sentenced women have been dismal. As indicated previously in this chapter, women in the Prison for Women suffered from the stereotypes of women offenders as morally bankrupt and in need of training that would make them obedient and subservient to the demands of men in general and specifically to their husbands (Dobash et al., 1986:23). Positive role models—as defined by men—generally referred to the fact that domestic work was the main (and sometimes only) type of program available to incarcerated women. They were taught appropriate homemaking skills, beautician skills, office skills, sewing, floral arranging and hairdressing. Few, if any, women were trained in other skills needed for them to become legitimately independent individuals upon release.

This approach continued until the 1980s. Treatment programs for incarcerated women "were still primarily in the context of good discipline, orderly habits, and traditional women's work . . . [P]hysical facilities . . . gradually improved but little else changed" (Carrigan, 1991: 471). However, the need for specific programs and services were identified during the late 1980s when numerous reports emphasized the continuing inadequacies in both the quality and quantity of women's programs provided at the federal Prison for Women (Berezins and Cooper, 1982; Sugar and Fox, 1990). A crucial factor in the demand for better programs came after six incarcerated women, all but one of which was aboriginal, committed suicide between December 1988 and February 1991. A Board of Inquiry into an attempted suicide recommended that consultants not employed by the federal government be hired to evaluate the nature of the programs offered to federally sentenced women at the Prison for Women.

Five major areas of programming within prisons have been identified by Pollock-Byrne (1990:88-89). The most common are known as maintenance programs, in which women inmates become involved in clerical, food service and cleaning roles. The second type of program, education, is important because many inmates lack basic educational and/or literacy skills. Vocational programs are necessary to train women in occupational requirements in order for them to become employed full-time upon their release. To date, most of these programs have centered upon traditional "female occupations," such as clerical work and flower arranging. The fourth type of programming involves the rehabilitation of women offenders. Rehabilitation programs can involve drug therapy and psychological treatment programs, but in the past they have been based upon the needs of male offenders. The fifth and final area of programming identified involves medical care. It is important to recognize the special needs of women offenders and their overall place in the improvement of the quality of women's lives.

All of these types of programs were identified as being necessary within the Prison for Women (*Creating Choices*, 1990:138-147). A recurring theme among many of the reports and commissions has been the fact that many needs of federally sentenced women go unattended or, at best, are only partially met. Kendall (1993; 1994) conducted an evaluation of therapeutic services at the Prison for Women over a 10-month period. While it was not part of the series of reports that contributed to the publication of *Creating Choices: Report of the Task Force on Federally Sentenced Women* (1990), it coincided with the efforts directed at creating new regional correctional facilities and, as a result, its results were used to help provide direction for the development of programs that would be implemented in the new facilities. In addition, its findings also contributed to the type of programs available to women inmates still held in the Prison for Women.

In her report, Kendall evaluated the counselling program and its role in the Prison for Women. In her interviews with staff members, the obvious benefits of counselling were noted, including stabilizing the effects of the prison environment, easier adjustment of the inmates, and crisis prevention. At the same time, some of the staff members voiced concern about whether the counselling practices were leading prisoners to engage in suicidal, self-injurious or volatile behaviour. The women inmates, however, gave overwhelming support to both the counsellors as well as the programs at the Prison for Women. This high level of satisfaction could in part be explained by the feminist-based therapy used by the counsellors. This approach led to counselling practices reflecting the issues inmates themselves identified as the most important: "assistance in taking control of their own lives, the opportunity to value and be valued by others, and space just to be themselves" (Kendall, 1994:20). These reflect the main principles of feminist therapy: personal autonomy and a mutually respected relationship with others.

Federally Sentenced Women and Their Children

In their survey of federally sentenced women, Shaw et al. (1991) discovered that of the 109 women, approximately 50 percent of the women incarcerated in the Prison for Women—and about 75 percent of federally sentenced women incarcerated in provincial institutions—have children. Overall, 64 percent of the women had children, with most reporting they had one or two children. Almost 50 percent of the women had children of school age (142 children), while another 24 percent identified having children below school age (52 children). The difficulties associated with the loss of living with their children are significant for incarcerated women as well as for their children (Belknap, 1996:105). Concerns about who will support their children and the loss of custody rights are great for incarcerated mothers. Trying to adjust to these issues from prison is difficult because there are many difficult legal, social and familial concerns to attend to (Shaw et al., 1991).

Research in the United States by Crawford (1990) demonstrated that a significant number of children of incarcerated women are cared for by relatives, and that a significant number of the women retain custody of their children. However, there are a number of problems that incarcerated women experience, most significantly, the effect of their incarceration upon their children. As Gabel (1995) has noted, a number of issues have been identified from research into the impact of having a parent incarcerated. The period of separation has led to trauma, disruption of personal and family bonds, and the deterioration of the family's social and economic situation. Behavioural problems are found in a "sizeable minority" of the children, with the greatest problems relating to family supports and coping mechanisms. Gabel (1995:39) stresses that the incarceration of mothers "may place even greater burdens on children if the children lose their primary caretaker (temporarily, or permanently)." A national study in the United States, for example, found that the children of incarcerated fathers are usually cared for by their mothers, while the children of incarcerated mothers are rarely looked after by their fathers (Glick and Neto, 1977). In this context, Baunach (1985) discovered that more than 50 percent of the incarcerated mothers in her study reported that their incarceration led to numerous problems with their children, such as emotional problems, aggressive behavior and school-related problems.

To address this issue, the Correctional Service of Canada chose to develop a **mother-child program**. While this is a new approach in Canada, similar programs have existed in the United States and Europe for a number of years. In addition, several provinces allow incarcerated women to keep their children with them until the age of two or three. The authors of *Creating Choices* (1990), however, discovered that federally sentenced women serving their sentence in provincial correctional institutions were usually able to maintain a relationship with their children through regular contact. For women in the Prison for Women, however, the geographical distances made regular contact difficult, except through telephone and/or mail.

The Correctional Service of Canada decided that the main basis for any decision-making regarding the mother-child program will be the best interests of the child. In addition, the goal of the program is to facilitate, maintain and encourage the mother-child relationship (Watson, 1995:25-26). Eligibility criteria for the mother include considerations such as (1) the existence of a positive, ongoing relationship between the mother and child; (2) the mother's physical and mental health; (3) the consent of court/child welfare authorities; and (4) the willingness

The Okimaw Ohci Healing Lodge, a minimum-security prison in Saskatchewan's Cypress Hills. The development of healing lodge facilities has been recommended as a means of serving the special needs of aboriginal inmates. *Canapress Photo Service (Kevin Van Paassen).*

of the mother to facilitate visits between the child and other significant family members (Watson, 1995:26). Not all mothers will be eligible to participate in the program when they enter a federal correctional facility. If an offender has been convicted of child abuse and/or neglect, she will not be allowed to participate until her custody rights are reinstated by the courts, and she has received treatment and/or has participated in a series of regular visits with her child or children (Watson, 1995:26).

The results of these programs for both women and men offenders have been extremely beneficial. Johnston (1995) reports that the Child Custody Advocacy Services (CHICAS) Project in Southern California was successful because women who had substance abuse problems went into treatment programs, enabling them to reunite with their children. The experience of being separated from their children is extremely difficult for women inmates, perhaps one of the harshest aspects of their incarceration. The availability of rehabilitation programs that can address their needs are essential, as it is through such programs that physical contact with their children can be reestablished.

Employment and Educational Programming

A significant limitation facing federally sentenced women has been their lack of access to both the quality and quantity of vocational and educational programs. Critics argue that the poor quality of these programs perpetuates the subordinate status of women in Canadian society. This has led to debate and some litigation concerning what women inmates are entitled to in terms of programs. Much of this debate has focused upon different services afforded federally sentenced women and men. The resulting differences have led to some litigation, the basis of which is grounded in the fact that the poor programs offered to women offenders deny them equal opportunity, particularly as they apply to equal protection and equal benefit of the law without discrimination on the basis of sex.

> [T]he vocational and educational programs available to males far exceed those available for females. Typically, women's programs are small in number and usually sex stereotyped. Thus, whereas men may have access to programs in welding . . . and plumbing, and to college programs, women may have cosmetology, and child-care, keypunch, and nurses programs, and often high school is the only education available to women (Pollock-Byrne, 1990:168-169).

Shaw (1991a; 1991b) reported the extent of this lack of programming in the "Survey of Federally Sentenced Women" and "The Release Study." In the "Survey of Federally Sentenced Women," 170 women were interviewed about their employment backgrounds and needs for education. Fewer than one-third indicated that they had formal qualifications beyond basic education prior to being sentenced, while the majority of the remaining women did not reach Grade 12 or its equivalent. In terms of work experience, most had found employment in the unskilled service sector. Just over 33 percent of the women had permanent employment, 40 percent indicated they had difficulty finding work, while 15 percent had never worked legitimately. Aboriginal women were different from the rest of federally sentenced women due to the fact that they were "particularly disadvantaged in terms of their educational backgrounds" (Shaw, 1991b:viii).

The researchers found the provision of training and educational facilities for federally sentenced women to be completely inadequate. Women offenders serving their sentences in provincial institutions had very little accessibility to vocational training facilities, and most worked at domestic chores. Only 17 of the offenders had taken training courses, and these were in the areas of hairdressing, first aid and dog training. Fifty-two women at the Prison for Women had taken training courses, but along with their provincial counterparts, they clearly indicated their need for employable skills in areas with good pay and career opportunities (e.g., laboratory technician training, computing, heavy machinery, carpentry, nursing and child care). As Shaw et al. (1991:viii) concluded, "what the women want are marketable skills with qualifications and certificates."

Overall, federally sentenced women serving their sentences in provincial institutions had only limited access to programs. Women located at the prison for women had more program choices, including alcohol and drug abuse programs, sexual and physical abuse programs, native spirituality and culture programs, as well as poverty and life skills programs. Most of them requested a variety of new programs, including work release and prerelease programs, as well as programs on health, legal advice, finances and child rearing. They also indicated that they wanted the choice whether to take part in any specific program, in particular those that related to addictions and mental health care, as well as to have some control over their involvement within each program.

In their report, "The Release Study," Shaw et al. (1991) studied 57 federally sentenced women who were on a conditional release program. With the exception of a few women who decided to be homemakers or who had reached retirement age, most indicated they wanted well-paid, full-time employment. Of the remaining women, 21 indicated they had found a good, permanent job with average pay and were satisfied with their current employment. The majority, however, told the researchers they had "more variable employment, low paid, seasonal, sometimes part-time in the absence of full-time work" (Shaw et al, 1991:16). Of the 21 women who stated they had a good job, only five indicated that they had never had any real previous work experience. The other 16 women were returning to jobs at a level similar to the jobs that they had prior to going to prison.

Many women informed the researchers that they felt the threat of losing their job was real if their record was discovered and/or if their employers learned of the fact that they were on a conditional release program. One woman informed the researchers that she had been dismissed from a well-paid, public sector job after complaints about her had been received and several others indicated they "had lost jobs or not found jobs when their record was disclosed" (Shaw et al., 1991:17).

Motiuk (1996) reported on the relationship between women and men offenders' employment need levels and conditional release failure. He discovered that when there was a high level of offender employment need, the more likely the inmate was to fail on a conditional release program. The Correctional Service of Canada now collects information concerning employment needs during the Offender Intake Assessment process. Not surprisingly, this process has identified approximately 75 percent of male offenders and 67 percent of women offenders as having needs in the area of employment. Overall, male offenders averaged 9.7 indicators on needs met, while women offenders averaged 8.5 indicators. This means that more relevant programs need to be provided to women offenders, programs that have been traditionally reserved for men offenders. However, receiving improved employment skills is usually associated with educational upgrading.

With the opening of the new regional facilities, it is hoped that they will have programs that will focus on living skills, spirituality, education, employment, vocational training and recreation (LeBlanc, 1994:12). These are considered essential ingredients for the reintegration of women into the community upon their release, and for providing them with a future career.

Risks and Needs of Federally Sentenced Women

During the late 1980s, concerns had been made about the ability of the correctional system to respond to the needs of federally sentenced women. These concerns included the problems of applying assessment instruments developed for male offenders to women inmates, the nature of therapeutic programs and the relevance of security classification (Adelberg and Currie, 1987; Berezins and Cooper, 1982; *Creating Choices*, 1990; Currie, 1986; Kendall, 1993). Since 1994, however, all federally sentenced women have had to complete the Offenders Intake Assessment (OIA) upon their arrival at an institution. In addition, psychological assessments are conducted to establish the needs of each offender. These assessments were originally developed to shift the focus of the psychological testing toward a holistic model of women's strengths and needs (Scarth and McLean, 1994). This led to the creation of the **Skills and Needs Inventory**, which involves a number of questions associated with both positive and negative strategies. Women are asked to identify and then describe their needs and strengths and the type of assessment they want. This approach is vastly different from prior approaches because it allows women offenders the chance to become personally involved in the assessment process.

Specifically, the Skills and Needs Inventory attempts to link social, cultural and economic factors with women's life experiences. Scarth and McLean (1994:34) report that the inventory has been extremely well-received by offenders, case-management workers and therapeutic staff. This method allows the offender to be less anxious, and in greater control of the process and therefore, it leads to the collection of better and more relevant information.

Another issue raised involves the use of appropriate security classifications for women offenders. This was not an issue until recently because there was only one federal institution for women and all offenders were classified as "high-risk." With the opening of the five new federal facilities for women offenders, the issue of security classification has become an area of discussion and debate. Shaw and Dubois (1995:5), for example, state that "women's violence has been formed largely as a response to an abusive situation or past abusive experiences." This argument has led to the demand that women offenders be given lower security classifications, an argument that has an impact on such areas as housing, program accessibility, and privileges. Blanchette (1997a) analysed this issue by comparing federally sentenced women on the basis of security level. She reports that, in her comparison of maximum-security with medium-security women offenders, there were reliable between-group differences on a variety of risk/need and suicide potential factors. She also found that, when compared to their medium-security counterparts, maximum-security inmates were higher risk, had greater needs and higher potential for suicide. Blanchette (1997b) also investigated the concern that when the security level increases, there is a corresponding increase in the risk and needs as well as suicide potential of women offenders. Her analysis revealed significant between-group differences in the areas of employment, marital/family relations, associates, substance abuse, community functions and attitude. She concluded (1997b:23-25) that there is a "heterogeneity of female groups by custody level" and that "the goal of assigning security classification is being met in an equitable manner."

Both studies conducted by Blanchette analysed women offenders as a unified group in comparison to male offenders. However, it is possible that there may be similarities and differences across and within groups. For example, Blanchette (1997b) looked at all women offenders in her study without looking at possible differences and similarities between aboriginal and white women offenders. It is possible that all racial groups have similar risk ratings but differ in all areas of needs with the exception of personal/emotional issues. For example, there could be a high concentration by racial group in various categories of need (e.g., one racial group could have higher needs in the areas of employment, marital/family, association/socialization, substance abuse or community needs). These differences could lead to recommendations that community reintegration efforts consider the offender's race as well as their gender.

Long-Term Incarceration for Federally Sentenced Women

On March 31, 1997, 88 federally sentenced women were serving long-term sentences (i.e., 10 years or longer) and/or life sentences. Fifteen were serving a sentence of 10 years or more, while the remaining 73 had been sentenced to life imprisonment or to an indeterminate sentence. This number is an increase from 62 in 1991 and 70 in 1994. Most of these women were convicted of a murder charge. In 1997, 17 federally sentenced women were convicted of first-degree murder, while 54 were serving a sentence for second-degree murder. Many of these women were serving their first federal sentence.

Long-term offenders are viewed as requiring special needs. Offenders serving less than 10 years have generally been found to have the capability to cope with imprisonment. For example, Zamble and Porporino (1988) found, in a sample of 41 federally sentenced men having completed at least seven years of their 10 year sentences, that they did not become more depressed, behave worse or lose contact with the outside world. In fact, they found that the inmates' emotional and behavioural states improved over time. Federally sentenced women, in contrast, have been designated as a population requiring special needs. This was largely the conclusion of the "Survey of Federally Sentenced Women," which discovered that women serving life sentences wanted greater accessibility to families, family counselling services and mental health services; earlier temporary releases; and greater access to retreats and recreational programs. They also indicated that they wanted one-to-one vocational training and that program accessibility should not be limited by security levels (Shaw et al., 1991).

Studies by Porporino (1990) and Hattem (1994) found problems with the Canadian system's response to these needs. Porporino, for example, found programming limitations for all long-term offenders— both women and men. He reported that inadequate planning of programs had been conducted in this area, and that the small amount of planning for release is usually delayed until offenders have served most of their sentence. Hattem (1994:43) stated that female long-term offenders are "denied access to programs or privileges (which they might have otherwise been entitled to) because of their sentence." This is, because a significant number of programs and privileges are based on an inmate's security classification, their long-term needs are largely ignored until they have served a substantial part of their sentence.

Sabath and Cowles (1990) found that a major difference in program planning between short- and long-term offenders is in the area of vocational skills training. For those offenders spending long periods of time in prison, many of the normal job training programs have little meaning. They feel frustrated when they are given little opportunity to receive training and/or to practise their skills productively while in prison. In this same context, Mitchell (1990) believes that if career planning is to be used as part of effective programming, it must be available relatively soon after the offender is institutionalized. This will give long-term offenders a sense of purpose and help their chances of receiving early release. Axon (1989) found in her American research that a variety of measures, among them chance of job assignment and consideration for early release, could be used as incentives to deal with the apathy found among long-term offenders.

In 1991, the Correctional Service of Canada released a study on inmates serving long sentences. The Task Force on Long-Term Offenders developed guidelines for looking after inmates serving long sentences. These included:

1. Involvement of the inmate in managing her or his sentence.

2. Personalizing programs and the decision-making process.

3. Developing programs adapted to the needs of this target group.

4. Promoting change for a successful reintegration into society.

5. Appealing for an increased involvement by family.

In an attempt to facilitate this process, the Report of the Task Force on Long-Term Offenders (1991) devised an operational framework that would divide sentences into four measurable segments. The four stages identified were: (1) adaptation, (2) integration in prison environment, (3) preparation for release, and (4) return to society. This idea was based on the recommendation that the Correctional Service of Canada "adopts a management model for long-term sentences, according to four stages . . . and that programs, modules, and services be developed according to the characteristics and needs of each stage."

Co-Correctional Facilities

The issue of **co-correctional facilities** (facilities serving male and female inmates together) was raised by Shaw (1990) when she discovered that 50 of the 102 women interviewed at the Prison for Women, as well as another 29 federally sentenced women located at a provincial correctional facility, were interested in serving their sentence at a co-correctional federal facility. The main reasons given included the hope that there would be a greater number of programs and services provided as well as a more "normal" environment, and that this would bring about positive changes among the women inmates. The perceived benefits of these facilities include the reduction and, hopefully, the elimination of gender-based programs by increasing women's access to educational, vocational and medical programs and services, as well as by decreasing the possibility that women will be sent to correctional facilities that are geographically distant from their homes. But do these benefits really enhance the conditions of women inmates?

The history of contemporary co-correctional facilities in North America can be traced to the opening of a state co-correctional facility in Fort Worth, Texas. During the next seven or eight years, in the United States, five federal and 15 state co-correctional facilities were opened. By 1990, the American Correctional Association reported that 45 percent of correctional facilities in the United States housed both women and men inmates. It was found that there were significant differences in the amount of interaction between women and men as well as in the availability of programs for women. Thirteen percent of these institutions allowed men and women to work together in prison industries during the day (American Correctional Association, 1990).

Most studies have attempted to assess the benefits accrued to women in terms of programming and services. The claims that women will be the beneficiaries of better programming have been found to be lacking. Women are typically given employment skills that place them in subservient roles to men; usually women have less freedom to move about the institution; women are more likely to be disciplined; and co-corrections rarely decreases the traditional women's programs (Chesney-Lind and Rodriquez, 1983; Schweber, 1985). Significant amounts of sex discrimination and sexual harassment have also been reported (Mahan, 1984; 1989).

> Critics have noted that co-corrections "normalizes in another way—it places women in a minority situation in which their needs are subordinated in a male-dominated environment. There is nothing about a co-correctional institution which prohibits management from deciding in allotting programs and services to focus on the majority—the men" (Ross and Fabiano, 1986:66-67).

SUMMARY

Federally sentenced women have experienced conditions quite different from the facilities and programs offered to incarcerated males. For a century, women inmates were forced to live in extremely confined quarters in Kingston Penitentiary. Later, when a separate facility was finally built, it lacked the appropriate gender-specific programs to assist women to reintegrate into society. Furthermore, all federally sentenced women were required to serve their sentence in Kingston, Ontario, although they came from all parts of Canada. In comparison, men were able to serve their sentences in their native regions, where they benefited from the maintenance of close family contacts. This issue of dislocation became a major concern during the 1980s and 1990s, resulting in new regional centres being constructed for federally sentenced women. These facilities were opened during the 1990s, but the Kingston Prison for Women remains open despite its symbolic image of women's oppression.

Federally sentenced women have also suffered over the issue of services and needs. Women have traditionally been forced to participate in gender-specific educational programs that force them to take a marginal economic position once they are released from incarceration. In recent years, however, a few court cases have led to improvements in this area, with the result that some programs are now the same as those offered to men serving time in federal institutions. However, a number of issues concerning federally sentenced women still need resolution—for example, the inmates' right to keep their children with them and the development of a security classification system different from that applied to male inmates.

DISCUSSION QUESTIONS

1. Do you think the number of spaces in federal institutions for women should be cut in half?

2. Do you think that women should receive the same types of security classification as men or that they should all be given the designation of "minimum security"?

3. Do you think children should be able to live with their mothers in a correctional facility?

4. Why do you think incarcerated women are given less opportunities than their male counterparts?

5. Should correctional facilities for women be run completely by women? What would be the benefits of such a system?

REFERENCES

Adelberg, Ellen and Claudia Currie (1987). *Too Few to Count: Canadian Women in Conflict with the Law*. Vancouver: Press Gang Publishers.

American Correctional Association (1990). *The Female Offender: What Does the Future Hold?* Arlington, VA: Kirby Lithographic Company.

Archambault Report (1938). *Report of the Royal Commission to Investigate the Penal System of Canada*. Ottawa: King's Printer.

Axon, Lee (1989). *Models of Exemplary Programs for Female Inmates*, Volume 1. Ottawa: Report to the Solicitor General of Canada.

Barry, Ellen M. (1991). "Jail Litigation Concerning Women Prisoners." *Prison Journal*, Volume 71, 44-50.

Basic Facts About Corrections in Canada (1977). Ottawa: Solicitor General of Canada.

Baunach, Phyllis Jo (1985). *Mothers in Prison*. New Brunswick, NJ: Transaction Books.

Belknap, Joanne (1996). *The Invisible Woman: Gender, Crime and Justice*. Belmont, CA: Wadsworth.

Berezins, Lorraine and Sheelagh Cooper (1982). "The Political Economy of Correctional Planning for Women: The Case of Bankrupt Bureaucracy." *Canadian Journal of Criminology*, Volume 24, 399-416.

Blanchette, Kelly (1997a). "Classifying Female Offenders for Correctional Interventions." *Forum on Corrections Research*, Volume 9, 36-41.

Blanchette, Kelly (1997b). *Risk and Need Among Federally Sentenced Female Offenders: A Comparison of Minimum-, Medium-, and Maximum-Security Inmates*. Research Report R-58. Ottawa: Correctional Service of Canada.

Boritch, Helen (1997). *Fallen Women: Female Crime and Criminal Justice in Canada*. Toronto: ITP Nelson.

Canadian Centre for Justice Statistics (1997). *Adult Correctional Services in Canada, 1995-96*. Ottawa: Statistics Canada.

Carlen, Pat (1983). *Women's Imprisonment: A Study in Social Control*. London: Routledge and Kegan Paul.

Carrigan, D. Owen (1991). *Crime and Punishment in Canada: A History*. Toronto: McClelland and Stewart.

Chesney-Lind, Meda and Noelie Rodriquez (1983). "Women Under Lock and Key." *The Prison Journal*, Volume 63, 47-65.

Clark Report (1976). *Report of the National Advisory Committee on the Female Offender.* Ottawa: Ministry of the Solicitor General.

Cooper, Sheelagh (1993). "The Evolution of the Federal Women's Prison." In Ellen Adelberg and Claudia Currie (eds), *Women in Conflict with the Law: Women and the Canadian Justice System.* Vancouver: Press Gang Publishers.

Crawford, J. (1990). *The Female Offender: What Does the Future Hold?* Washington, DC: American Correctional Association, St. Mary's Press.

Creating Choices: Report of the Task Force on Federally Sentenced Women (1990). Ottawa: Correctional Service of Canada.

Currie, Claudia (1986). *Developing Tools for the Study of the Female Offender: A Review of the Literature.* Ottawa: Correctional Service of Canada.

Dobash, Russell, R. Emerson Dobash and Sue Gutteridge (1986). *The Imprisonment of Women.* New York: Basil Blackwell.

Faith, Karlene (1993). *Unruly Women: The Politics of Confinement and Resistance.* Vancouver: Press Gang Publishers.

Fauteux Report (1956). *Report of a Committee Appointed to Inquire into the Principles and Procedures Followed in the Remission Service of the Department of Justice of Canada.* Ottawa: The Queen's Printer.

Gabel, Stewart (1995). "Behavioral Problems in the Children of Incarcerated Parents." *Forum on Corrections Research*, Volume 7, 37-39.

Glick, Ruth and Virginia V. Neto (1977). *National Study of Women's Correctional Programs.* Washington, DC: U.S. Government Printing Office.

Hannah-Moffat, Kelly (1994). "Unintended Consequences of Feminism and Prison Reform." *Forum on Corrections Research*, Volume 6, 7-10.

Hattem, Tina (1994). "The Realities of Life Imprisonment for Women Convicted of Murder." *Forum on Corrections Research*, Volume 6, 42-45.

Heidensohn, Frances M. (1985). *Women and Crime.* New York: New York University Press.

Heney, J. (1990). "Reduction of Self-Injury: A Mental Health Priority." *Forum on Corrections Research*, Volume 2, 3, 10-12.

Johnson, Holly (1993). "Images and Realities: Profiles of Women Offenders." In Ellen Adelberg and Claudia Currie (eds.), *In Conflict with the Law: Women and the Canadian Criminal Justice System.* Vancouver: Press Gang Publishers.

Johnson, Holly (1986). *Women and Crime in Canada.* Ottawa: Solicitor General of Canada.

Johnson, Holly and Karen Rodgers (1993). "Getting The Facts Straight: A Statistical Overview." In Ellen Adelberg and Claudia Currie (eds.), *Too Few to Count: Canadian Women in Conflict with the Law,* Second Edition. Vancouver: Press Gang Publishers.

Johnston, D. (1995). "Child Custody Issues of Women Prisoners: A Preliminary Report from the CHICAS Project." *The Prison Journal*, Volume 75, 2, 222-239

Kendall, Kathleen (1994). "Creating Real Choices: A Program Evaluation of Therapeutic Services at the Prison for Women." *Forum on Corrections Research*, Volume 6, 19-21.

Kendall, Kathleen (1993). *Program Evaluation of Therapeutic Services at the Prison for Women*. Ottawa: Correctional Service of Canada.

LeBlanc, Therese (1994). "Redesigning Corrections for Federally Sentenced Women in Canada." *Forum on Corrections Research*, Volume 6, 7-10.

Lefebvre, Linda (1994). "The Demographic Characteristics of Offenders on Day Parole." *Forum on Corrections Research*, Volume 6, 7-10.

Lieber, Francis (1964). "Translator's Preface." In G. Beaumont and A. de Tocqueville, *On the Penitentiary System in the United States and Its Application in France*. Carbondale, IL: Southern Illinois Press (originally published in 1833).

Loucks, Alex and Edward Zamble (1994). "Some Comparisons of Male and Female Serious Offenders." *Forum on Corrections Research*, Volume 6, 22-25.

MacKenzie, D.L., J.W. Robinson and C.S. Campbell (1989). "Long- Term Incarceration of Female Offenders: Prison Adjustment and Coping." *Criminal Justice and Behavior*, Volume 16, 223-238.

MacLeod, Linda (1986). *Sentenced to Separation: An Exploration of the Needs and Problems of Mothers Who are Offenders with Children*. Ottawa: Ministry of the Solicitor General.

Mahan, Sue (1989). "The Needs and Experiences of Women in Sexually Integrated Prisons." *American Journal of Criminal Justice*, Volume 13, 228-239.

Mahan, Sue (1984). "Imposition of Despair. An Ethnography of Women in Prison." *Justice Quarterly*, Volume 1, 228-239.

Mann, Coramae Richey (1984). *Female Crime and Delinquency*. Tuscaloosa, AL: University of Alabama Press.

Mitchell, Barry (1990). "The Management of Life Sentence Prisoners in England and Wales." *The Prison Journal*, Volume 80, 96-108.

Morris, Allison (1987). *Women, Crime and Criminal Justice*. Oxford, England: Basil Blackwell.

Motiuk, Larry (1996). "Targeting Employment Patterns to Reduce Offender Risk and Need." *Forum on Corrections Research*, Volume 8, 22-24.

Oliver, Peter (1994). "'To Govern By Kindness': The First Two Decades of the Mercer Reformatory for Women." In J. Phillips, T. Loo and S. Lewthwaite (eds), *Essays in the History of Canadian Law*. Toronto: Osgoode Society.

Pollock-Byrne, Joycelyn (1990). *Women, Prison and Crime*. Monterey, CA: Brooks/Cole.

Porporino, Frank J. (1990). "Differences in Response to Long-Term Imprisonment: Implications for the Management of Long-Term Offenders." *The Prison Journal*, Volume 80, 73-96.

Rafter, Nicole Hahn (1983). "Prisons for Women, 1790-1980." In Michael Tonry and Norval Morris (eds.), *Crime and Justice: An Annual Review of Research*, Volume 5. Chicago: University of Chicago Press.

Ross, Robert R. and Elizabeth A. Fabiano (eds.) (1986). *Female Offender: Correctional Afterthoughts*. Jefferson, NC: McFarland.

Sabath, Michael J. and Ernest L. Cowles (1990). "Using Multiple Perspectives to Develop Strategies for Managing Long-Term Inmates." *The Prison Journal*, Volume 80, 58-72.

Scarth, Karen and Heather McLean (1994). "The Psychological Assessment of Women in Prison." *Forum on Corrections Research*, Volume 6, 32-35.

Schweber, Claudia (1985). "Beauty Marks and Blemishes: The Co-Ed Prison." *The Prison Journal*, Volume 64, 3-15.

Shaw, Margaret (1994). "Women in Prison: A Literature Review." *Forum on Corrections Research*, Volume 6, 13-18.

Shaw, Margaret (1991a). *Survey of Federally Sentenced Women: Report of the Task Force on Federally Sentenced Women on the Prison Survey*. Ottawa: Corrections Branch, Ministry of the Solicitor General of Canada.

Shaw, Margaret (1991b). *The Federal Female Offender: Report on a Preliminary Study. User Report 1991-93*. Ottawa: Corrections Branch, Ministry of the Solicitor General of Canada.

Shaw, Margaret (1990). *Survey of Federally Sentenced Women: Technical Report 1*. Ottawa: Correctional Service of Canada.

Shaw, Margaret and S. Dubois (1995). *Understanding Violence by Women: A Review of the Literature*. Ottawa: Correctional Service of Canada.

Shaw, Margaret with Karen Rodgers, Johane Blanchette, Tina Hattem, Lee Seto Thomas and Lada Tamarack (1991). *The Release Study: Survey of Federally Sentenced Women in the Community*. Ottawa: Supply and Services Canada.

Solicitor General of Canada (1997). *Basic Facts About Corrections in Canada*. Ottawa: Solicitor General of Canada.

Stojkovic, Stan and Rick Lovell (1997). *Corrections: An Introduction*, Second Edition. Cincinnati: Anderson.

Sugar, Fran and Laura Fox (1990). *Survey of Federally Sentenced Aboriginal Women in the Community*. Ottawa: Native Women's Association of Canada.

Vachon, Marla Marino (1994). "It's About Time: The Legal Context of Police Charges for Female Offenders." *Forum on Corrections Research*, Volume 6, 3-6.

Watson, Lisa (1995). " In the Best Interest of the Child: The Mother-Child Program." *Forum on Corrections Research*, Volume 7, 25-26.

Wetherell, Donald G. (1979). "To Discipline and Train: Adult Rehabilitation Programmes in Ontario Prisons, 1874-1900." *Histoire Sociale/Social History*, Volume 12, 23, 145-165.

Wheeler, Patricia A., Rebecca Trammell, Jim Thomas and Jennifer Findlay (1989). "Persephone Chained: Parity of Equality in Women's Prisons." *The Prison Journal*, Volume 69, 88-102.

Zamble, E. and F. Porporino (1988). *Coping Behavior and Adaptation in Prison Inmates*. New York: Springer-Verlag.

The Future of Corrections in Canada

FORECASTING THE FATE OF CORRECTIONS IN CANADA

What will corrections in Canada look like in the next decade? Forecasting future correctional issues is difficult because there can be significant policy changes at any stage of the criminal justice system that can have a tremendous impact on the correctional enterprise. After all, changes in the sentencing provisions of the criminal code give the impression that the federal government is committed to offering judges the possibility of sentencing offenders to alternatives that largely involve nontraditional sanctions.

It is still not known whether these changes in sentencing will have a positive impact on the correctional population by reducing the number of individuals incarcerated, but it is an attempt to deal with the problems facing correctional administrators today. There are policies that could have a significant impact upon corrections, but it is unlikely that they will be implemented in the near future. These changes are referring to the implentation of fundamental social structural transformations in those rural and urban communities and neighborhoods across Canada from which the majority of the correctional population is drawn. At the present time, such policies are unlikely, but they are probably the best approach for dealing with the crisis facing our correctional system.

At the present time, the near future of corrections in this country involves three issues: (1) intermediate punishments, (2) the reintegration of offenders, and (3) restorative justice. Of the three, the issue of intermediate punishments is most real for provincial governments. In most provinces, various types of intermediate punishments are being employed. While it is too soon to discuss their successes and/or failures, it is possible to discuss general issues. It should be noted that much of the enthusiasm for intermediate punishments by government officials stems from their presumed cost-effectiveness. However, these arguments have been brought into perspective by studies that show that they are more expensive than most people realize. Moreover, if the use of intermediate punishments continues to increase, any cost savings will be diminished to the point of having no cost savings whatsoever. Increases in technical violations, court appearances, revocations and incarceration can all lead to costs more than doubling. In addition, the recidivism rates of those individuals placed on intermediate punishments have tended to be the same or higher than those on regular programs. This is largely due to the greater surveillance of program participants; it should be realized that most of these are for violations of the technical conditions of the release orders. Generally speaking, then, the use of intermediate punishments does not reduce or deter criminal behaviour any more than regular programs.

The federal government continues to operate in the area of reintegrating criminals. As Box 7.1 indicates, the reintegration ideology is part of the official policy of the Correctional Service of Canada. In this approach, the emphasis is upon the recognition and treatment of the problems facing offenders and assistance in the prevention of repeat criminal behaviour. However, if this ideology is to be successful, greater efforts have to be made at the operational level to attain the operational goals.

Perhaps the most encouraging development is in the area of restorative justice. In this approach, the victim and offender as well as their supporters are able to meet and (hopefully) work out their differences. In essence, restorative justice focuses on the harmful effects of offenders' actions and involves both victims and offenders in the process of reparation and rehabilitation. Restorative justice operates according to several propositions. According to Van Ness and Strong (1997), these propositions include the following:

(1) Justice requires that we work to restore victims, offenders and communities who have been injured by crime.

(2) Victims, offenders and communities should have opportunities for active involvement in the restorative justice process as early and as fully as possible.

(3) In promoting justice, government is responsible for preserving order and the community for establishing peace.

Restorative justice, therefore, emphasizes repairing the harm created by a criminal act and reducing the likelihood of future harm. This is achieved by encouraging offenders to take responsibility for their actions and for the harm they have caused, by providing some form of compensation to the victims and by promoting the reintegration of both victims and offenders back into the community. Box 7.2 outlines the major issues facing restorative justice.

Box 7.1   Reintegration

Reintegration

The Service can carry out this program for each offender only through effective partnerships with courts, police, other federal departments and agencies, provincial governments, municipalities and voluntary organizations.

According to the Correctional Service of Canada operates under the 1992 *Corrections and Conditional Release Act,*[2] the purpose of federal corrections is as follows:

The purpose of the federal correctional system is to contribute to the maintenance of a just, peaceful and safe society by:

(a) carrying out sentences imposed by courts through the safe and humane custody and supervision of offenders; and

(b) assisting the rehabilitation of offenders and their reintegration into the community as law-abiding citizens through the provision of programs in penitentiaries and in the community.

Guiding Principles

The Act also sets out 10 guiding principles for the Service including the following:

1. that the protection of society be the paramount consideration in the corrections process;

2. that the Service enhance its effectiveness and openness through the timely exchange of relevant information with other components of the criminal justice system, and through communication about its correctional policies

and programs to offenders, victims and the public;

3. that the Service use the least restrictive measures consistent with the protection of the public, staff members and offenders;

4. that offenders retain the rights and privileges of all members of society, except those rights and privileges that are necessarily removed or restricted as a consequence of the sentence;

5. that the Service facilitate the involvement of member of the public in matters relating to the operations of the Service;

6. that correctional policies, programs and practices respect gender, ethnic, cultural and linguistic differences and be responsive to the special needs of women and Aboriginal peoples, as well as to the needs of other groups of offenders with special requirements; and

7. that offenders are expected to obey penitentiary rules and conditions governing temporary absence, work release, parole and statutory release, and to actively participate in programs designed to promote their rehabilitation and reintegration.

Source: Arden Thurber (1998). "Understanding Offender Reintegration. *Forum on Corrections Research*, Volume 10, Number 1, page 15.

Box 7.2 Restorative Justice

Four Questions About Restorative Justice

1. What is restorative justice?

- It is a *different way of thinking* about crime and our response to it.
- It focuses on the *harm caused by crime:* repairing the harm done to victims and reducing future harm by preventing crime.
- It requires offenders to take *responsibility* for their actions and for the harm they have caused.
- It seeks *redress* for victims, *recompense* by offenders and *reintegration* of both within the community.
- It is achieved through a *cooperative effort* by communities and the government.

2. How is restorative justice different from what we do now?

- It *views criminal acts more comprehensively:* rather than defining crime only as law-breaking, it recognizes that offenders harm victims, communities and even themselves.
- It *involves more parties:* rather than giving key roles only to government and the offender, it includes victims and communities as well.
- It *measures success differently:* rather than measuring how much punishment has been inflicted, it measures how much harm has been repaired or prevented.
- It recognizes the importance of *community involvement and initiative* in responding to and reducing crime, rather than leaving the problem of crime to the government alone.

3. How does restorative justice respond to crime?

- It emphasizes *victim recovery* through redress, vindication and healing.
- It emphasizes *recompense by the offender* through reparation, fair treatment and habilitation.
- It establishes processes through which parties are able to *discover the truth* about what happened and the harms that resulted, to *identify the injustices* involved and to *agree on future actions* to address those harms.
- It establishes evaluation processes through which the community and government may consider whether *new strategies to prevent crime* are needed.

4. How does restorative justice seek to prevent crime?

- It builds on the *strengths of community and the government.* The community can build peace through strong, inclusive and righteous relationships; the government can bring order through fair, effective and parsimonious use of force.
- It emphasizes the need to *repair past harms* in order to prepare for the future.
- It seeks to *reconcile* offenders with those they have harmed.
- It helps communities learn to *reintegrate* victims and offenders.

Source: Daniel Van Ness and Karen Heetderks Strong (1997). *Restorative Justice.* Cincinnati: Anderson, pages 42-43.

PRIVATE PRISONS

While private prisons are now a major factor in the adult correctional services in the United States, they have not enjoyed much success in Canada. In fact, their presence has largely been confined to the operation of juvenile facilities in a number of provinces. For example, the New Brunswick provincial government contracted the American-based private correctional corporation, Wackenhut Corrections Corporation, to build and operate its new youth facilities in the spring of 1995. The involvement of Wackenhut in the facility was ultimately limited to constructing the new facility due to objections voiced by guards and others concerned with the quality of treatment. The rationale given by the provincial government in its attempt to contract out the operation of the juvenile correctional facility was that costs would be reduced by about 15 percent. In recent years the Ontario government has explored the possibility of issuing contracts to a private correctional organisation to operate provincial correctional facilities.

There are three types of private correctional institutions. Perhaps the most common one is that of a contractor-owned and -operated facility. In this configuration, a government pays the private organisation for their services, typically on a per diem basis for each inmate held. Another type of private correctional facility is an institution owned by a government who, in turn, contracts a private organisation to operate it. In this system as well, payment will usually be made on a per diem basis for each inmate. These contracts have also included a guarantee of a minimum payment by the government, so that if the number of inmates falls below a certain level, the contractor is guaranteed a certain amount of pay. A third type of private correctional facility is the privately built facility that is operated by a government. In these cases, a private organisation finances and builds the facility and then leases it to the government, usually for a certain number of years.

The situation in Canada can be compared to that in the United States. In the United States, at the end of 1990, there were 44 secure adult correctional facilities under contract with private correctional organisations, and this amounted to a total of 15,000 beds. The largest providers were the Correctional Corporation of America and Wackenhut. In 1991, the Correctional Corporation of America operated 14 adult secure correctional facilities with a total of approximately 4,800 beds. Wackenhut managed eight adult secure correctional facilities with about 3,200 beds. While these numbers have been slowly increasing during the 1990s, it must be remembered that the largest number of adult correctional facilities in the United States still are operated by the federal and state governments. Government agencies were responsible for the operation of more than 3,500 jails and 1,400 federal and state prison facilities.

The possibility of privatising secure adult correctional facilities represents a rather new development in the history of Canadian corrections. However, this does not mean that private companies are not active in the correctional area. For example, as long ago as 1983-84, the Correctional Service of Canada held contracts with 175 privately owned, nonprofit halfway houses and other aftercare facilities, which received $10.5 million for their services (Solicitor General of Canada, 1985). In addition, in an attempt to lower costs, the federal and provincial governments today contract with private organisations for many of their service needs. In addition, private organisations work under both provincial and federal governments to administer community service sentences as well as treatment. Other examples include private probation services, particularly in the area of enforcing home confinement orders.

This type of private industry involvement in the adult correctional system has not been considered a significant issue by most Canadians or the federal government, but two issues that are considered significant in the areas of private sector involvement in Canada include facility management and operation, and the expansion of the role of private enterprise in prison industries. The issues related to these two areas are just now emerging and will no doubt lead to controversy and debate in the near future. This is due to concern about the costs of administering corrections today as well as maintaining and increasing the quality of treatment programs. According to Stojkovic and Lovell (1997:628), these two areas "promise to generate more difficult questions in the coming years—and the resolution of certain of these questions will require the attention of a wide array of public officials, interest groups, and members of the public."

Perhaps the more pressing of these questions in Canada today involves the issue of whether private interests should operate federal and/or adult correctional facilities. Particularly significant are administrative issues, legal issues and financial issues. Administrative issues typically focus upon accountability. There is concern regarding the quality of care and the maintenance of appropriate standards within the correctional facility. Legal issues generally involve the question of liability. As the National Institute of Justice in the United States (1985:77) has pointed out, since "private facility management contracts are a recent phenomenon, no body of case law has yet emerged to clarify the respective liabilities of public and private agencies. There is, however, no legal principle to support the premise that public agencies will be able to avoid or diminish their liability merely because services have been delegated to a private vendor." Advocates of private prisons argue that it is within the law to contract the operation of secure adult correctional facilities. According to McDonald (1990:53), "the state does not own the right to punish . . .that such a move violates no fundamental principle within a democracy. It merely administers it in trust, on behalf of the people and under the rule of law." Finally, financial considerations must be taken into account. It is plain that one of the major objections to privatisation would include concerns over sacrificing prisoners' interests for profit. Advocates of private prisons argue that this concern is not justified— that the rights now accorded to prisoners by the courts would protect them from any violation of their legal rights by private contractors.

Legislative changes would have to be made in Canada to allow private corporations to manage federal correctional facilities. This could be accomplished with relative ease as long as there was no or very little opposition from interested parties. However, given the opposition in New Brunswick when they attempted to privatise the operation of their juvenile facility, it appears likely that any similar move in the adult sector would end up the subject of protracted debate.

TECHNOLOGY

One of the fastest growing aspects of the correctional system is the sophisticated technology involving the surveillance of inmates and offenders who are on some form of conditional release program in the community. Many conditional release programs involve a sentence of home confinement that is enforced with some type of electronic monitoring. This type of program is exceedingly popular in the United States, where electronic monitoring was put into operation in all states by 1990 (Renzema, 1992). These programs can involve large numbers of participants. For example, during most of the 1990s, the state of Florida typically has had in excess of 13,000 offenders on home confinement at any given time. While these programs are in operation (either permanently or experimentally) in various forms across Canada at different levels of jurisdiction, they involve much lower numbers of participants.

The possibility of home confinement coupled with electronic monitoring should be of great interest to correctional officials in Canada (particularly federal correctional administrators) because these programs have been developed largely to control prison overcrowding, a significant issue in Canada's federal correctional system today (see Chapter 1). With the introduction of home confinement, the correctional system could save the costs associated with incarcerating offenders (usually low-risk offenders), as inmates with permanent jobs are released back into the community. Under this system, the client is not costing the system much money, and is working within the community, keeping family ties intact and avoiding the stigma associated with incarceration. Once an electronic monitoring program becomes part of home confinement, it provides a higher level of surveillance over offenders and increases the certainty of detection of violations.

The first electronic monitoring programs focused only on low-risk offenders, namely those convicted of alcohol-related traffic infractions. These programs were successful in reducing recidivism rates, but subsequent evaluations discovered that the clients selected for the programs were the most likely to succeed anyway (Lilly et al., 1987; 1993). Very few detailed evaluations are available concerning the general success or failure of these programs. Renzema (1992), for example, points out the scarcity of the literature on this topic, especially as it relates to the issues of recidivism and cost-effectiveness. One of the most significant studies to date involves a case study of the development, implementation and growth of a program in Arizona (Palumbo et al., 1992). This study points out that, much like private corrections, home confinement was first viewed by officials as a means to significant cost reductions by releasing low-risk offenders back into the community. However, researchers discovered that this program actually ended up costing the Arizona state government more money than what was originally estimated. In addition, program participants had a recidivism rate (for technical violations) 34 percent higher than those placed on "normal" parole release. As Baumer and Mendelsohn (1991) commented after reviewing the literature on this topic, "the incapacitative and public safety appeal of this sanction has probably been overstated" largely due to the fascination with the technological aspects of this program. They conclude that the strength of this program lies with the control of low-risk offenders (who would normally be given accelerated release parole or probation) on early release parole and that it will not play a significant role other than this in the correctional system.

SUMMARY

Correctional decisionmakers appear to have taken a unique perspective toward determining the future direction of corrections in Canada. Instead of relying upon deterrence-based policies (e.g., longer sentences) or high-technology solutions (e.g., electronic monitoring), they have chosen to pursue a policy reflecting reintegration and restorative justice. This means that Canada, unlike the United States, has chosen to deal with overcrowding and large correctional populations by distinguishing offenders according to different risk levels and by implementing programs that attempt to "heal" the relations between the victim and offender.

Such a move indicates that offenders can be best handled by determining and understanding their risks and needs, and by having trained staff deal with these needs appropriately. Whether this is true in the long term remains a question; in the short term, it appears that the new policies introduced by the Corrections and Conditional Release Act have been able to decrease the amount of recidivism while offenders are on the various conditional release programs. In addition, the emphasis upon restorative justice should divert a number of offenders away from correctional facilities. To date, the early results of restorative justice programs, such as community justice forums, have indicated great success.

Nevertheless, any future long-term successes are likely to lie in the treatment of offenders in the community. These programs have the potential to place offenders into programs that address criminogenic needs. Deterrence-based punishments do not target the needs of offenders, but instead focus on surveillance and punishment. Community resources will no doubt become a major component of the correctional system in the future, assisting with the reintegration of offenders as well as increasing the levels of public safety.

REFERENCES

McDonald, Douglas C. (1990). "Private Penal Institutions." In Michael Tonry (ed.), *Crime and Justice: A Review of Research,* Volume 16. Chicago: The University of Chicago Press.

Lilly, J. Robert, Richard A. Ball, G. David Curry and John McMullen (1993). "Electronic Monitoring of the Drunk Driver: A Seven-Year Study of the Home Confinement Alternative." *Crime & Delinquency,* Volume 39, 462-484.

Lilly, J. Robert, Richard A. Ball and Jennifer Wright (1987). "Home Incarceration with Electronic Monitoring in Kenton County, Kentucky: An Evaluation." In Belinda R. McCarthy (ed.), *Intermediate Punishments: Intensive Supervision, Home Confinement and Electronic Surveillance.* New York: Criminal Justice Press,

Palumbo, Dennis J., Mary Clifford and Joann K. Snyder-Joy (1992). "From Net-Widening to Intermediate Sanctions: The Transformation of Alternatives to Incarceration from Benevolence to Malevolence." In James M. Byrne, Arthur J. Lurigio and Joan Petersilia (eds.), *Smart Sentencing: The Emergence of Intermediate Sanctions.* Newbury Park, CA: Sage.

Renzema, Marc (1992). *Electronic Monitoring Primer: Version 0.90.* Kutztown, PA: Tracking Systems Corporation.

Solicitor General of Canada (1985). "Prisons for Profit." *Liaison,* Volume 11, 11-19.

Stojkovic, Stan and Rick Lovell (1997). *Corrections: An Introduction,* Second Edition. Cincinnati: Anderson.

Glossary

A

accelerated review: A form of conditional release that stipulates that some offenders who are serving their first term of imprisonment in a federal institution may be released on full parole after they have served one-third of their sentence.

Archambault Commission: A government commission (1936) that reported that rehabilitation should become the focus of the Canadian correctional system.

Auburn system: see **congregate system**

B

benefit of clergy: A practise of the Middle Ages that exempted clergy members from many punishments, later extended to citizens who could demonstrate religiosity be reading a bible passage.

Brown Commission: A government commission (1848) that recommended that the separate system should be introduced into the Canadian correctional system to complement the Auburn system. It also exposed conditions of brutality within the Kingston Penitentiary.

C

case management ISP: A type of intensive supervision probation in which participants are classified according to their risk of reoffending as determined by a risk classification instrument.

Clarke Report: A report by a government commission that argues that federal legislation be revised to eliminate discrimination on the basis of sex or religion.

clemency: A form of early release in which a senior government official was allowed to release inmates before the termination of their sentence.

co-correctional facilities: Correctional facilities that house men and women inmates together.

collective incapacitation: The amount of crime reduction achieved through traditional offense-based sentencing, in which offenders are sentenced according to prior record and seriousness of the act.

conditional release: An offender's release from a correctional facility, by which he or she serves part of his or her sentence in the community under the supervision of a designated official.

congregate system: A prison system in which inmates were allowed to congregate for meals and while working.

D

Daubney Committee: A federal governmental committee (1987) that recommended that conditional release be maintained and improved upon.

day parole: Parole in which an offender is allowed to participate in community activities in preparation for release but has to return to a secure facility (such as a halfway house) overnight unless otherwise authorized by the National Parole Board. Day parole can be granted six months before an offender can apply for full parole.

deterrence: The inhibition of criminal activity achieved through the fear of state-imposed penalties.

doctrine of free will: The idea that humans rationally and freely choose to engage in the social contract that allows the government to impose sanctions on those who break the law.

doctrine of the social contract: The idea that society is held together by a bond between citizens and government, in which governmental authority protects citizens, but citizens relinquish some individuality so the government can do so.

E

earned remission :   Remission (three days per month) earned by inmates for good behaviour while institutionalized. This remission cannot be lost once earned.

F

"faint hope" clause: Section 745 of the Criminal Code of Canada, which allows offenders serving at least 15 years of a sentence to apply for a reduction in the amount of time they have to wait before their parole eligibility date.

false negatives: In criminal justice contexts, the incorrect release of offenders who subsequently commit a crime in the community.

false positives: In criminal justice contexts, the incorrect placement of offenders who are predicted to recidivate but do not.

Fauteux Report: A report by a government commission (1956) that introduced the medical model of rehabilitation into the federal Canadian correctional system.

full parole: Parole in which inmates serve the remainder of their prison sentence under supervision in the community. Most offenders can apply for full parole after serving one-third of their sentence.

G

general conditions: Conditions of probation that are imposed on all probationers, such as reporting changes in residence and not leaving a certain jurisdiction without permission.

general deterrence: The inhibition, resulting from the punishment of certain offenders, of the desire to become involved in criminal behaviour among the general population.

Goldenberg Report: A report released by a government committee (1974) that recommended that parole be extended to the greatest number of possible offenders.

good time: Remission gained through good behaviour while institutionalized, allowing inmates to be released earlier than the end of their original sentence. Usually inmates earn two days for each day of good behaviour.

Great Law: A Quaker law stipulating that hard labour is an effective punishment for crime and that capital punishment should be abolished

H

Hugessen Report: A report released by a government committee (1973) that recommended that criteria for the parole decision should be made more clear.

I

incapacitation: Custodial control of convicted offenders that ensures their inability to commit crimes that affect the general public.

intensive supervision parole: Community-based criminal sanctions that emphasize close monitoring of offenders while they are in the community under the control of federal government officials.

intensive supervision probation (ISP):   Probation in which there is increased surveillance and monitoring of offenders while on probation. It usually involves a low client-to-probation-officer ratio and a graduated return to the community in terms of surveillance and control.

J

judicial reprieve: A form of probation in which a judge temporarily delays the imposition of a sentence as a result of good behaviour.

K

Kingston Penitentiary: The first penitentiary to open in Canada (1835). It was operated by the Ontario Provincial government until 1867, when it was taken over by the federal government.

M

Macdonnell Commission: The Royal Commission on Penitentiaries (1914), which recommended that federally sentenced women be sent to their provinces of origin and supervised by provincial authorities.

mandatory supervision: A program implemented in 1970 that allowed all inmates being released as a result of earned or statutory remission of 60 days or more to be placed under the authority of the National Parole Board.

marginal deterrent effect: The extent to which crime rates response to incremental changes in the threat of sanctions.

Mercer Reformatory: The first separate institution for female offenders in Canada, opened in 1880.

mother-child program: A prison program in which incarcerated women are allowed to keep their children with them until the age of two or three years old.

N

Nickle Commission: A government commission (1921) that investigated allegations of sexual misconduct in the Prison for Women, the first inquiry specifically appointed to investigate issues concerning federally sentenced women.

O

Ouimet Report: A report by a government commission (1969) that suggested that the federal Canadian correctional system should pursue offender change within a community setting and that imprisonment should be a last resort for offenders.

P

panopticon: An institution invented by Jeremy Bentham in which offenders would be placed and given the time to contemplate their criminal actions. This was the forerunner to the modern prison (from the Greek word meaning "all-seeing").

parsimony: The idea that the punishment should involve a sentence that places the least restrictive control on the offender.

penitentiary: A place for the incarceration of criminals designed to protect offenders from moral contamination and to restore them to a proper way of living by improving their character.

postsentence report :   A report, usually completed by a probation officer, used to give information for sentence decisionmaking involving an offender.

prison diversion: A type of intensive supervision probation in which judges send convicted offenders to programs according to certain standards established for them by probation officials.

Prison for Women: A separate facility for federally sentenced women opened in Kingston, Ontario, in 1935.

probation: A community-based sanction in which the offender is released into the community under certain conditions and under supervision. The probationer has to meet certain general and/or specific conditions, such as reporting to a designated individual once each month.

probation: A court-ordered alternative by which an offender is placed under the control, supervision and care of a probation staff member in lieu of imprisonment, so long as the probationer meets certain standards of conduct.

proportionality: The idea that there has to be a rank ordering of crimes on the basis of their relative seriousness proportionate to the rank ordering of the severity of punishments.

R

R. v. Daniels: A case in which the court decided that an inmate's right to life and security would be violated if she had to serve any part of her sentence at an institution in which there was a high risk of inmate suicide.

R. v. Gayle Horii: A case in which the court decided that an inmate was allowed to remain in a facility that offered programs and that being transferred away from such programs on the basis of gender would be a violation of her rights under the law.

recidivism rate: The number of offenders who, during a designated time period after being released from a correctional facility, are rearrested for committing another offense or violating the conditions of their parole.

reform era: The era (c. 1700s) in which reform efforts for prisons were introduced in England and the United States that were aimed at making punishments more humane.

rehabilitation era: The era (1935-1960) in Canada when rehabilitation emerged as the dominant correctional ideology.

rehabilitation: The application of corrections to improve the condition of offenders so they no longer want or need to commit crimes.

reintegration era: The era (1960-present) in Canada in which reintegration of the offender emerged as the dominant correctional ideology.

reintegration: The application of corrections stressing the acquisition of skills and opportunities for offenders to participate in community settings.

reintegrative shaming: A process suggested by Braithwaite whereby offenders are shamed in response to their offenses, but are also accepted back into the community.

remand: Nonsentenced admission to custody, such as when an offender is awaiting trial or being held for an immigration hearing.

remission: Early release from incarceration for good behaviour.

risk assessment: An assessment of an inmate's risk that considers the factors of offence type, criminal history, social problems, performance on earlier release, mental status, the offender's relationships and employment, psychological reports, expert opinions and information from victims.

S

selective incapacitation: The amount of crime reduction achieved through sentencing in which offenders are sentenced according to their risk of committing future crimes.

separate system: A prison system emphasizing solitary confinement, manual labour in cells and the separation of inmates from one another.

shock incarceration: A deterrence-based punishment patterned after the military-style discipline used in armed forced boot camps. These programs are typically short (no more than six months) and involve young adults.

SIR Scale: The General Statistical Information on Release Scale, a 15-point scale used to discriminate between high-risk and low-risk cases. It is a core component of the reintegration ideology as it assists federal officials in determining the needs of each offender.

Skills and Needs Inventory: An inventory involving questions associated with positive and negative strategies, asking offenders to describe their needs and strengths and the type of assessment they want. This inventory is used by the federal government to collect information on inmates for classification and placement purposes.

specific conditions: Conditions of probation that relate to the needs and risks of a particular probationer.

specific deterrence: The inhibition of one's desire to become involved in future criminal behaviour resulting from punishments suffered personally.

split sentence: A short period of incarceration followed by a period of time on probation.

statutory release: Conditional release that requires offenders to serve the final one-third of their sentence in the community. Offenders serving indeterminate sentences are not eligible for statutory release.

statutory remission: Remission in which 25 percent of a sentence is credited to inmates when sentenced. This remission can be taken away as a result of problematic behaviour.

substantive equality: An approach used for federally sentenced women that focuses on situational diversity, recognizing the specific needs of male inmates and female inmates.

suppression effect: A reduction in the number and seriousness of crimes although offenders continue to participate in criminal activity.

T

technical violation: A violation of a condition of parole.

temporary absence: A conditional release program in which offenders may leave a correctional facility for a specific program purpose.

ticket-of-leave: The earliest system of parole. Inmates who were of good behaviour were released early in order to return to the community. Parolees were required to report monthly to the local police until the end of their sentence.

U

utilitarianism: see **doctrine of free will**

Name Index

A

Abadinsky, H., 99
Adelberg, E., 178
Albert, G., 113
Allen, H., 35, 48, 70, 140
Alpert, G., 58
American Correctional Association, 133
Andrews, D., 11, 12, 42, 43, 44, 45, 46, 47
Apospori, E., 58
Applegate, B., 44, 45, 47
Augustus, J., 140
Austin, J., 53, 85, 87
Axon, L., 181

B

Baehre, R., 74
Ball, M., 43
Banks, J., 149
Barnes, H., 70, 98, 99
Barrett, S., 108
Barry, E., 155
Baunach, P., 175
Beattie, J., 73
Beaumont, G., 72
Beccaria, C., 54, 66
Beck, A., 55
Beirne, P., 67
Belcourt, R., 11, 13, 112
Belknap, J., 168, 174
Bentham, J., 54, 66, 67
Berezins, L., 173, 178
Bernard, T., 38
Besserer, S., 10, 13, 15, 16, 135, 136, 137, 138, 139

Birkenmayer, A., 10, 13, 15, 16, 135, 136, 137, 138, 139
Blanchette, K., 179, 180
Blumstein, A., 38, 55, 85
Boe, R., 18, 19, 21, 22, 23, 24
Boldt, E., 145
Bonta, J., 11, 12, 43, 44, 47, 48, 118
Boritch, H., 10, 166
Bottomley, A., 106, 124
Braiker, H., 36
Braithwaite, J., 57, 58, 59
Brockway, Z., 99
Brodeur, J.-P., 176
Brown, G., 119
Bursik, R., 58
Byrne, J., 54, 121, 150

C

Camp, C., 43, 53
Camp, G., 43, 53
Carlen, P., 161
Carrigan, D., 73, 75, 78, 81, 167, 173
Carter, R., 98, 149
Chaiken, J., 37, 39
Chaiken, M., 37, 39
Chan, J., 52, 53
Chesney-Lind, M., 182
Clark, J., 40
Clear, T., 47, 69, 83, 87
Clinard, M., 57
Cohen, S., 48, 68, 83, 87
Conklin, J., 41, 42, 54, 56
Conley, J., 71
Conrad, J., 35
Cooper, S., 164, 165, 173, 178
Cormier, R., 117, 118

Cowles, E., 181
Crawford, J., 174
Crofton, W., 98, 99
Cullen, F., 41, 42, 43, 44, 45, 47, 48
Currie, C., 178

D

Daniels, C., 171
de Tocqueville, A., 72
Dickie, I., 11
Dinitz, S., 35
Dobash, R., 68, 160, 172
Dubois, S., 179
Duffee, D., 83

E

Edmison, J., 77
Ekstedt, J., 76, 77
Ericson, R., 52
Erwin, B., 121
Evans, S., 48

F

Fabiano, E., 182
Faith, K., 164
Ferres, J., 75
Finckenauer, J., 56
Finkler, H., 111
Fogel, D., 84, 85
Foran, T., 1, 2, 4, 5, 6, 9, 12, 29
Foucault, M., 68
Fowler, G., 40
Fox, L., 173
Frankel, M., 85
Frase, R., 49
Frideres, J., 10, 14
Fry, E., 161, 165, 169

G

Gabel, S., 174, 175
Geerken, M., 39
Geis, G., 57
Gendreau, P., 42, 44, 45, 46
Gibbs, J., 54
Gilbert, K., 41, 42, 43
Gillis, C., 114, 115
Glick, R., 175
Goggin, C., 44, 45, 46

Goldkamp, J., 47
Gosselin, L, 77
Gottfredson, D., 42
Grant, B., 11, 12, 14, 112, 114, 115
Grasmick, H., 58
Green, D., 57
Greenwood, P., 37-39, 47
Griffiths, C., 76, 77, 134

H

Hagan, J., 21, 145, 146
Hann, R., 107, 111, 117, 118
Hannah-Moffat, K., 169, 170
Hanson, R., 118
Harman, W., 107, 111, 117, 118
Hattem, T., 180
Hawkins, G., 58
Hawkins, R., 113
Heidensohn, F., 161
Heney, J., 159
Henslin, J., 9
Hill, M., 140
Horii, G., 172
Horney, J., 58
Hudson, B., 70
Hylton, J., 52, 53

J

Jackson, G., 84
Jackson, M., 75
Jaffray, S., 80
Jacobs, J., 56
Jobson, K., 103
Johnson, H., 157
Johnson, R., 68, 71

K

Kelleher, J., 108
Kelly, A., 150
Kendall, K., 174, 178
Kittrie, N., 81
Krisberg, B., 53, 85, 87

L

LaPrairie, C., 118
Latessa, E., 48, 140, 144, 145
Laurier, W., 100
Lavigne, B., 13

Law Reform Commission of Canada, 14,
    111
LeBlanc, T., 178
Lefebvre, L., 97, 158
Lieber, F., 165
Lipsey, 42, 46, 47
Liska, A., 55
Losel, F., 46
Loucks, A., 158
Lovell, R., 76, 142, 143, 160

M

MacKenzie, D.L., 57, 158
Macleod, L., 159
Maconochie, A., 98
Mahan, S., 182
Makin, K., 114
Manitoba Aboriginal Justice Inquiry, 114
Mann, C., 155
Marshall, D., 111
Marshall, I., 58
Marshall, W., 108
Martinson, R., 42, 44, 85
Mathiesen, T., 85
McCarthy, B.J., 50
McCarthy, B.R., 50
McGee, R., 98
McLean, H., 178, 179
McMahon, M., 52, 53
Melossi, D., 68, 72
Messerschmidt, J., 67
Miethe, T., 50
Miller, F., 101
Miranne, A., 39
Mitchell, B., 181
Mitford, J., 84
Moore, M., 60
Morash, M., 57
Morgan, K., 148
Morris, A., 158, 161
Morrison, P., 3, 5, 14, 25, 30
Motiuk, L., 11, 12, 13, 88, 178
Moylan, J., 75
Mugford, S., 59

N

Nagin, D., 56
National Advisory Commision on
    Criminal Justice Standards and
    Goals, 51
Nelson, A., 9

Nelson, K., 98
Neto, V., 175
Nuffield, J., 102, 105, 111, 117

O

O'Leary, V., 83, 87
O'Reilly, M., 165, 166
Ormond, D., 77
Ouimet, R., 84, 104

P

Palmer, T., 42
Pattavina, A., 54
Pavarini, M., 68, 72
Pepino, N., 112
Petersilia, J., 47, 48, 53, 54, 121, 124,
    133, 146, 148, 149
Peterson, M., 36
Pfohl, S., 49
Pollock-Byrne, J., 160, 173, 176
Porporino, F., 112, 180
Posner, C., 79

R

Reed, M., 3, 5, 9, 14, 25, 28, 30, 93, 96,
    135, 136
Richards, K., 142, 143
Ritti, R., 38
Roberts, J.V., 9, 25, 28, 93, 96, 135, 136
Robinson, D., 11, 13, 117
Rodgers, K., 157
Rodriquez, N., 182
Rosencrance, J., 146
Ross, B., 42
Ross, R., 182
Rothman, D., 68
Rowe, C., 55
Rucker, L., 57

S

Sabath, M., 181
Savage, E., 140
Scarth, K., 178, 179
Schissel, B., 21
Schoom, M., 74
Schwartz, M., 41, 78, 82, 88
Schweber, C., 182
Scott, J., 48

Scull, A., 68
Senna, J., 140
Serin, R., 88, 117, 118
Shaw, M., 12, 157, 158, 159, 166, 167, 170, 174, 176, 177, 179
Shields, I., 43
Shipley, B., 55
Shoom, S., 74
Shover, N., 57
Siegel, L., 55, 57, 140
Simonsen, C., 35, 70
Solicitor General of Canada, 5, 6, 12, 13, 14, 94-95, 102, 105, 106, 107, 108, 111, 117
Spelman, W., 47
Spohn, C., 146
Standing Committee on Justice and the Solicitor General, 14
Stanley, D., 113
Statistics Canada, 6
Stojkovic, S., 76, 142, 143, 160
Strong, K., 188, 190, 192
Subcommittee on the Penitentiary System in Canada, 77, 86
Sugar, F., 173

T

Taft, D., 70
Teeters, N., 70, 98, 99
Thurber, A., 191
Tittle, C., 55
Travis, L., 41, 78, 82, 88
Tunnell, K., 57
Turner, S., 53, 54, 121, 124, 133, 146, 149

V

van Dine, S., 35
Vito, G., 48, 143
Van Ness, P., 188, 190. 192
Verdun-Jones, S., 134
Visher, C., 36, 37, 38, 39
von Hirsch, A., 39, 85

W

Waldrum, J., 118
Walker, S., 98, 140, 141
Waller, I., 125
Walsh, A., 145
Ward, L., 11
Watson, L., 175, 176
Weisburd, D., 57
Welch, S., 146
Wetherell, D., 164, 166
Wheeler, P., 155
Williams, K., 58
Wilson, D., 46, 47
Wilson, J.Q., 36
Wotherspoon, T., 10

Y

Yu, J., 55

Z

Zamble, E., 158, 180
Zedlewski, E., 55, 88

Subject Index

A

Aboriginals, 14-15
    age, 9
    education, 11
    employment, 12
    parole, 111-112
    probation, 136
    temporary absences, 111-112
Accelerated review, 95
Act Respecting Penitentiaries and the Directors Thereof, 74-75
Age-crime curve, 18
Annual Report of the Commissioner of Penitentiaries, 81
Archambault Commission, 80, 162, 167
Auburn system, 69, 71-72

B

Benefit of clergy, 140
Board of Directors of Federal Penitentiaries, 75
Board of Inspectors for Asylums and Prisons, 74
Boot camps, 57, 150
British Columbia Penitentiary, 75
Brown Commission, 74
Burnaby Correctional Centre for Women, 172

C

Canadian Correctional Association, 162
Canadian Penal Congress, 78
Canadian Sentencing Commission, 107, 125

Child Custody Advocacy Services Project, 176
Chinnery Report, 163
Clark Report, 167, 168
Clemency, 100
Collective Incapacitation, 36-37
Commission on Systemic Racism in the Ontario Criminal Justice System, 112
Conditional release programs, 3, 29-30, 95-98
Congregate system, 71-72
Co-correctional facilities, 182
Corrections and Conditional Release Act, 88, 93-94, 108, 113, 115, 126
Creating Choices, 169-170, 173-176, 178
Criminal Law Reform Act of 1984, 86

D

Daubney Committee, 107, 108, 126, 163
Day parole, 29, 94
Detention, 112-115
Deterrence, 54-59
    general deterrence, 56
    specific deterrence, 55
Dorchester Penitentiary, 75
Double-bunking, 4

E

Electronic monitoring, 195-196
Elizabeth Fry Society, 84
English Anglican Code, 70
Exchange of Services Agreements, 2, 168

F

"Faint hope" clause, 118-120
False negatives, 88
False positives, 88
Fauteux Committee, 81-82, 101-104,
    162, 167
Federally sentenced women, 155-182
    children, 174-176
    dislocation, 170-172
    employment, 12, 176-178
    long-term incaceration, 180
    risks and needs, 178-180
    services, 172
Free will, 66
Full parole, 29, 94

G

Good time, 102
Goldenberg Report, 105
Great Law, 70

H

Hugessen Report, 105

I

Incapacitation, 35-37
    collective incapacitation, 37
    selective incapacitation, 37-42
Incarceration costs, 4-6
Intensive supervision parole, 121-124
Intensive supervision probation, 53-54,
    149-150
    case management ISP, 150
    prison release ISP, 150

J

John Howard Society, 84
judicial reprieve, 140
Judicial Review of Parole Eligibility, 119

K

Kingston Penitentiary, 6, 72-73, 75, 164,
    165, 167, 183

L

Ladies Society for Promoting the Refor-
    mation of Female Prisoners, 161
Law Reform Commission of Canada, 85,
    86, 105, 142

M

Macdonnell Commission, 162, 166
MacGuire Report, 163
Mandatory supervision, 104-106
Manitoba Penitentiary, 75
Matsqui Medium Security Prison, 172
Mercer Reformatory, 165
Meta-analysis, 46
Minimum parole, 103
Minnesota Sentencing Guidelines
    Commission, 50
Mother-child program, 175

N

National Congress of Penitentiary
    Reform and Reformatory
    Discipline, 140
National Inmate Survey, 11, 14
National Parole Board, 1, 2, 30, 82, 93,
    94, 96, 101, 104-110, 112, 113,
    127, 128
Needham Report, 163
Net-widening, 87-88
New Brunswick Penitentiary, 72
Nickle Commission, 167

O

Ouimet Report, 83-84, 104, 162
Outerbridge Report, 84

P

Panopticon, 66-67
Parole
    faint-hope clause, 118-121
    principles, 108
    programs
        accelerated review, 96
        Intensive supervison parole,
            121-124
        recidivism, 116-118

Parole Act, 101
Parole hearing
 risk assessment, 109-110
 statistical probability of reoffending, 110
Parsimony, 49
Penitentiaries, 65
Penitentiary Act, 106
Penitentiary Branch Report, 76
Pennsylvania system, 71
Postsentence report, 144
Presentence report, 144-146
Prison diversion, 149
Prison for Women, 158, 162-163, 166, 167, 168, 170, 171, 172, 173, 174, 175, 177, 183
Prisoners, profile 9-16
 age 9-10
 criminal history, 13-14
 education, 11
 employment, 12
 ethnicity, 14
 family, 12-13
 financial status, 12
 gender, 10
 race, 14
 type of offence, 15-16
Prisons and Reformatories Act, 168
Privatization of prisons,
Probation, 28-29, 133-135, 146-150
 caseloads, 147
Probation officer, 144
Probation supervision, 146-147
Probationers
 age, 135
 history, 140
 sentence of, 136-137
Proportionality, 48

R

R. v. Daniels, 171-172
R. v. Gayle Horii, 172
R. v. Richards, 142
RAND Corporation, 37-39, 121, 124
Recidivism, 41-42, 116
Reform era, 70
Rehabilitation, 41-48
 Era, 78-82
 need, 43
 responsivity, 43
 risk, 43

Reintegration, 48-53, 82-88
Reintegrative shaming, 58-59
Remand, 25
Remission, 99
 earned, 103
 statutory, 103
Remission Service, 100
Risk assessment, 109
Royal Canadian Mounted Police, 25
Royal Commission of Inquiry, 73
Royal Commission on Status of Women, 162

S

St. Vincent de Paul Penitentiary, 75
Scared Straight, 56
Selective incapacitation, 37
Separate system, 71
Shock incarceration, 56
SIR Scale, 117-118
Social contract, 66
Split sentence, 134
Statutory release, 30, 95
Stoney Mountain Penitentiary, 14, 75
Suppression effect, 42

T

Task Force on Long-Term Offenders, 181
Task Force on Reintegration of Offenders, 86
Technical violation, 115
Temporary absence, 25, 95, 112
"Three strikes and you're out" laws, 40-41
Ticket-of-Leave Act, 100, 101

U

Utilitarianism, 66

W

Walnut Street Jail, 71
Women in corrections, 155-183